P9-CNG-880

For quite a long time, computer security was a rather narrow field of study that was populated mainly by theoretical computer scientists, electrical engineers, and applied mathematicians. With the proliferation of open systems in general, and of the Internet and the World Wide Web (WWW) in particular, this situation has changed fundamentally. Today, computer and network practitioners are equally interested in computer security, since they require technologies and solutions that can be used to secure applications related to electronic commerce. Against this background, the field of computer security has become very broad and includes many topics of interest. The aim of this series is to publish state-of-the-art, high standard technical books on topics related to computer security. Further information about the series can be found on the WWW at the following URL:

http://www.esecurity.ch/serieseditor.html

Also, if you'd like to contribute to the series and write a book about a topic related to computer security, feel free to contact either the Commissioning Editor or the Series Editor at Artech House.

Recent Titles in the Artech House Computer Security Series

Rolf Oppliger, Series Editor

Computer Forensics and Privacy, Michael A. Caloyannides
Demystifying the IPsec Puzzle, Sheila Frankel
Electronic Payment Systems for E-Commerce, Second Editon, Donal O'Mahony, Michael Peirce, and Hitesh Tewari
Information Hiding Techniques for Steganography and Digital Watermarking, Stefan Katzenbeisser and Fabien A. P. Petitcolas, editors
Non-repudiation in Electronic Commerce, Jianying Zhou
Secure Messaging with PGP and S/MIME, Rolf Oppliger
Security Fundamentals for E-Commerce, Vesna Hassler

For a listing of related *Artech House* titles turn to the back of this book.

Computer Forensics and Privacy

Michael A. Caloyannides

Artech House
Boston • London
www.artechhouse.com

Library of Congress Cataloging-in-Publication Data
Caloyannides, Michael.
    Computer forensics and privacy / Michael Caloyannides.
      p. cm. – (Artech House computer security series)
    Includes bibliographical references and index.
    ISBN 1-58053-283-7 (alk. paper)
    1. Computer security.   2. Data protection.   3. Forensic sciences.
    I. Title.   II. Series.
  QA76.9.A25 C345   2001
  005.8—dc21   2001022883

British Library Cataloguing in Publication Data
Caloyannides, Michael.
  Computer forensics and privacy. — (Artech House computer security series)
  1. Computer security
  I. Title
  005.8
  ISBN 1-58053-283-7

Cover design by Wayne McCaul

Microsoft® screen shots reprinted by permission from Microsoft Corporation.
Netscape Communicator browser window © 1999 Netscape Communications Corporation.
Used with permission. Netscape Communications has not authorized, sponsored, endorsed, or approved this publication and is not responsible for its content.
Qualcomm's Eudora screen shots used with permission.

© 2001 ARTECH HOUSE, INC.
685 Canton Street
Norwood, MA 02062

International Standard Book Number: 1-58053-283-7
Library of Congress Catalog Card Number: 2001022883

10 9 8 7 6 5 4 3 2 1

This book is dedicated to the memory of my late father, Akylas, whose sense of honor was never intimidated by abusive governmental authority, and to my two children, Melody and Brian, who did not yet understand why I spent so much time writing this book on the computer as opposed to playing computer games with them.

Contents

Part I
Computer Forensics

1

Introduction

If you give me six lines written by the most honest man, I will find something in them to hang him.

—Cardinal Richelieu

In any country's court of law, physical evidence is as compelling as—and often more compelling than—personal testimony by a credible eyewitness. The well-known Miranda warning given to criminal suspects in the United States—"anything you say can and will be used against you"—applies to those apprehended in any country, and applies to criminal proceedings as well as civil litigation. Furthermore, what "can and will be used against you" refers not only to what an individual says but also to any "incriminating" material brought to bear in his or her case.

Up until about a decade ago, documentary evidence was mostly on paper. Even "computer evidence" amounted to reams of printed pages. This is no longer the case. The electronic version of a file that was created and stored in a computer can be far more damaging to an individual or organization, because it contains not only the documentary evidence but also "data about the data" (such as when it was created, when it was revised, how it was revised, using whose software, and so on).

There is nothing "personal" about a personal computer (PC) other than who paid the bill to buy one. Quite the contrary, it is often the most sought-after piece of supporting evidence used in building a case. A PC is not at all private in the eyes of the law; besides, most countries do not have laws

3

protecting privacy. If a PC's data storage (hard drive, floppy disks, tape backups, CD-ROMs) is confiscated or subpoenaed—and this is done with increasing regularity today—then anything in it "can and will be used against you."

Most individuals and companies have always been careful with what they commit to paper or say over the telephone; in litigious contemporary societies cognizant of assorted discrimination laws, individuals have also learned to be reserved and discreet with respect to what they say to one another, especially within a company or other organization. Yet those same individuals treat electronic mail as if it were a private channel that enjoys some magic protection from unintended recipients; language that one normally would not commit to paper (such as gossip, off-color jokes, innuendo, and biases which could evoke an emotional reaction in a judge or jury that negatively affects the verdict, and even plans that are of questionable legality or outright illegal) are routinely confided to personal and corporate computers through electronic mail. Yet electronic mail and computer records are far more permanent than any piece of paper, and electronic mail is far more likely to reach unintended recipients than a plain old message in a mailed envelope. Also, whereas there can only be a single "original" of a paper document (that can haunt a company or an individual in court), a copy of a computer record is as admissible a piece of evidence as the original record.

Society today favors more informality than in years past. This extends from personal associations to corporate communications; today's organization tends to encourage creativity, esprit de corps among employees, and candor. Whereas in the past there was a fairly rigid hierarchy in the typical organization and one had to go through layers of filtering to reach upper management, e-mail has effectively allowed employees to bypass the hierarchy and protocol and contact people directly; this is ostensibly done "in confidence," when in fact the exact opposite is true because of the permanence and indestructibility of e-mail.

One often hears that statistical analyses can be presented to support just about any preconceived notion; this is so because of selective inclusion and exclusion of data that is made possible by the fact that there is a lot of data to select from to make one's case. The same applies even more so to computer evidence: There is usually so much data in a confiscated or subpoenaed computer that, if judiciously selected, can present a judge or jury with what may appear on the surface to be compelling evidence about this or that.

One might tend to dismiss the threat posed by information that can be accessed via personal and corporate computers as applying to others but not oneself. As this book will show, nothing could be further from the truth. *It applies to anyone using a computer (and that is practically everyone) for any purpose.* In addition, it is of direct interest to lawyers and future lawyers, to corporate officials, to employees with access to employers' computers, to sole proprietors and individual entrepreneurs, to law enforcement officials, to politicians, to medical doctors and other healthcare providers, to college students, to information technology specialists, to hackers and aspiring hackers, to mental health professionals, and many others.

It is important to add that investigation of the contents of a personal computer does not require physical access to that computer; in most cases, it can be done (and has been done by assorted hackers and software companies) while one is "on-line" (i.e., connected to the Internet or to any other network). In many cases it can even be done while a computer is off-line, by someone using commercially available equipment costing a few hundred dollars. While evidence obtained without physical access to a targeted computer may not hold up in court in some nations, it still provides the creative investigator with a wealth of information about the targeted person.

Interestingly, in the United States at least, what little "privacy" exists for data stored in computers within one's premises does not exist for data stored off-site with third parties, such as on the Internet; legislation is premised on the assumption that, even though information is increasingly stored in networks off site, there is no legal expectation of privacy for such information.

Unlike, say, classical mechanics or advanced mathematics, information technology is evolving at an unprecedented rate. Even so, a concerted effort has been made to keep this text pertinent in the face of new advances; this is done by explaining the fundamentals (which do not change) and by providing directly relevant sources of information that the interested reader may access to stay up to date on the latest.

This book is intended for either of two opposing camps:

1. For the law enforcement professional who needs the technical and procedural background to conduct a forensic examination of a computer in order to obtain evidence for a substantive crime, such as murder, so that the evidence will hold up in court.

2. For the professional or businessperson who does not want to have his or her proprietary business information or intellectual property stolen by an unscrupulous competitor or by a thief.

The book will also be useful to attorneys defending wrongly accused individuals when the "evidence" is in computer files, and to law-abiding citizens in democratic societies or freedom fighters in repressive regimes who do not want to be unfairly targeted by overzealous prosecutors. It will also provide peace of mind to individuals whose laptop may be among the hundreds of thousands of laptops stolen every year, who do not want their personal medical and financial information to become public.

Since computer infiltration is a "measures and countermeasures" type of activity, both of the above camps would benefit from both the Computer Forensics and the Computer Privacy and Security sections (Parts I and II) of the book. The forensics camp needs to know what roadblocks can be placed by the privacy-minded professionals so as to devise counter-countermeasures, and the privacy-minded professionals need to know what the actual threats are before they can even begin to think about ways of negating them.

No background in information technology, beyond a typical working familiarity with computers, is assumed. This book is intended to stand on its own two feet, and material aimed at furthering understanding of some of the technical issues discussed is explained in easy-to-follow appendices.

As with any tool, such as a kitchen knife or a hunting rifle, or technique, such as the use of chlorine to wipe out bloodstains, computer forensics and counterforensics can be used for both legal and illegal purposes. *The author does not condone any illegal use of the techniques presented here.*

This book deals with computer forensics, as distinct from network forensics. Computer forensics pertains to anything and everything that can be found in an individual's computer. Network forensics, on the other hand, pertains to evidence that exists elsewhere such as logs kept by Internet service providers (ISPs) and other remotely located networked computers. Network forensics is most relevant in the investigation of remote hackings, remote denial-of-service attacks, and so on. Even so, since most computers today are connected to the Internet at one time or another, this book also covers those aspects of network forensics that affect anyone connecting to the Internet.

2

Relevance of Computer Forensics

2.1 General Explanation

What is computer forensics? Rather than getting embroiled in complex legal definitions and semantics, suffice it to say that computer forensics is the collection of techniques and tools used to find evidence in a computer.

If the evidence is obtained by or on behalf of law enforcement officials, it can be used against a person in a court of law. In the case of totalitarian regimes, it can seal an individual's fate without the intercession of the courts. If the evidence is obtained by an employer or other party with which the individual has a contractual association, it can be used against the individual in administrative proceedings. Evidence obtained by a third party can also be used in the commission of a crime, such as blackmail, extortion, impersonation, and the like.

It is noteworthy that the computer in question does not have to be owned by the user; it can be owned by an employer, or by a totally unrelated party, as in the case of Internet cafés and school and public library computers.

2.2 Computer Forensics and You

2.2.1 As an Employee

Recently, a Northwest Airlines flight attendant hosted a message board on his personal Web site on the Internet. Among the various postings were a few anonymous messages by Northwest employees, then in contract negotiations with the airline, urging coworkers to participate in sickouts (which are illegal under U.S. federal labor laws) so as to force the airline to cancel profitable flights during the 1999 Christmas season. Indeed, over 300 Northwest Airlines flights were cancelled during that time.

Interestingly, Northwest Airlines obtained permission from a federal judge in Minneapolis to search 22 flight attendants' hard drives in computers located not only in union offices but in the flight attendants' own homes, so as to find the identities of those who had incited the sickouts.

Other companies, too, have sued in an effort to find the identities of posters of anonymous messages whose content was deemed by the companies to be disagreeable; they include Varian Medical Systems and Raytheon. ·

The result of such lawsuits is that the suing companies get the courts to subpoena computer records and data-storage media; if what is subpoenaed belongs to a third party (such as an Internet bulletin board), that third party often complies right away without even bothering to notify the person who posted the contested message(s).[1]

The bottom line is that individuals who post electronic messages that are deemed disagreeable by an employer can have their identities revealed—to the extent that this is technically possible—and their personal computers subpoenaed.

An employer can be (and often has been) held liable for the actions of his or her employees, whether those actions involve computers or not. Electronic mail sent by employees even within the same company can be used as evidence against an employer to show, for example, lax enforcement of anti-discrimination laws, patterns of biases, assorted conspiracies, and the like. In an effort to prevent such legal liability, employers can (and often do) legally monitor employee activities involving company computers just as they can (and often do) monitor employees' phone calls on company telephones. It is interesting to ponder how this practice might extend to the increasing numbers of employees who are allowed to work from home using their own personal computers.[2]

---

1. America Online (AOL) and Microsoft® notify chat room posters 14 days before they comply with a civil subpoena. Most others give no such notice.

2. Allowing employees to work at home is not an entirely altruistic practice on the part of employers, although it certainly benefits workers who need to stay at home for such valid reasons as risky pregnancies, illnesses, caring for sick children, and so on. From an employer's perspective, with off-site workers there is less need for expensive office space and ancillary office equipment.

2.2.2 As an Employer or Corporate Executive

Many have heard by now of the embarrassing, to Microsoft, e-mail presented as evidence in the U.S. government's antitrust case against the company, which allegedly made references to "cutting the air off" the competing Netscape Internet browser.

Numerous other companies had electronic files subpoenaed during legal civil discovery processes which proved to be damaging to those companies; a $22.5 million judgment was reportedly leveled against Autodesk Inc., for example, in a case in which company e-mail appeared to support allegations of theft of trade secrets made by Vermont Microsystems Inc. Sloppy deletion of evidence usually hurts more than it helps; in Autodesk's case, evidence of partially deleted evidence was reportedly found on an employee's work and home computers to support Vermont Microsystems' case.

Even effective deletion of electronic evidence is not necessarily a viable way out for a company. Hughes Aircraft Company lost a wrongful-termination case brought by Garreth Shaw, a former attorney of the company, largely because of company-deleted e-mail; in this case, Hughes allegedly had a policy of routinely deleting electronic messages older than three months, but Shaw's attorney successfully argued that Hughes should have suspended the policy when it knew that it was being sued. Sprint Communications Corporation settled a case of alleged patent infringement involving Applied Telematics Inc., after a court found that Sprint had destroyed pertinent electronic evidence.

Encryption of files by individual employees in a manner that the company cannot decrypt can also get an employer in legal trouble. According to John Jessen, CEO of Electronic Evidence Discovery of Seattle, Washington, if electronic evidence that a company cannot decrypt is subpoenaed, that company could be charged with "purposeful destruction of evidence."

A company has an obvious vested interest in ensuring that no employee steals its competitive edge, which exists in the form of proprietary designs, marketing plans, customer lists, innovative processes, and the like.[3] Corporate espionage is a fact of life [1]. According to the American Society of Industrial Security, in Alexandria, Virginia, theft of intellectual property, accomplished mostly by electronic means, costs U.S. businesses more than $250 billion every year.

---

3. The reader may recall the 1993 accusation by General Motors that one of its former senior employees and seven others had allegedly stolen thousands of proprietary documents before joining a competing foreign automaker. GM was awarded $100 million in damages.

2.2.3   As a Law Enforcement Official

Computers can be used to commit crimes and to store evidence of a crime that has nothing to do with computers. The former category includes cyber-fraud, illegal tampering of others' computers through networked connections, and the like. The latter could pertain to any crime whatever, including murder.

Fraudulent-credit-card-generating software is openly available on the Internet, as is software to create fake AOL accounts (e.g., http://www.geoci-ties.com/SiliconValley/Lakes/3285/fake.html). The amount of fraud perpetrated on-line is rivaled only by the amount of fraud perpetrated off-line.

Criminal prosecutors can, therefore, often find evidence in a computer which can be presented in a court of law to support accusations of practically any crime, such as fraud, murder, conspiracy, money laundering, murder, embezzlement, theft, drug-related offenses, extortion, criminal copyright infringement, hidden assets, disgruntled employee destruction of employer records, dummy invoicing, and so on.

Unless the law enforcement individuals know enough about how to collect the required data and also to maintain the requisite chain of custody in a manner that will hold up to challenges by a presumably competent defense, chances are that—in many regimes at least—such evidence will be dismissed by the court.

2.2.4   As a Private Citizen

Anyone accessing the Internet—and that is a few hundred million individuals worldwide, a number that is rapidly growing—is vulnerable to ending up with files on his or her computer that were never solicited by him or her and yet whose possession may be illegal under local law. This can happen in several ways:

- While "browsing the Web," we have all come across Web sites that flash assorted images of nubile females in scanty clothing as part of ads that show up on the screen. These images can (and often do) get stored in one's hard disk automatically. If the subjects in the ads turn out to be underage, or (in some countries) if the photographs are considered explicit, they can be deemed to be "evidence" of the computer owner's having downloaded and possessed illegal material.

- When e-mail with attachments is received on a PC—even unsolic-ited e-mail that is deleted without being read—the attachments can stay in the computer despite the deletion of the e-mail message itself. One must take special steps to delete those attachments, or to configure personal e-mail software to delete attachments when the e-mail that brought the attachment in is itself deleted.

- It has been documented numerous times that when one is on-line—on the Internet or any other internal network—it is eminently possible for a savvy hacker at a remote site (which can be thousands of miles away) to have free run of one's computer and to remove, modify, delete, or even add files to that computer. This obviously includes being able to feed the computer incriminating evidence.

In all of the above cases, it would take an Internet-savvy defense lawyer to convince a typical judge, with average computer knowledge, or a jury of non-technical-minded peers that such illegal data files "just happened" to be in the accused individual's computer. If the files are deleted by a semi-savvy hapless user, the situation might look even worse, because such files can often be discovered through computer forensics; at that point, the accused person will have to defend himself or herself against the charge not only of having downloaded and possessed illegal material but also of having taken active steps to delete the evidence. Individuals who never connect their computer on-line are not immune from hostile computer forensics.

2.2.5 As a Trial Lawyer

Given that a rapidly increasing percentage of legal cases (both criminal and civil) involves computer-based evidence, the legal training of yesteryear is insufficient. Today, a lawyer must be extremely well versed in the ins and outs of computer forensics in order to competently defend a client.

The lawyer must be able to answer the following questions, to his or her own and the client's satisfaction:

1. Could the computer data used against the accused have been altered, damaged, corrupted, or in any way modified while being obtained and handled?

2. Are all procedures used in the forensic examination "auditable," in the sense that a qualified expert can track and attest to their soundness?

3. Is any of the information that may have been obtained by the prosecution during the forensic examination of the computer

covered by the confidentiality protection of the attorney-client privilege?

4. Can the prosecution demonstrate a chain of custody of the data that precludes any possibility that such data could have been contaminated in any way?

5. Could a computer virus, "Trojan," "worm," or other such software have been activated after the data was copied, causing it to be altered?

6. Can the prosecution prove that the accused was the sole user of the computer in question?

7. Could the data used as evidence in the client's computer have been placed there without that individual's knowledge?

Of course, numerous case-specific questions must be answered as well.

Even if computer-based evidence is not brought to bear against a lawyer's particular client, a competent lawyer may well wish to subpoena the "other" party's computer-based records, if appropriate, in order to argue a case in his or her client's favor. Situations where this could be relevant include, for example, cases of wrongful termination, discrimination, harassment, conspiracy, breach of contract, tort, libel or defamation, copyright infringement, violation of applicable securities regulations, and so on.

2.2.6 As an Insurance Company Executive

Insurance companies have an obvious interest in discovering evidence of fraudulent claims of any kind (e.g., auto insurance, medical insurance, workmen's compensation), as well as evidence of crimes and conspiracies that may have resulted in subsequent claims (e.g., arson, willful destruction of property in order to obtain insurance compensation, professed loss of insured valuables). Evidence for such crimes is very likely to reside—however fragmented—in claimants' computers.

2.2.7 As a User of a Third Party's Computer

It is becoming increasingly common for those who travel to use Internet-connected computers available for a fee at such places as hotels, convention centers, Internet cafés, and so on. Some Internet-connected terminals are also available at no charge in schools and universities, booths by ISPs that want to sell ISP subscriptions, public libraries, and so on.

The one fact that must be kept in mind is that the user of others' computers must have absolutely no expectation of privacy. Every keystroke can be—and often is—captured, and this includes login passwords and encryption/decryption keys in addition to the full content of messages and attachments.

2.3 Privacy Without Culpability

The statement "If you have done nothing illegal, you have nothing to fear" is simply not the case—anywhere! Parroted by numerous persons in positions of power over many generations to justify invasions of privacy, it is simply not true, for the following reasons.

- One may genuinely believe that one is doing nothing wrong, but given the myriad of laws on the books, their inconsistency from state to state and nation to nation, and the fact that they change all the time, one cannot know for sure.

- One may be doing nothing wrong now, but the law in many nations can change at a future time and be applicable *retroactively,* with no statute of limitations.

- One may be wrongly accused, and to prove one's innocence may take financial resources that far exceed one's means, with no guarantee of success. Witness the number of individuals in the United States who have been exonerated through DNA forensics *after they had been executed;* the situation can be reasonably expected to be far worse in the many nations that have fewer safeguards against the miscarriage of justice than the United States has.

- One may be framed by law enforcement; sadly, as was illustrated in a recent case in Los Angeles when a handcuffed suspect was shot to death by police officers who then framed him for a crime, such gross abuses of police authority can occur even in the most democratic countries, let alone in states where police power goes unchecked.

The right to privacy is not a "cover for crimes," as some law enforcers would assert. Think about the following points.

- There are some activities, such as sexual relations, going to the bathroom, and so on, that civilized people want to keep private. The presumption that the only reason one would want to keep some activities private is fear of incrimination is, therefore, patently false.

- Given that different people hold different religious and other beliefs, it is often very dangerous for one to allow locally unpopular beliefs to be known by others.

- Civilized countries require police to have warrants before any search or seizure; the same goes for interception of telephone conversations. This does not mean that individuals living in their homes and talking on their telephones have "something to hide"; it means that society has decided that the right to privacy supersedes any desire by the police to monitor someone's house, bedroom, bathroom, and office. A warrant is issued (in theory, at least) by an impartial judge after police have made a compelling case for such. The idea that citizens should surrender privacy in order to "prevent crime" is why the U.S. Constitution includes the Fourth and Fifth Amendments. The founding fathers of the United States recognized that government would find it easier to take citizens' rights away than to solve specific law enforcement problems. As all totalitarian regimes know and practice, it is easier to treat all people as criminals than to catch the criminals. However, in general, violating citizens' privacy does little or nothing to prevent crime.

As stated eloquently in a pseudonymous Usenet posting in December 2000, the statement "If you are doing nothing wrong, you have nothing to worry about" implies an invalid presupposition. The incorrect presupposition with this statement is that privacy is about hiding something. There is no way to answer the "nothing wrong" question without resolving the incorrect presupposition. Privacy is not about hiding something; it is not about culpability—it is about keeping things in their proper context. Why do we need to keep things in their proper context? For a host of reasons: One is that certain actions performed in the context of one's home (taking a bath or shower, or having sex, for instance) are legal, but when performed in the context of a public place are (usually) illegal. The difference is the context. The action is the same. When one removes the context, things that one does with impunity every day can suddenly become illicit or against the law.

Reference

[1]   Winkler, I., *Corporate Espionage*, Rocklin, CA: Prima Publishing, 1997.

3

Business and Administrative Issues

3.1 The Market for Computer Forensics

The market for information services security in the United States is expected to reach $1.05 billion in hardware, $2 billion in software, and $950 million in services in 2001, according to *Computer World*. It increased by about $1 billion from 1997 to 1998 and that rate of growth is on the rise. Frost and Sullivan, the respected market research firm, provides comparable figures. By 2002, the figure for Internet software security alone is estimated to reach $7.4 billion, according to International Data Corporation, based on a survey of 300 companies with more than $100 million in revenue. These figures do not include the information security needs of the defense community, or those of the many law enforcement entities in the United States.

The demand for computer forensics can be reasonably assumed to track the explosive growth of the corresponding commercial sector; computer crime is proportional (though not linearly so) to the increasing commercial use of the Internet and of computers in general. Computer forensics is a mature and rapidly expanding cottage industry. While initially computer forensics was used mostly by law enforcement, it is now a standard tool used by criminal defense attorneys as well as by companies trying to identify insider misdeeds, and by lawyers for the prosecution as well as for the defense in civil proceedings. Often, computer users practice computer forensics on their own computing system in order to recover data that has been inadvertently deleted.

Computer crime (and, hence, the need for computer forensics) has, predictably, increased with the rise of virtual offices and telecommuting. To law enforcement's delight, e-mail has proved to be fertile ground for data detectives because of the social tendency to treat e-mail like a phone call instead of like a written record. Indeed, computers, the Internet, and e-mail have created the most surveillance-friendly medium ever devised.

The current market in computer forensics provides support to:

- Law enforcement, in its attempt to uncover enough evidence to seek a conviction under the law;

- The legal profession, in defending a client in civil or criminal proceedings, by finding supporting evidence;

- The legal profession, in finding evidence to support civil legal action against a defendant;

- Private parties (individuals or companies) in their effort to identify the perpetrator of a suspected attack on their computer(s) and/or network(s);

- National defense establishments.

3.2   Computer Forensics Practitioners

Unlike, say, neurosurgery or research in fluid mechanics, both of which take a thorough schooling in the respective sciences in addition to a considerable amount of practical experience, computer forensics can be done—and, sadly, is often done—by persons with a minimal amount of either education or experience.

As a result, in addition to the truly qualified professionals in the field, a vast cottage industry has sprung up that peddles its services to law enforcement, to lawyers, to private detectives, to employers, to individuals snooping on their spouse's on-line activities—in short, to anybody who asks for such services.

Because of the vast number of entities in the field, the list in Section 3.3.2 is partial and selection is random. No judgment is either made or implied with respect to each entry's relative degree of expertise; some may well be among the best. Similarly, exclusion from the list does not imply a judgment of incompetence; the author's interest was in keeping the list to a manageable size.

Since some readers may have a need for computer forensic services, Appendix A lists numerous providers of such services as well as organizations providing training in computer forensics.

3.3   Forensics Software Tools

3.3.1   Purpose of Forensics Tools

Recommended standards for legally acceptable procedures for using forensic software for law enforcement purposes have been published by the International Association of Computer Investigative Specialists (IACIS).

Forensics tools must do three things:

1. Obtain an exact copy of the original magnetic media to be investigated, without altering the original in any way.
2. Do a query-like search of the copy.
3. Ensure that the processes and procedures used can stand up to scrutiny by the opposition's legal team. (For an overview of the process, see "Discovery of Computer Data" at http://wings.buffalo .edu/Complaw/CompLawPapers/printup.html.)

3.3.2   Commonly Used Forensics Software

Most computer forensics tools are for Windows®-based platforms, simply because most computers today utilize Windows.

The main programs used, and a brief critique of each, are listed here.

- **Byte Back** by Tech Assist, Inc., http://www.toolsthatwork.com/. Copies IDE drives effectively but seems to have problems with SCSI drives.
- **Encase** Version 2.08 by Guidance Software, http://www.guidance-software.com/. A popular suite of computer forensics products that is reasonably self-contained and complete and has its own graphical user interface. It is reportedly the tool of choice in law enforcement at the local and state levels in the United States, because of its ease of use and effectiveness. It has no option to use "direct access" on IDE drives. In tests it failed to image all of the sectors on some SCSI drives, according to http://www.scmagazine.com/scmagazine/ 2000_09/survey /products_01.html. Also, it does not allow image to

tape or disk-to-disk copy. Even so, it is one of the most widely used software programs by U.S. law enforcement.

- **Expert Witness** by ASR Data, http://www.asrdata.com/. See comments for Encase; this is a similar product by a competing provider. Initially made for the Macintosh OS.

- **Drivespy** by Digital Intelligence, http://www.digitalintel.com/.

Software for making legally acceptable copies of disks on which all analysis is made includes:

- **Safeback** Version 2.0 by NTI (New Technologies Inc.), http://www. sydex.com/sydex.html; http://www.forensics-intl.com/. Considered a classic in copying disks, but was reported not to have been able to image all sectors of some SCSI drives (e.g., Seagate ST3450N). Provides mirror-image backup of hard disks and diskettes; can image to tape. Also contains numerous other computer forensics utilities.

- **Linux "dd"** Version 6.1. Free. Effectively images IDE and SCSI drives. Can copy images to another drive or tape. Requires considerable skill on the part of the user because of the Unix operating system.

Lesser-known computer forensics software includes:

- **IP-Filter.** Uses "fuzzy logic" concepts to automatically identify patterns of e-mail addresses and URLs. By NTI (New Technologies Inc.), Gresham, Oregon, 503-661-6912. Considered a world leader in forensic computer operations, training, and software. Founded in 1996 by Michael R. Anderson (formerly with the IRS). http://www.secure-data.com/.

- **Drive Image Pro** Version 3.0 by PowerQuest Corp., http://www.power-quest.com. Unable to handle drives without a valid partition table. This is a serious handicap in computer forensics.

- **Norton Ghost 2000** Personal Edition by Symantec, http:// www.symantec.com/. This is primarily intended to allow users to copy their own drives for archival and backup purposes. Effectively copies both SCSI and IDE drives, but cannot copy a drive's image to tape. As a laptop backup tool it is not effective, because—assuming that one does not physically remove the internal drive—a laptop can only be imaged to another drive connected to the PCMCIA or USB ports, neither of which are supported by the software since it does not have DOS drivers for PCMCIA or USB. Also, it cannot handle drives with damaged partitions.

- **Filter-I.** Cleans binary information for further processing to examine plain text lurking in slack (portion between end of file and end of cluster) and in unallocated space and swap files.

- **Text Search Plus.** To keyword search through reams of data uncovered with Filter-I and IP-Filter.

- **Norton Disk Edit** by Symantec. Used mostly to piece forensically extracted data together.

- **Data Custodian** by Electronic Evidence Discovery, Inc., http://www.eedinc.com/.

- **Anadisk** by Sydex Corporation, Eugene, Oregon. Rebuilds magnetic traces of data from damaged disks, sector by sector.

- **QuickViewPlus** by Verify Inc., Sunnyvale, California. To view graphics.

- From the Federal Law Enforcement Training Center (FLETC): Custom software for computer forensics by Steve Choy and Bill Haynes.

- **DIBS (Disk Imaging Backup System).** Introduced into the United States by London-based Lee and Allen Computer Forensic Investigations.

- **Recover98** Version 2.5 by Phoenix Software POC: Robert Burns. Allows recovery of forensic information in Windows 95, 98, NT4.0, and NT5 (beta). Compatible with SCSI, RAID, IDE, and removable media. FAT12, 16, 32, and NTFS.

- **Financial Crime Investigator,** computer forensic tool. Anthem Corp., 12020 Sunrise Valley, Suite 200, Reston, Virginia (703-620-1212). Reportedly the first program of its kind to use "expert systems" technology.

- **EMD (Electronic Media Discovery).** Dockery Associates, LLC, http://www.finder.com/medical.html.

- **PERU** (portable evidence recovery unit), by Computer Forensics Company, London, England, with offices in New York and Hong Kong. Used in numerous prosecutions by British police units.

- Custom Computer Forensics Software Tools. Per-Se Technologies (a unit of Atlanta-based Medaphis Corporation). POC: Lewis Larson, managing director of Secure Solutions.

- Access Data Systems' (a Utah company) software for breaking the password protection of some commercial-application-generated files. See http://www.accessdata.com/. Specifically for PKZip, Win-Zip, Word, Excel, WordPerfect, Lotus1-2-3, Paradox, Q&A, -Pro, Ami Pro, Approach, QuickBooks, Act!, Pro Write, Access, Word Pro, DataPerfect, dBase, Symphony, Outlook, Express, MSMoney, Quicken, Scheduler+, Ascend, Netware, and NT server/ workstation.

- **SnapBack DatArrest** Version 4.12 by Columbia Data Products. Its strength is in handling SCSI drives. Has no option for writing disk images to hard drives and is reported to be constrained by BIOS on IDE drives.

- **Crak Software,** http://www.crak.com/. Another maker of software for cracking password-protected documents generated by some popular commercial software.

- **AFS (Authentec Forensic Software)**. By Authentec International Co.

- **Recover98** Version 3.1.2. Allows the recovery of files from magnetic media, even with a corrupted file system or virus. From LC Technology International, Inc., http://www.lc-tech.com/.

- **Recover98** Express Version 1.1.5. Allows one to quickly undelete files, even those that have even been removed from the Recycle Bin. (For Win95/98.)

- **RecoverNT** Version 3.1. Intended to recover files from a hard drive, even after the disk has been formatted. (For Win 95/98/NT/2000.)

3.3.3 Specialized Forensics Tools for Unix Systems

One commonly used set of free forensics tools for Unix is The Coroner's Toolkit (TCT), available from http://www.fish.com/tct/ and from http://www.porcupine.org/forensics/. It can also be used for a small amount of data collection and analysis from non-Unix magnetic media. It runs under:

- FreeBSD2-4*
- OpenBSD 2*
- BSD/OS2-3*

- SunOS 4-5*
- Linux 2*

A mailing list on TCT can be joined by sending a message to majordomo @porcupine.org with the phrase "subscribe tct-users" (without the quotes) in the main body of the message.

An excellent technical introduction to Unix forensics is Dan and Wietse's "Forensic Computer Analysis: An Introduction," available at http://www.porcupine.org/forensics/column.html.

3.4 Administrative Limitations of Law Enforcement

Information technology has been advancing at an unprecedented rate. Not surprisingly, law enforcement has been left behind, especially at the local (as opposed to national) level, for the following reasons:

- When budgetary constraints require that a choice be made between acquiring or upgrading a capability in computer forensics and buying another patrol car, most local police departments choose the latter.

- The demand for information technology experts is such that salaries in the private sector far exceed those in government; this has resulted in a "brain drain" from government, and the trend is unlikely to change in the foreseeable future.

- Effective countermeasures that negate computer forensics can readily be used by individuals involved in serious offenses, such as organized crime, narcotics trafficking, and terrorism. This leaves only the suspected perpetrators of less far-reaching crimes as being viable targets of computer forensics.

- Internet activity, which has roughly doubled every year for the last decade, is now so vast that identifying "suspect" activity in an ocean of trivia is, realistically, quite difficult and requires resources that exceed the limitations of most law enforcement organizations.

- The transnational nature of the Internet makes the identification and prosecution of Internet-based crime a daunting prospect that is usually beyond the scope and jurisdiction of any local law enforcement organization.

Selected Bibliography

Bentley, J., *Programming Pearls*, Reading, MA: Addison-Wesley, 1999.

Garfinkle, S., et al., *Practical Unix and Internet Security*, Sebastopol, CA: O'Reilly and Associates, 1996.

McKemmish, R., "Forensic Computing," Donald MacKay Churchill Fellowship Report, 1998, http://www.aic.gov.au/publications.

McVoy, L. W., and S. R. Kleiman, "Extent-Like Performance from a Unix File System," *USENIX*, Winter 1991.

Stoll, C., *The Cuckoo's Egg: Tracking a Spy Through the Maze of Computers Espionage*, New York: Pocket Books, 1990.

4

Where Incriminating Data Is Stored and How It Gets There

4.1 When Deleting Does Not Delete

4.1.1 General

Our computers' hard disks contain a mirror of our lives. E-mail, love letters, tax returns, and privileged communications with our lawyer are all saved in our computer, for our benefit and for the benefit of a computer forensics investigator.

To begin with, even if one went to the heroic measures needed to make a sensitive file truly disappear from magnetic media, there is a high likelihood that copies and earlier versions of that file exist in numerous other places; these copies can have unrecognizable names, or names that are invisible in the normal default directory lists. To make things worse, chances are that there will be fragments of earlier copies of such sensitive files scattered all over one's magnetic media.

If one is using Windows rather than DOS, one pays a high security price for the convenience of a graphical user interface. Unbeknownst to the user, most Windows-based applications create temporary files on the hard disk at unadvertised locations and using unrecognizable names, so that—should the computer "crash" for any reason, such as a power failure—the user will not lose files that he or she worked so laboriously to create. Since Windows and its application software are not clairvoyant and cannot tell whether or not a computer will crash, they usually create and save such temporary files "for good measure"; if the computer does not crash—as is typically the case—these temporary files remain in one's computer.

At a minimum, a security-conscious user should take the following preliminary precautions in Windows-based platforms:

1. Find (by experimenting) the actual location (folder name) where your particular software saves temporary files. If the software allows you the option, change it to another folder in a RAM disk (see Sections 9.1.1–9.1.4 on enhancing the security of Windows installations through the use of RAM disks). This way, the temporary file will not be written on the hard disk; this is not enough, however; one must still worry about the "swap file," discussed in detail in Section 4.2.3.

2. Disable "allow background saves" and "save auto-recovery info," if possible in Microsoft Word. This can be done using Tools/Options/Save.

3. Disable the "allow fast save" option. The reason for this is as follows: In order to reduce the time it takes to save a file that one is working on, every time one pushes the "save" button, Microsoft Word merely appends the changes to the originally saved document. A savvy recipient of this saved document (in the form of a floppy disk or an electronic attachment to an e-mail) will have the benefit not only of the last version of the file but also of all the interim versions, which the creator of the document usually does not want to share.

4. Do not "delete" a file using the normal DOS or Windows command, because that makes it very hard to find its remnants so as to remove it securely in the manner described later in this section.

5. Use "save as" rather than "save." If the latest version of a file by any one name is shorter than the previous version, then the "extra" data from the previous version will stay in the last "cluster" used by that file when it was saved (between the "end of file" of the new, shorter file and the "end of cluster" of the old, longer file). If you use "save as" with a different name each time (such as "File1," "File2," etc.), then that problem won't come up and you can securely delete all of these individual files later on.

The point being made is that secure deletion of any one file is not a simple proposition; it must be viewed only as part of the secure cleanup of an entire disk and never as a secure removal of a single file (the latest copy).

But let us assume that, somehow, one "feels confident" that the only file that needs to be deleted has been identified and that the issue is how to make it disappear. (Disappear from whose eyes? The nosy maid's? The computer hacker's? The computer forensics firm's? The eyes of someone even more sophisticated? This issue will be discussed later in Part II.)

For starters, what must disappear is not just the file itself but all information about the file, such as its name (which was hopefully chosen with some care so as to be nondescript and not incriminating in itself) and the date it was created, which are stored separately in a computer disk.

Using the "delete" command achieves absolutely nothing. It merely changes a single character in the disk's file-allocation table to indicate to the computer that the spaces taken by that file could be overwritten in the future if necessary; the file remains in the disk in its full glory. (If "delete" really worked, then the many versions of "undelete" would not, right?)

Using "format" does not remove sensitive files either, contrary to popular belief. All that "format" does is to write on the file-allocation table, which contains the 64,000-plus pointers to the exact locations of the clusters on the disk, where the various files are. It merely sets those pointers to zero. Even if one uses the "full" or long version of "format," the computer only tries to read each cluster to find if it should be marked in the file-allocation table as "bad"; the files themselves are not overwritten at all.[1]

It follows that, to remove a sensitive file (and its separately stored name and date stamp), one must overwrite it. Overwriting a known file is easy, assuming that there is only one copy of it with no temporary or other copies of it, and no evidence of it in the swap file. Removing the file name and its attributes is not.

4.1.2 Removing File Names and Attributes

A modern filing system, such as a log-structured file system (LFS), obtains its performance by writing new blocks of data at the end of a log and not by

---

1. So-called low-level formatting of a hard disk sets to zero all sector contents. Most IDE hard disk manufacturers do not provide a utility for doing this, only some SCSI hard disk manufacturers do. Low-level formatting of a hard disk will defeat software-based means of recovering data from such a disk, but may or may not defeat microscopic examination of the magnetic particles of a disk.

changing the old ones. This makes secure removal of the old logs extremely difficult. As an example, one freely available software program, PGP, which also claims to overwrite files, assumes incorrectly that the data can be simply overwritten through the operating system's file system; this is not the case a lot of the time.

Windows 95 and 98 create a new directory entry when renaming a file; both the new and the old name stay on the disk. Unlike Windows 3.1x and Windows NT, on Windows 95 and 98 the old directory entry is simply marked as being deleted and a new one is added. Going into DOS and renaming the old file will not solve the problem, because the Windows long name is not overwritten when the file is renamed.

This makes the secure removal of directory names of sensitive files quite a chore. The only way to remove a file name in Windows 95 and 98 requires the following steps:

1. Lock the drive so as to prevent any software from accessing it to change the file system entries.

2. Read the whole file of all file system entries into memory.

3. Clear the old and undesirable names from that file.

4. Overwrite that entire portion of the disk.

5. Write the modified file system from step 3 back onto disk.

6. Unlock the disk to enable normal access.

In short, secure file deletion in Windows platforms is a major exercise and can only be a part of a secure "wipe" of one's entire hard disk. Anything less than that is likely to leave discoverable electronic evidence behind.

Most individuals are not inclined to go through the process of doing this secure file removal manually. As a result, commercial and freely available software have become available that do secure file (and file name and attributes) removal.

Not all do what they claim to do. To begin with, it is almost pointless to depend on the many available software programs that place an icon on one's desktop that claims to "securely delete" whichever file one "drags and drops" into that icon.

Some software that claims to overwrite file names when a file is erased cannot be depended on because all it does is delete the file and then creates a large number of temporary files with random names into the directory in the hope that these new files will overwrite the one that is to be removed.

The following is a list of the various secure-file-deletion software that this author has experimented with; some of these software pieces have a different primary function (such as encryption, in PGP and ScramDisk's cases) but do offer "secure" file wiping as well.

- **DiskCleaner.** A user-friendly wiping software from ksolway @poboxes.com with a good help file tutorial. As can be seen in Figure 4.1, it attempts to clean a lot of errant information in one's magnetic media and its author has been very prompt in responding to e-mailed questions. This writer did not, however, have luck in wiping a swap file that was not in the default directory; file names were also not wiped but can be wiped by doing a disk defragmentation after the wiping.

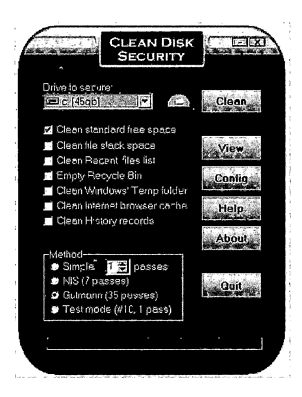

Figure 4.1 DiskCleaner wiping options. (Courtesy of Kevin Solway.)

- **BCWipe.** Seems to remove the file names when using the "delete directory" feature.

- **PGP.** Effectiveness depends on which version one is using. Generally unreliable in removing file names.

- **Eraser.** Wiping of the file name is unreliable when overwriting a file, but is reliable when it is part of the process of wiping the entire free space of a disk. Eraser is this author's favorite disk-wiping software.

- **ScramDisk.** Fairly good in cleaning after its own messes but not as a general cleaning tool for other files' electronic trails.

- **Cyberscrub.** Appears to remove file names. There have been unsubstantiated allegations by a competitor (Evidence Eliminator) that this software product has intimate ties with law enforcement.

- **Evidence Eliminator.** Appears to successfully remove file names. Caution: There have been allegations that some bootleg copies pretend to function when in fact they do not. Also, it does not work as well in Windows 2000 unless the user does a lot of manual customizing with respect to it.

- AccessData's **SecureClean.** Appears to successfully remove file names. It is this author's second-favorite disk-wiping software. More bug-free than most. Figure 4.2 shows the intuitive and comprehensive interface.

- **Spytech Eradicator.** By Spytech software.

- **SCORCH.COM.** To be used instead of the DOS "del" command, and "SCOUR," available from http://www.bonaventura.free-online .co.uk/ for DOS-based wiping.

Software that successfully removes file names can only do so as part of an entire disk cleanup operation, which *must* include defragmenting a disk before and after the disk-wiping operation.

Given the various weaknesses of individual wiping software, one would be well advised to:

- Use two (or preferably more) different disk-wiping software in sequence.

- Defragment the disk before using any disk wiping as well as after. Defragmenting is *not* a substitute for, but an adjunct to, disk wiping.

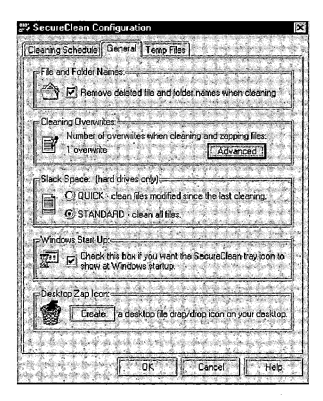

Figure 4.2 AccessData's SecureClean. (Courtesy of AccessData Corp.)

- Use "EnCase" to double check if a file that is supposed to have been removed has in fact been removed along with all references to it.

A more complete list of software is available from http://www.fortune-city.com/skyscraper/true/882/Comparison_Shredders.htm and includes information about shredders' other qualities (or lack thereof), such as availability and pricing.

Some software available for disk wiping has not been specifically evaluated. This includes:

- **Shredder** 2.0, by Strafor Systems;

- **Cover Your Tracks** 3.0, by FatFree Software http://www.ffsoftware.com/;

- **Shiva, Destroyer of Files,** by Isis Software http://isis-software.com/;
- **Nuker,** by Genio.

Since disk cleaning takes many hours, it is self-evident that a security-conscious user cannot apply it against an imminent threat. If one is in such an environment (e.g., a totalitarian regime), one must do disk cleaning on a *very* regular basis, in the assumption that the door could be broken down by an intruder at any time.

4.1.3   Magnetic Microscopic Examination of Disks

The best reference on Class 2 and 3 attacks (explained below) is a somewhat dated paper (1996) http://www.cs.auckland.ac.nz/~pgut001/secure_del. html by Peter Gutmann of the Department of Computer Science of the University of Auckland, pgut001@cs.auckland.ac.nz, titled "Secure Deletion of Data from Magnetic and Solid State Memory." An excellent collection of stunning photographs of microscopic remnants of "erased" magnetic recordings can be found at Digital Instruments' Web site http://www.di.com/.

In general, the forensic analysis of magnetic media using conventional microscopy is becoming increasingly difficult because of the ever-increasing density of magnetic storage in off-the-shelf commercial media in use today by practically all computers. Today's densities approach 1 gigabit per square inch, which means that the intrinsic size of magnetic features is smaller than the wavelength of even blue light. That is why a new technique, magnetic force microscopy (MFM), which uses the power of scanning probe microscopy, is needed to do forensic analysis on such media. This technique allows one to "see" features as small as 50 nanometers (1 nanometer is 0.000000001 meter).

Albert Bell Isle of Cerberus Systems identifies three classes of computer forensic threats to files. Class 1 attacks use forensic software only. They can be defeated by disk overwriting of:

- All copies of a file (including fragments of it);
- The entire file-allocation table and names files and their attributes;
- The swap file.

Class 2 attacks use special amplifiers and signal processing and can recover with variable degrees of success some overwritten files. The degree of success depends on specifics, such as how many times a file has been over-written and with what data patterns, the physics of the magnetic media in question, and so on.

Class 3 attacks use MFM; they are expensive and can potentially get around many kinds of overwriting. Basically, they make a magnetic duplicate of the disk being investigated, and a detailed analysis is then made on this duplicate. This technique can work without damaging the protective coating of the surface of the hard disk being investigated and is very effective. According to Gutman, "[E]ven for a relatively inexperienced user the time to start getting images of the data on a drive platter is about 5 minutes. To start getting useful images of a particular track requires more than a passing knowledge of disk formats, but these are well documented, and once the correct location on the platter is found a single image would take approximately 2–10 minutes depending on the skill of the operator and the resolution required. With one of the more expensive MFM's it is possible to automate a collection sequence and theoretically possible to collect an image of the entire disk by changing the MFM controller software."

The latest variant uses magnetic force scanning tunneling microscopy (STM); it is more sensitive and may damage the surface of the disk being investigated. According to Gutman, "there [were, as of 1996], from manufacturers sales figures, several thousand STMs in use in the field, some of which have special features for analyzing disk drive platters, such as the vacuum chucks for standard disk drive platters along with specialized modes of operation for magnetic media analysis. These STMs can be used with sophisticated programmable controllers and analysis software to allow automation of the data recovery process. If commercially available STMs are considered too expensive, it is possible to build a reasonably capable STM for about $1,400, using a PC as a controller." There is also a new patent on Magnetic Disk Erasers in Japan (see http://www.research.ibm.com/journal/rd/445/patents.html).

From the attackers' perspective, an assessment is likely to be made as to the possibility of using any less expensive alternate ways of obtaining the same data, such as those discussed in Chapters 5 and 6.

4.2   Places Where "Evidence" Can Hide

Unfortunately (for the privacy-conscious professional), sensitive material can hide in far too many places, all of which must be considered. For an understanding of where and why, some minimal technical background is necessary.

4.2.1   Cluster Tips, or Slack

Whereas LP music records of yesteryear stored the music in a single long, spaghetti-like grove, computer disks are divided into a large number of completely separate bins that information is stored in. At the risk of oversimplifying the issue, each such bin is called a "cluster" (because it consists of a bunch of smaller bins called "sectors," but that is irrelevant for the purposes of this discussion).

The size of each bin (that is, how much data can fit into each cluster) depends on both the total capacity of the disk and on the operating system being used (that is, whether it is DOS, Windows 95, Windows 98, or Windows NT), and also on what each user has selected, in cases where there is a choice. The size of each such cluster can vary from 256 bytes (a byte is essentially one alphabetical symbol or number) all the way up to over 65,536 bytes (always a "power of 2," i.e., 2 multiplied times itself).

Both DOS and all versions of Windows share one rule: They will not allow any one such cluster to have data from more than a single file (a "file" can be a piece of software, a user-created document, or an image). Of course, a file may well require numerous clusters; as an example, let us assume that the cluster size is 512 bytes and that a file takes 768 bytes; this will require one and a half clusters. It is important to understand what happens to the remaining half cluster.

Windows will never write less than one clusterful of data onto a cluster; if it only needs to write half of it, it will mark the end of where that file ends (the "end of file" mark) and fill the rest of the cluster with whatever data happens to be floating about in portions of the computer's electronic memory (random access memory, or RAM).

The security nightmare that results is obvious: Passwords that were manually typed and went to RAM, never intended to be immortalized for posterity in one's disk, may well end up in this "dead space" between the "end of file" and "end of cluster" and stay there for the benefit of whoever can retrieve that information.

The larger the cluster size, the bigger the problem. If a cluster is 32,768 bytes big and it is used to save a puny file of, say, 1,000 bytes, then there will be some 31,768 bytes of whatever happened to be in RAM memory at that instant ending up being placed on the disk. This space between end of file and end of cluster is known as "cluster tips," or "slack" in the computer forensics trade. It is one of the most productive areas of a computer forensics investigation of a computer.

Indeed, there is very little, if anything, that a computer user can do to prevent sensitive data from getting placed on one's hard disk in the slack. About all one can do is to use special software (available freely worldwide, as well as commercially) to "erase" any and all data placed on a disk.

4.2.2   Free Space

As we have discussed, when a computer file is deleted using the normal "delete" command in DOS or the "Trash bin" in Windows, the file is in fact not deleted at all. All that happens is that the portion of the disk that keeps a record of which file is where makes a note of the fact that this particular file is no longer desired and that the space that it occupies on the disk could be taken in the future by other files if necessary.

In the course of using a disk, whether a hard disk or the humble floppy disk or most any other magnetic storage media, one ends up having an entity with a lot of ostensibly deleted information that is very much present for the benefit of a computer forensics investigator. This "free space" is a goldmine of information for the forensics investigator and a major headache for the computer user. About the only way to get rid of those files is to do the electronic equivalent of erasing them, which is done by overwriting those clusters with assorted patterns of nonsense data.

But even that is not enough. The name of the thusly "erased" file is stored in a different location of one's disk; if the name is incriminating (say, "freedom.doc" in a totalitarian regime), the user can end up in trouble if the disk is analyzed by a forensics investigator. Changing the name of the file (from "freedom.doc" to "long_live_the_leader.doc") is not enough, either. As we have stated, computers are a forensics investigator's dream because, in addition to the files themselves, they contain data about the data. Such data could include when the file was created, when it was modified, what software was used, and so on. The security-conscious user must see to it that this data about the data is also erased.

4.2.3   The Swap File

The swap file is an important topic in itself and is treated fully in Section 4.3. In the way of a summary, it is the portion of a hard disk that Windows uses for temporary storage of data that would normally be stored in the volatile RAM but does not fit there. As such, this file can include just about anything, specifically including passwords that were never intended to end up on a hard disk, drafts that were never saved to disk, and so on. The more RAM one has, the less one needs a swap file, Microsoft admonitions to the contrary notwithstanding. If one has enough RAM, one does not need any swap file at all; fortunately, one can easily set the swap file size to zero in such a case.

Removing the swap file is not much different from removing any file. One should find it and wipe it (i.e., overwrite it a number of times). Its location can be anywhere one wants it to be and is called "win386.swp" in Windows 95/98 for historical reasons. Overwriting it cannot be done from within Windows. One can boot, for example, from DOS, find it, and use a good overwriting utility to wipe it.

4.2.4   Spool and Temporary Files

As files are sent by a user to the printer, they are usually "spooled" to a queue (a file created for the occasion on one's hard disk). As soon as they are printed, they are "deleted" from this queue, which means that they remain in the hard disk in that spool file for a forensics investigator to find until and unless that disk space is overwritten intentionally or in the normal course of storing other files on the hard disk.

4.2.5   Application-Software-Created History Files

Many software applications have the habit of creating a history file of what a user has done with that application. A typical example is the hugely popular Netscape Navigator/Communicator, which creates a file called "netscape.hst"; interestingly, this file:

- Is not needed by anything and can be safely deleted (at which point Navigator/Communicator will create a new one from that point in time on, unless active measures are taken by the user to prevent this—see Chapters 10 through 14);

- Records everything a user has done with Netscape Navigator/Communicator on-line or off-line since the software was installed;

- Is mildly encrypted so that the average user is kept in the blind as to its function.

Microsoft system software and applications have comparable tendencies to create assorted history files. Unless the user knows their names and locations, chances are that they are not deleted or modified. Even some security-related application software, such as the ConSeal personal firewall, creates a history file showing the dates and times for every time a user went on-line with that software; there is no option to preclude this from happening; the user must manually overwrite it.

4.2.6 Data in the Registry Files

The registry file is an important topic in itself and is discussed in Section 4.4.

4.2.7 Data from Sloppy Use of Personal Encryption Software

The installation ritual of most application software involves numerous in-between steps, such as decompression, creation of temporary files, and so on, all of which are stored in a temporary folder that is often specific to each such software application. Once installed, these files are sometimes deleted (made invisible in the directory), but often they are not. In all cases, they are left behind for the benefit of the forensics investigator, unless the user takes active steps to overwrite all such files. In fact, the ones left behind undeleted are the worst offenders, in the sense that most users assume that what is left behind is still needed by the newly installed application, and such users will not remove them either securely or otherwise.

4.2.8 CMOS Memory

When a computer is first turned on, it has no idea what to do with itself; it does not know if it has magnetic media, let alone anything about the magnetic media, it does not know the date or time, it does not know how much memory (RAM) it has, it does not know whether to try to go to a hard disk first or to a floppy or to other media (such as CD-ROMs), and so on. All this information has to be stored *somewhere* other than a disk (which the computer initially does not even know if it has or where it is), or the user would have to enter it manually every time. CMOS (complementary metal oxide semiconductor) memory is an electronic memory that consumes very little power so that it can survive for many years with just a small external battery, even if the computer is unplugged. CMOS memory also stores any "bootup passwords" that some users enable. In theory, unless an aspiring user knows the magic password selected by the authorized user, he or she will not be able to get past this step. In practice, one can remove the battery keeping the information in CMOS alive, whereupon, when the computer is turned on, the unauthorized user will be asked to enter his or her own choice of a new password (in addition to manually having to enter the system-related data, which can be done within a few minutes).

Additionally, many computer manufacturers, tired of users forgetting their CMOS passwords and asking for technical support, have provided for "backdoor entry" passwords that users can use to gain access to the respective manufacturers' computers. Needless to say, these backdoor keys have been posted on the Internet for anyone who wants them (see Section 14.6).

4.3 The Swap File

4.3.1 General

The swap file (or "paging file," also known as "virtual memory") is a major source of forensic information for a computer investigator. To an individual interested in maintaining the privacy of his or her computer files (e.g., an attorney with clients' privileged files, a physician with patients' confidential medical data, a businessman whose laptop contains his company's proprietary designs), it is a relatively easy threat to remove, although most users are only vaguely aware of it.

Basically, the swap file is a large space on a hard disk (typically a few hundred megabytes; i.e., a few hundred million alphabetical letters' worth), where Windows places anything that currently resides in RAM memory (the electronic memory that "evaporates" when the power is turned off, as opposed to disk memory, which stays) that it does not need at any particular instant, so as to make room in memory for other data that is needed. An instant later, different data may be needed in memory, and Windows will juggle what is in RAM and in the swap disk file so that it has in RAM memory what it needs at any particular moment. This way, a user with limited physical memory (RAM) can "run" more with less such memory.

From the perspective of the security-conscious reader, this file is an unmitigated disaster, because it can end up including just about anything, such as passwords typed on a keyboard and never intended to be stored on disk, copies of sensitive files, and so on. Even if a user securely deletes all evidence of a sensitive file (see Chapters 8 through 14), the swap file—if not specifically wiped—may well contain a copy of that same file or portions of it.

The amount of space allocated to the swap file on a disk is determined by Windows itself (in the default situation), but can be altered by the individual user. One would reasonably think that the more physical RAM memory one has, the less swap file size is needed; amusingly, Windows feels otherwise and assigns more swap file space when one has more RAM.

One can specify exactly how much swap file space one wishes to have (if any). Go to Start/Settings/ControlPanel/System/Performance/Virtual Memory and specify what amount one desires, if any. One can ignore admonitions by Windows about allowing Windows alone to decide this. In general, one would be well advised to have as much RAM memory as possible (at least 128 MB for Win3.1x; at least 256 MB for Win95/98/NT/2000), and to completely disable any virtual memory. Doing so still leaves the hard disk with the last version of the swap file (called win386.swp). This must be securely removed. If one has elected to allow numerous programs to run in the background (e.g., virus checkers, software firewalls), then one's RAM requirements can exceed the minimums suggested above; a good way to find just how much RAM one is actually using under normal circumstances is to run a small utility called "SWAPMON" by Gary Calpo of Flip Tech International, available on the Internet at http://www.pinoyware.com/swapmon/index.shtml.

Even if one elects to have some disk space allocated to the swap file (not a good idea from a security perspective, as per above), it is strongly recommended that the user and not Windows (which is the default setting) fix the amount, despite admonitions to the contrary by Windows. This is so because it is far easier for security utilities that "wipe clean" the swap file to do this on a fixed-size swap file than on one whose size changes all the time. The reason for this is obvious: If the size of the swap file is fixed, then wiping it (that is, overwriting it) is straightforward; if its size changes all the time, then it is quite possible that its last size is smaller than its previous size; wiping the smaller-size swap file will leave evidence in the disk space that accommodates the difference between the last swap file and the previous one untouched and available to any forensics investigator.

The procedure for setting a fixed swap file is similar to that shown below for setting no swap file: The user simply selects the same value for minimum and maximum size of the swap file.

4.3.2   Securely Wiping the Swap File

Securely wiping the swap file can *only* be done from DOS, never from within Windows. When Windows is started, it opens up the swap file with exclusive access and prevents any other application from accessing it, so as to prevent the system from crashing.

Do not trust any wiping software that runs under Windows and claims to wipe the swap file; many such programs try to do this by allocating very large amounts of memory and hoping that the operating system will write it to the disk, thereby—hopefully—overwriting the swap file; this is unacceptably insecure. Some well-written disk-wiping files, however, wipe the swap file well because they "drop down" to DOS before wiping the swap file. An example of this is Access Data Corporation's Secure Clean.

Since no one wiping program can be entirely trusted, a security-conscious user is well advised to use two different such programs in tandem, preferably one of them from within DOS. Possibilities for wiping the swap file from DOS include:

1. Using a DOS version of pgp, type

   pgp -w win386.swp

2. Using RealDelete (available from http://www.bonaventura.free-online.co.uk/realdelete/), type

   realdel [win386.swp] /per /garb

   The brackets are needed to wipe a file as a foreground task and the additional switches select personal security level—just one over-write in this case—and a random data overwrite.

3. Using Scribble, type

   SCRIBBLE /A/K c:\windows\win386.swp

   The /K switch allows the file to remain as an entity after it is wiped clean.

Since a swap file is typically a few hundred megabytes long, this wiping will take a few minutes to complete.

Windows NT allows one to delete and overwrite with zeros the swap file automatically as part of a shutdown. According to Microsoft's own Resource Kit, one must edit the registry[2] (type regedit at the "run" blank space) and go to:

HKEY_LOCAL_MACHINE\System
\CurrentControlSet

\Control
\Session Manager
\Memory Management
ClearPageFileAtShutdown REG_DWORD
Range 0 or 1
Default 0
Set it to 1.

Note that Windows NT will not overwrite the entire swap file, because some of it is being used by NT. To overwrite the entire file one must do so outside Windows (whether NT or any other version). This can be done manually or through the use disk-wipe software both commercially and freely available. (See Chapters 9 through 12.)

Do not change the size of the swap file by editing the Registry. To create a new paging file or to change the size, go to Control Panel/Performance/Virtual Memory/Change.

4.3.3   One Refinement for Windows 98

Windows 98 manages memory and virtual memory (i.e., the swap file) in a far more advanced manner than Windows 95. As an example, Windows 98 tends to write the swap file on the disk when it is not really needed, merely in anticipation of what might be needed; this is done during times when there is relatively little computing activity going on.[3]

The "tweak" needed to reduce such swap file activity is to add the following line to the [386Enh] portion of the SYSTEM.INI file (which is in the Windows subdirectory):

ConservativeSwapfileUsage=1

To do this, use any text editor to edit the SYSTEM.INI file, find the [386Enh] portion of it, and insert the above line.

---

2. Caution: Back up the registry before doing any editing. How to do this depends on which version of Windows one is using. For Windows 95/98, for example, one can do this with Start/Run SCANREGW. In Windows NT, one can create an emergency backup disk with Start/Run RDISK /S. See Section 7.3 for details.

3. For the technically curious, this is the Page_File-Call_Async_Manager feature, so as to give the appearance of faster performance.

This enhancement is recommended only for Windows 98 systems that have at least 128 MB of RAM, which is highly recommended both for security and for computational efficiency.

4.4 The Registry

4.4.1 Why the Registry Is a Major Source of Forensics Evidence

The user of Windows wants the computer to remember such things as which little icons one wants on the screen and where, what resolution monitor one is using, if a modem is connected to the computer and on which port, and so on. It would be very annoying and time consuming to have to enter such information every time one turned on one's computer.

In the Windows 3.1x days (Windows 3.1, 3.11, and Windows for Workgroups), all this information was stored in two easily accessible and readable files: WIN.INI and SYSTEM.INI. These files were (and are) readily readable and editable with any text editor.[4]

With Windows 95/98/NT, these two files were replaced by what seems like a bottomless pit full of data, which is hard to read and much harder to edit, called the registry. There is no file called "registry" per se. Instead, the registry is the collective name for two very unique files called USER.DAT and SYSTEM.DAT, with the former being the biggest threat. What is unique about them is the following:

1. To even view them, one needs special software (graciously provided by Microsoft) called REGEDIT or (in the case if Windows NT, which also accepts REGEDIT) REGEDT32; the latter does not recognize all the data types that REGEDIT does.

2. What one sees on these files is not what is there. Entries that have been removed with the above two software pieces are, in fact, not removed at all. Appearances notwithstanding, they are very much there, but have merely been marked as "no longer current"; yet a forensics investigator will find them extremely easily. Entries that have been edited out by REGEDIT do not get removed.[5]

3. Even if one does, in fact, remove offending entries in the registry (using techniques to be presented below), the slate is not wiped

---

4. If one uses a word processor for this function, one should make sure that the edited end results are saved as "text only" and not as formatted documents.

clean; a forensics investigator can still easily find those entries. This is so because Windows takes it upon itself to store backup copies of the registry, "just in case" the computer's registry is corrupted and needs to be restored from a known working version (such as the backup copy). Removing the backup copies is doable but not recommended because Windows does, in fact, crash for many reasons, and a working copy of the registry is a godsend, without which one would most likely have to reinstall everything on the affected hard disk, Windows and applications software, from scratch. For this reason it is extremely important to always have around a (nonincriminating) fully functioning copy of the registry.

4. Windows and many applications software pieces take it upon themselves to store far, far more in the registry than any privacy-minded person would ever want. This includes but is not limited to:

   a. One's name, address, company affiliation, phone number, and so on (entered by an unsuspecting individual when installing Windows and/or many application software pieces);

   b. What has been browsed on the Internet recently (if Microsoft's Internet Explorer is used as a Web browser), regardless of who used that computer to do the browsing;

   c. Who uses the computer and what each user's preferences are;

   d. All the software that has ever been installed and what the user did with each (most software programs that one "uninstalls" do not bother to remove their paper trails);

   e. Serial numbers and passwords, in many cases, of applications software;

   f. Traces of messages downloaded from Usenet newsgroups (if one lives in a totalitarian regime and patronizes newsgroups dealing with freedom and equal rights, one may not want "evidence" of that to remain in the computer);

---

5. They are not removed until the registry becomes as large as 500 KB, which comprises a vast amount of ostensibly removed sensitive information, or until one types REGEDIT/ OPT from within DOS. This is controlled through the line "Optimize=1" in the scan-reg.ini file in one's subdirectory. The reason that REGEDIT does not actually remove entries and compress the registry (even though it pretends that it does) is that the registry is too long; it would take some time for Windows to compress it to fill the hole every time an entry in it is removed.

g. Plaintext passwords in files that were supposed to be encrypted; look in content.ie5 and history.ie5.

Any and all of this information can be retrieved not only by a forensics examiner but also by any half-decent hacker while a user is on-line, on the Internet or any other network (unless special precautions such as those discussed in Chapters 10 through 14 have been taken). This is clearly unacceptable.

4.4.2   Where Private Information Hides in the Registry

As previously stated, the registry consists of two key files: USER.DAT and SYSTEM.DAT. USER.DAT contains all sorts of personal information, as can be easily verified, usually to one's shock, by opening it with Notepad or Wordpad. One can then do a "wildcard" search (meaning a search for any desired sequence of letters) for whatever one wishes to exclude from there, such as personal letters and proprietary business topics. Do *not* edit this file with either Notepad or Wordpad.

Do not attempt to edit or "clean up" the registry unless you first:

- Back it up.
- Know how to restore it from such a backup, in case you inadvertently mess it up.

How to do this is spelled out in Section 4.4.3. In Windows 95/98, it is a good idea to run Registry Checker from the Startup/Programs/Accessories/System Tools menu before shutting down, to be alerted to any registry problems before shutting down.

4.4.3   Backing Up the Registry and Restoring a Corrupted One

4.4.3.1   Windows 95 (Except Win95a) and 98

Method 1

From within Windows, enter Start/Run scanregw. Alternately, from within DOS, one can type scanreg/backup. Neither is a particularly useful approach, however, because one cannot really see what is in the registry but is not visible through the standard registry editor REGEDIT.

Method 2

Since system.dat and user.dat are hidden system files, make them visible and editable by typing (from DOS)

attrib –s –h –r *.dat

in the subdirectory where they are.

Simple backup system.dat, user.dat, and index.dat by typing, for example:

copy system.dat system.dax2
copy user.dat user.da2
copy index.dat index.da2

4.4.3.2   Windows NT

Start/Run rdisk/s. This will ask for a floppy disk to be inserted, onto which the computer will save the entire Windows NT registry.

Restoring the registry from the disk is done by following the standard Windows NT restore process (see Windows NT documentation), which amounts to starting a reinstallation but opting for a registry restoration when the option is offered.

4.4.4   Cleaning Sensitive Data from the Registry

Do *not* try to edit the registry file "as is" with any text editor or even hex editor, because of the high likelihood of corrupting it. Instead follow the instructions here.

Method 1

1. Start/Run regedit.
2. Search for and remove any and all references to sensitive material, making sure not to remove default settings needed to run Windows. Specifically, the "secret file" that Media Player uses to store a list of recently played items is in

    HKEY_CURRENT_USERS\Software\Microsoft\MediaPlayer\
    Player\Recent\URLList

    Delete all values except "Default."

A related concern is information in the file index.dat. It, too, can be examined using Notepad or Wordpad.

The biggest concern may well be with the most recently used (MRU) list kept in the registry, which essentially records the latest batch of activities done on the computer. This has no socially redeeming value other than potentially entrapping the user. One should delete all values except those showing a "Default" as a value in each and every one of the following keys:

> HKEY_CURRENT_USER\Software\Microsoft\Windows\
> Current Version\Explorer\Doc Find Spec MRU

> HKEY_CURRENT_USER\Software\Microsoft\Windows\
> CurrentVersion\Explorer\FindComputerMRU

> HKEY_CURRENT_USER\Software\Microsoft\Windows\
> CurrentVersion\Explorer\PrnPortsMRU

> HKEY_CURRENT_USER\Software\Microsoft\Windows\
> CurrentVersion\Explorer\RunMRU

> HKEY_CURRENT_USER\Software\Microsoft\Windows\
> CurrentVersion\Explorer\StreamMRU

Not all of the above keys may exist in every computer. Again, do *not* delete the "Default" value. Also, do not remove any files that list all the folders in your disk drive; if you do, you won't really lose anything, but the settings/preferences will revert back to default settings.

3. Boot into DOS.

4. Type: regedit /e registry.txt. The "/e registry" suffix in this command exports the registry into a text file called registry as a single text file that one can use to see what is in the suspect registry and also to restore the registry if it gets inadvertently corrupted.

5. Look at the text file called registry with Wordpad or Notepad to ensure that nothing inappropriate remains there.

6. Now type: regedit /c registry.txt.

Restoring a registry file this way without editing it should remove references to files that were "edited out" (but not truly removed) with REGEDIT.

Method 2

To compact the registry in order to actually remove entries that have been edited out with REGEDIT, go to DOS first (by clicking on the "Command Prompt" icon in the Start/Programs list, or, better yet, by turning the computer off and booting into DOS) and type Scanreg/opt.

Scanreg/fix from within DOS should also clean up fragments in USER.DAT.

Caution: Windows maintains backup copies of the registry as user.da0, system.da0, user.da1, system.da1, and so on. Cleaning up the primary registry does not clean up these backups. It is not a good idea to delete these backups, just in case one has damaged the registry inadvertently and it has to be restored from a working backup.

After one has ascertained that the new cleaned-up registry works properly, then one can force backups of it as shown above. This still does not wipe the forensics slate clean, since deletion and overwriting do not usually remove what was there before. One must then go through the process of wiping the disk clean as shown in detail in Chapter 9, which includes overwriting the slack or cluster tips, the free space, and the file names.

This is all very tedious and, as a result, unlikely to be followed by most individuals on a regular basis. A convenient alternative is for one to use software available either commercially (such as the disingenuously named Evidence Eliminator from www.evidenceeliminator.com in the United Kingdom, or Window Washer from http://www.webroot.com/) or other

Figure 4.3 Easily customizable Window Washer. (Courtesy of Webroot Software, Inc.)

such software. Window Washer, in particular, is very convenient and self-explanatory to use; it allows for an extensive amount of customization and one can download numerous plug-ins at no additional cost that take care of cleaning after bits left behind by a large number of programs. Figure 4.3 conveys the flexibility of customizing this software.

Evidence Eliminator seems to have done the most thorough job of covering all of the bases, although there is a cloud of suspicion about it in connection with the allegation that, in the case of "blacklisted registration numbers" (the number that one enters to convert it from the "one month free trial" version to the paid version), it may pretend to do its advertised functions but in fact does not. While it may well be a very good program of this genre, some Usenet postings allegedly written by that company did a disservice to its reputation.

5

Specialized Forensics Techniques

5.1 Digital Watermarking

The ease with which digitized information can be distributed worldwide and on a massive scale through the Internet extends to copyrighted material, which brings up a host of legal and ethical issues. Any material, copyrighted or not, can be digitized, stored, and sent to the world today: music, text, photographs, images, speech, and so on.

Not surprisingly, owners of intellectual property and copyright holders take great offense at losing revenue and credit for their work. This book does not take sides as to who is right and who is wrong in such situations but limits itself to the technical facts. Some recent cases worth mentioning are:

- Napster and Gnutella software, allowing individuals to trade copyrighted music on-line. The former involves technology that required users to go through specific servers; the latter works on a direct one-on-one basis.
- DeCSS software, which allows individuals to break the (weak) encryption used by the Hollywood studios in DVD disks. As many may know by now, the U.S. courts ruled in favor of the Motion Picture Association of America (MPAA), which represented the Hollywood studios.

Unless some means can be found whereby a copy of a copyrighted item can be shown to be an illegal copy, effective prosecution is unlikely. Furthermore, the legal costs of prosecuting an individual for an item that would have cost $20 or so to buy are disproportionate, because it is very hard to prove where an unpaid-for copy came from[1]; as a result, there is hardly ever any such prosecution except against mass-production entities that make a business out of profiting from others' intellectual property.

Quite clearly, there is a growing need for "digital watermarking" technology that can:

- Show the origin of the work that was copied;

- Show that it is copyrighted and/or someone else's intellectual property, to preempt the "I didn't know" defense;

- Show, if possible, the exact pathway that the unauthorized copy took from the original authorized owner to the present unauthorized one, so that the correct individual(s) can be held responsible for the breach of trust.

A digital watermark has to be "robust," meaning that it should survive efforts to remove it. For example, if the work being protected is an image, the digital watermark should not be "washable" with the extensive image-enhancement operations that any user of an image-processing software, such as Adobe Photoshop, can do (such as cropping, resampling, filtering, color and contrast changes, and so on).

Technically, this is a tall order: Some image-saving formats (such as JPEG) are intentionally "lossy" in the sense that they obviously remove a lot of "information" from an image, massively reducing the size of the digital file; to their credit, they do so with an impressively low reduction in the visual appeal of the image.

A similar situation exists with music files: MP3 reduces the amount of digital storage required without a (to most of us) perceptible difference in quality. Asking that a digital watermark (1) be preserved despite such drastic

---

1. The author intentionally avoids the word "piracy," a term that evokes images of drunken savages with swords, roaming the high seas, attacking peace-loving vessels, plundering, raping, and killing. The use of the term to characterize a teenager's possession of an unpaid-for copy of a computer game was an ingenious act of posturing by self-serving software makers who wanted to capitalize on the negative connotations of the word. "Unauthorized copy" is a far more accurate term

reductions in the digital storage requirements (and hence the information content) of a digital file and (2) be imperceptible to our ears and eyes so that the sound file or image appeals to our senses, is very difficult.

The technology behind digital watermarking is not different from that of steganography, used to hide the mere existence of messages, which is discussed at length in Section 14.5.

The two classes of techniques used amount to:

1. Modifying part of the file [e.g., changing the least significant bit of some pixels (picture elements) or sound files];

2. Modifying the entire file by spreading the digital watermark (or steganographically hidden message) over the entire file.

Some of the most sophisticated digital watermarks involve two such marks: the first one that is simple to spot and remove, whose purpose is to mislead a transgressor into thinking that "the" watermark has been removed; and a second one that is much harder to identify, intended to catch the transgressor.

Commercial digital watermarking products are offered by the following companies, among others:

- Aliroo, http://www.aliroo.com/;

- ICE Company, http://www.digital-watermark.com/;

- Digimarc, http://www.digimarc.com/;

- Fraunhofer Institute for Computer Graphics, http://syscop.igd.fhg.de.

Numerous new companies are entering this potentially lucrative field. Indeed, the Hollywood-based entertainment industry has been proceeding very aggressively toward the establishment of numerous digital watermarking schemes. The Galaxy Group of consumer electronics companies (IBM, NEC, Hitachi, Pioneer, and Sony) has already agreed on a new digital watermarking standard. Numerous venture capital firms, such as a new Korean firm, TrusTech, are doing likewise.

Not to be outdone, watermarking-negation schemes have also been proliferating, and several software packages exist that can in many cases negate a digital watermark. These packages include:

- **2Mosaic_0.1,** http://www.cl.cam.ac.uk/~fapp2/watermarking/image_ watermarking/2mosaic/. This software can take a JPG image that has been watermarked, divide it into many smaller ones, none of which are big enough to contain enough information to prove the existence of the original watermark, send them via the Internet, and then reconstruct them at the other end.
- **UnZine** (available for Win9x). This product removes the digital signature from a digitally copyrighted image.
- **StirMark.** This software removes most of the watermarks available commercially. It is available from http://www.cl.cam.ac.uk/~fapp2/ watermarking/image_watermarking/stirmark/index.html.

For technical papers on digital watermarks, the interested reader is referred to the following documents:

1. J. Brassil, et al., "Electronic Marking and Identification Techniques to Discourage Document Copying," AT&T Bell Labs, Murray Hill, NJ.
2. S. H. Low, et al., "Document Marking and Identification Techniques," University of Melbourne.

5.2   The British RIP Law and the U.S. Carnivore Device

The effectiveness of any measure is not measured with a yes/no verdict but is a question of degree and, ultimately, cost effectiveness.

The Regulation of Investigatory Powers (RIP) is a new British law that authorizes British authorities to intercept Internet communications and to seize decryption keys used either to protect the confidentiality of such communication or to protect the confidentiality of data stored in individual computers. RIP dictates that every electronic communication be sent to the Government Technical Assistance Center (GTAC), which is being established in the London headquarters of the British security service MI5 (analogous to the U.S. FBI). The official text of this law can be found at http://www.legislation.hmso.gov.uk/acts/acts2000/20000023.htm. See also http://www.idg.net/ic_238302_2340_1-1483.html.

"Carnivore" was the disingenuously chosen name for a computer-based tool used by U.S. federal law enforcement authorities; it was renamed DCS1000 in early 2001. It is intended to be attached to an ISP's circuits—with ISP permission—where it scoops up a large amount of traffic; subsequently, law enforcement personnel identify and read the portion of that collected traffic that pertains to a targeted individual for whom a duly executed court warrant has been obtained. See http://www.robertgraham .com/pubs/carnivore-faq.html and http://www.cdt.org/security/carnivore/.

Other countries are likely to have equivalent laws and devices that have not received any publicity, notably including the use of force without the authority of any law. All of these laws and devices will be largely ineffective in their intended purposes for the following technical reasons:

1. Internet communications can defeat interception simply by establishing end-to-end encryption between one's computer and the "host" computer to which one is connected.

    a. This is already routine in the case of SSL connections to Web sites that handle most individuals' on-line purchases using credit cards. It is simple to extend SSL connections to the entire connection, as is the case with servers such as http://www.privacyx.com/, http://www.zeroknowledge.com/, and others.

    b. The forthcoming Internet protocol IPv6 will allow any two computers to negotiate and use session-specific encryption for each session and to automatically destroy those keys immediately thereafter, thereby rendering them inaccessible to law enforcement.

2. Any individual in the world can establish an Internet account with an out-of-country ISP. Such ISPs are not bound by the provisions of any one country's laws to provide local authorities with data such as a targeted subscriber's e-mail. Of course, in a totalitarian regime that has the technical means to monitor *all* telephone communications leaving the country (including satellite and cellular ones), a call to an out-of-country ISP would be alerting.

3. It is routine nowadays for individuals to have numerous ISPs and to change some or all of them at a moment's notice and very frequently, especially since many are free today. With the proliferation of ISPs, it is not cost-effective for law enforcement to target each and every one of them (either with a RIP-authorized hardwired connection or with a Carnivore device).

4. The use of publicly accessible terminals (Internet cafés, public libraries, terminals at airports and in hotel lobbies) in conjunction with just-created new free Internet accounts at out-of-country

servers will make it impossible for law enforcement to identify who is communicating with whom. If encryption is added to the brew, then the content will also be inaccessible.

5. Strong and properly used steganography (see Section 14.5) makes it very hard for law enforcement to identify the mere existence of encrypted traffic. If the messages are brief and have a pre-agreed-upon meaning (e.g., a Usenet message that states "For Sale: One dining room table and four chairs," could have the pre-agreed-upon meaning "Let's meet at location number 1 at 4 P.M."), then detection will be impossible.

6. One-time-pad encryption, openly known for a very long time (see Chapter 13), can easily be used so that the key to be surrendered to law enforcement yields an innocuous decrypted message while another key, whose existence will not be acknowledged, would be needed to yield the real message.

7. Outgoing PGP-encrypted e-mail, if properly configured, cannot be decrypted by the sender and only by the recipient, who may be in another country. The in-country person could only decrypt incoming PGP-encrypted e-mail, over which he or she has no control and for which is therefore unlikely to be legally accountable.

8. A British group consisting of a number of anonymous senior cryptographers and computer scientists (http://www.m-o-o-t.org) is working on the creation of a system that will defeat both Carnivore and RIP's implementation. (According to this Web site, "M-o-o-t is an open design project to defeat RIP and make it look silly and to allow U.K. citizens to communicate and to store information without worrying about it; it will also defeat Carnivore and the Australian and proposed NZ and Council of Europe laws.") It will be a CD-ROM from which the computer will boot and will have its own operating system (and hence not use the computer's hard disk at all so that nothing is saved that can be found through forensics later).

9. The technically represented hacker group "Cult of the Dead Cow" demonstrated an uninterceptable means of Internet communications on July 4, 2001; this means is based on peer-to-peer networking.

In conclusion, it is evident from the foregoing that:

1. Laws and devices will "catch" the unsophisticated target of computer forensics but not the technically sophisticated one who,

presumably, is (or should be) of most interest to law enforcement. Mundane petty-crime catching does not realistically justify national-level massive resources and expenditures when it is clear that the real threats (terrorists, spies, narcotraffickers, and so on) will be able to defeat any such broad-scope surveillance systems.

2. As time goes on and technical sophistication percolates downward, more and more targets of computer forensics will be out of the reach of law enforcement.

3. From an economic perspective, the costs of implementing technical means of wholesale-interception of Internet traffic will rapidly reach the point of diminishing returns because of the combined effect of encryption, steganography, increasingly vast amounts of traffic, practically achievable anonymity, and the global nature of the Internet.

In view of the foregoing, the logical inference is that the deployment of massively expensive surveillance techniques like the United Kingdom's RIP Act, the United States' DCS1000 and others, and other countries' equivalents, is either not well thought out or is intended for large-scale control of a country's own citizens, and not for the professed reason of catching terrorists and narcotraffickers.

Finally, one must consider the fact that both of these (and related) tools have far more technical capability than the capability that is allowed by applicable laws in the respective countries.

Selected Bibliography

A vast amount of background material and references on digital watermarking is available. Over 60 pages of references can be found in an annotated bibliography on information hiding by Ross J. Anderson and Fabien Peticolas of the University of Cambridge Computer Laboratory, http://www.cl.cam.ac.uk/~fapp2/steganography/bibliography/.

Some of the most relevant entries in this work are provided here.

Anderson, J., (ed.), *Information Hiding: First International Workshop*, Lecture Notes in Computer Science, Vol. 1174, Isaac Newton Institute, Cambridge, England, May 1996, Berlin: Springer-Verlag.

Bender, W., et al., "Techniques for Data Hiding," *IBM Systems Journal*, Vol. 35, Nos. 3 and 4, pp. 313–336. A good survey of techniques used in data hiding.

Hsu, C., et al., "Hidden Digital Watermarks in Images," *IEEE Trans. on Image Processing,* Vol. 8, No. 1, January 1999, pp. 58–68. This document discusses JPEG image watermarkings that survive cropping, enhancement, and lossy JPEG compression.

Minitzer, F., et al., "If One Watermark Is Good, Are More Better?" *Intl. Conf. Acoustics, Speech and Signal Processing,* Vol. 80, 1999, pp. 2067–2070, http://citeseer.nj.nec.com/mintzer99one.html. The document shows why the order in which watermarks are applied is important.

Paskin, N., "Towards Unique Identifiers," *IEEE Proc.,* Vol. 87, No. 7, July 1999, pp. 1197–1207. This is a good tutorial on the overall subject, including definitions and requirements.

Schneider, B., et al., "Subliminal Channels in the Digital Signature Algorithm," *Computer Security Journal,* Vol. 9, No. 2, 1993, pp. 57–63. Discusses covert communications channels that a user of a digital signature algorithm can use.

Solachidis, V., et al., "Circularly Symmetric Watermark Embedding in 2-D DFT Domain," *Intl. Conf. Acoustics, Speech and Signal Processing,* Vol. 80, 1999, pp. 1653–1656, http://citeseer.nj.nec.com/solachidis99.circularly.html. This document shows a watermarking means that is robust to rotation and scaling.

6

Modes of Data Insertion and Acquisition

6.1 Physical Possession of the Computer

The fact that physical possession of a computer by an investigator allows that investigator to search for all evidence in the computer is self-evident and needs no further elaboration. It is the basic premise behind computer forensics as practiced by law enforcement. If there is any unencrypted information left behind in the confiscated data storage media, and if the forensics investigation is thorough enough, that information will be found. Physical possession does not have to be clandestine; when computers are taken to be serviced, service technicians have full access to them.

6.2 Physical Access to the Computer

Physical access to a targeted computer is just as good as full possession of it, if such access allows one to make a full magnetic copy of the computer's hard disk(s). In legal proceedings, it must be shown that the disk(s) copied could not have been contaminated by the copying process, and the disks must be removed from the targeted computer and placed in another one over which the forensics investigator has full control. Safeback (see Section 3.3.2) is one of the standard pieces of software used to make a track-by-track and sector-by-sector copy of a targeted disk onto another disk of equal or greater capacity.

If the purpose of the forensics investigation is to collect data without having to show it in court, then disks can be copied even without removal from a computer, as long as the investigator has taken steps to ensure that there is no booby-trapped software running that would delete or modify disk(s) that are copied by a stranger.

Similarly, physical access can allow for surreptitious data collection, by law enforcement or anyone else. The commercial sector is full of devices that transmit information fed into them. An interceptor who has somehow obtained physical access to someone else's premises (or just to that person's computer, such as when it was taken in for repair) could elect to combine a data-interception device with a small radio transmitter that transmits the intercepted data out to a receiver.

The only limits as to how to send out the data that has been collected from a targeted computer are one's imagination, nerve, and pocketbook.

6.3   Keystroke-Capturing Hardware Device

A commercial device is openly available worldwide from a New Zealand firm, KeyGhost Ltd. (http://www.keyghost.com/); surreptitiously placed on the target computer, it looks like a small adapter on the cable connecting the keyboard to the computer. This device requires no external power (and hence lasts indefinitely) and no software installation (and hence cannot be detected by any software). Numerous versions are available, as shown in Figure 6.1. Figure 6.2 depicts the keystroke-capturing device itself, with adapters for different computers. It comes with the requisite adapters and manual "out of the box," for installation by nonspecialists, as shown in Figure 6.3.

The high-end models, which sell for around $250, can store 500,000 keystrokes, or about 80,000 words (approximately the size of a 160-page paperback book). Special versions of the device can capture and store one to four million keystrokes. An upcoming KeyGhost mini will look like a normal keyboard extension cable.

For an extra $50 or $60 more, one can buy a standard or Microsoft Natural keyboard with the device built inside it, thereby making it totally invisible, as shown in Figure 6.4.

The captured keystrokes are stored in the device in 128-bit encrypted form (i.e., unbreakable for all practical purposes). Unlike the software-based keystroke-capturing commercial and freeware products discussed in Section 6.4, a hardware-based keystroke capture works even if one boots a computer from a floppy disk, and is independent of the operating system used. It can

Model	Capacity	Ghost Playback	Encryption	Fast Download Adapter	Casing
Keyghost II Professional SE	2,000,000 Keystrokes	Yes	128 bit	Yes	EMC Balun
Keyghost II Professional	500,000 Keystrokes	Yes	128 bit	Yes	EMC Balun
Keyghost II Standard	97,000 Keystrokes	Yes	None	No	EMC Balun
Keyghost Mini Covert	120,000 Keystrokes	No	N/A	Yes	PS-2 Plug
Keyghost II Security Keyboard (Pro)	500,000 Keystrokes	Yes	128 bit	Yes	Keyboard
Keyghost II Security Keyboard (Std)	97,000 Keystrokes	Yes	None	No	Keyboard

Figure 6.1 Versions of KeyGhost keystroke-capturing device. (Courtesy of KeyGhost Ltd.)

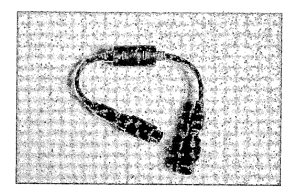

Figure 6.2 KeyGhost device with adapters.(Courtesy of KeyGhost Ltd.)

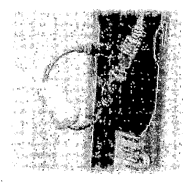

Figure 6.3 Installation of KeyGhost device. (Courtesy of KeyGhost Ltd.)

be placed on password-protected computers without having to defeat such passwords. In fact, a device such as this can also capture the initial BIOS

Figure 6.4 Invisibly modified keyboard to capture keystrokes. (Courtesy of KeyGhost Ltd.)

password optionally used by any computer. If the entire data storage area of the device is filled up unretrieved, it will proceed to overwrite the oldest stored data.

The information captured by the device can be retrieved by anyone who can get physical access to the computer by entering the appropriate installer-selected password; since this can be up to 12 characters long, it is highly unlikely that such passwords can be typed accidentally. Alternately, the device itself (cable or keyboard) can be swapped with a normal one that looks the same, and taken to another computer where its contents can be retrieved at leisure.

6.4 Keystroke-Recording Software

Numerous software packages are openly available on the Internet, some for a fee and many for free, that record all keystrokes. Those listed here are downloadable from http://www.cotse.com/winnt.htm:

- Playback.zip
- Win95pwgrabber.zip
- Keycopy V.1.01
- Keylogger V.1.5
- 9x_int09.zip
- achtung.zip

Other openly available keystroke-logging software includes:

- **Internet Tracker** 2.1. Intended to track stolen computers; reports on a computer's activities by e-mail.
- **The Investigator** 3.0. This records all keystrokes and sends the data out to whomever the surreptitious installer specified. It is sold for $99 by "WinWhatWhere," and is popular with employers for monitoring employees. According to CMP's Tech Web, this software has been purchased, among others, by the U.S. State Department, the U.S. Mint in Denver, Exxon, Delta Airlines, the accounting firm Ernst and Young, the U.S. Department of Veteran Affairs, and Lockheed Martin.

The following software-based keystroke-capturers can be obtained from http://winfiles/cnet.com/apps/98/access-control.html.

- **Gotyour Keystrokes** (freeware). Developed as a tool for parental control.
- **SpyAgent Professional** (shareware, $34.95). Powerful full-featured software.
- **NetSpy** (shareware, $19.95). Also allows the snoop to see what Web sites were accessed by the targeted computer, as well as e-mail, even if it is subsequently deleted. Currently supports Netscape Navigator, Internet Explorer, AOL, and Prodigy.
- **Desktop Detective** (shareware, $29). Full-featured snooping utility.
- **Spytech Shadow** (shareware, $29.95). Emphasizes visual screen monitoring rather than text capture and records full visual screens every few seconds.

Additionally, one can purchase software such as "KeyKey," from http://www.keykey.com/index1.html and from http://cyberdetective.net/keykey.htm. For Windows 95/98, NT, and 2000, this product asserts that it hides itself from antimonitoring software and records date/time stamps; it sells for $19.95. KeyKey's versatility is evident from Figure 6.5, which shows the reporting options available to the surreptitious installer of that software; notice that these options include e-mailing of the captured keystrokes.

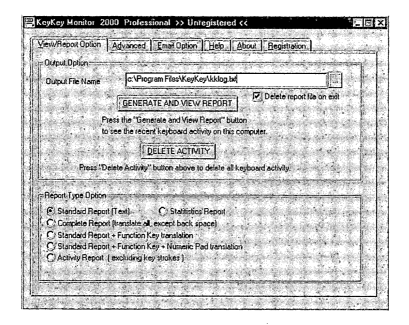

Figure 6.5   KeyKey's keystroke-capturing reporting options. (Courtesy of Mikko Technology.)

KeyKey's "professional" version comes with a Screen Capture package; as this name suggests, it surreptitiously captures, stores, and can transmit what someone is viewing on the screen as well, as shown in Figure 6.6. Notice that the options include capturing screenfuls at preset intervals of time, or when the mouse or keyboard is used in any mode defined by the surreptitious installer.

6.5   Internet or Network Connections

A serious security threat results from merely being on-line. Unless one has taken drastic steps to defend against a wide assortment of hacking attacks (see Chapters 8 through 14), one is highly likely to become the target of trolling hackers who delight in identifying and exploiting security weaknesses of anyone who stays on-line long enough. Such attacks can be minimized by:

- *Using a good firewall.* (See Section 12.16.)

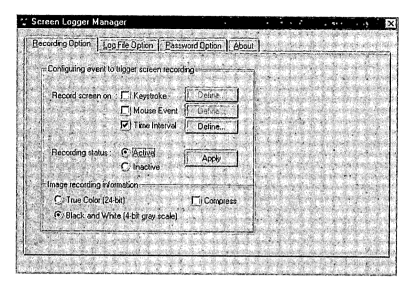

Figure 6.6 KeyKey screen-capturing options. (Courtesy of Mikko Technology.)

- *Not staying on-line for long.* Hacking attacks probe one's weaknesses based on one's dynamically assigned (meaning that it changes every time one goes on-line) Internet Protocol (IP) address. An IP address is the unique identifying address of anyone connected to the Internet; it is the equivalent of one's telephone number. Since there are more Internet users than there are IP addresses, an Internet service provider has a pool of such IP addresses from which it selects at random to assign to each user when that user goes on-line; when this user goes off-line, that IP address is assigned to someone else. The longer one stays with a single IP address, the longer a hacker has to probe for weaknesses. Users of high-speed connections (cable modems and xDSL lines) would be well advised to disconnect their computers from the network when not actually using them.

- *Using virus/Trojan/worm protection software* and keeping it current; this means checking for updates once a day or, if one uses a computer sparingly, prior to each new use.

Unless a user has taken drastic and current measures to prevent access to his or her computer by others on a network or the Internet, there is a vast repertoire of ways whereby a knowledgeable person can extract data from a user's computer while that user is on-line. The extent of what can be remotely extracted in this manner ranges from literally everything on one's hard disk to nothing, depending on what protective measures have been taken along the lines of those described in Part II of this book.

6.5.1 Internet Service Providers or ISP Security Breaches

The primary security threat to a computer connected to the Internet is not the malicious remote Web site or the malicious remote hacker—although both of these dangers are very real—but one's own Internet service provider. The ISP is always in a position to know what one does on-line, who one connects to, the content of incoming and outgoing e-mail, who one communicates with and when, and so on. The only exceptions are:

- When a user elects to connect to remote Web sites with SSL encryption (see Section 12.7.1), which provides end-to-end encryption between the user and such sites; the ISP is incapable of knowing what data is moving back and forth.

- When a user elects to use a virtual private network (VPN) connection to the remote site, as per Section 12.4. Comments made above about SSL encryption apply here as well.

- When a user elects to use encryption to hide the contents of e-mail and attachments. This still does not hide the "from whom" and "to whom" information, unless the user has also elected to use multiple concatenated remailers (see Section 11.5.2); in this case, the ISP knows that a remailer is being used.

While the methods above do provide the protection shown, they also raise the user's profile in the eyes of the suspicious ISP, as someone who is "hiding something."

If one wants to "have cake and eat it too," then steganography is the only way out (see Section 14.5), as long as it is employed judiciously so that its use is not alerting.

It is not "paranoia" to assume that an ISP has a financial interest in a user's on-line activities: A company called Predictive Networks is promoting a scheme that would pay ISPs to track users' every move on the Internet so as to sell detailed profiles to numerous buyers who want to target their advertising. (See http://home.mpinet.net/pilobilus/CS01.html, http://www. vortex.com/privacy/priv.09.13, and http://www.predictivenetworks.com/.)

6.5.2 Telephone Taps

Anything that an ISP can see can also be seen through a tap on the communications medium used by an individual to connect to the Internet, be that a telephone line, a cable modem, an xDSL line, or a wireless link; most any wireless link (e.g., cellular phone, Ricochet modem) eventually becomes a wired connection, more practical for someone to intercept.

6.5.3 Remote Web Sites

The litany of ways whereby remote Web sites can extract information from one's computer on-line is almost endless. (See Chapters 10 through 14 for protective measures.) Rather than enumerating the vast number of such threats, Chapters 10 through 14 approach the topic from the perspective of wholesale negation of them.

"Cookies" (see Chapter 10) have been correctly blamed for allowing Web sites that the individual accesses to track the individual's Web-browsing habits. (A "cookie" is simply a small amount of data sent by the accessed Web site to the individual's computer and stored in that computer; such data is supposed to be readable only by the site that sent it, but in fact can be read by any Web site that elects to do so.)

In fact, a Web site does not need to store anything at all in an individual's computer to track that individual's browsing habits. As a user accesses any Web page, that site has to know the user's IP address in order to send the information requested. If that site elects to record the IP address for posterity, then it can easily tell if a user has visited that site before. This is only true for users with fixed IP addresses (such as most users with xDSL or cable modem access who have not deployed protective measures) but is not true for dial-up users because such users get a different IP address every time they dial up their ISP to connect to the Internet.

The most recent culprit is a device known as CueCat, which has been mailed gratis to numerous individuals in the United States. CueCat is a digital bar-code scanner promoted by a Denver, Colorado, organization, which has a personal tracking feature within it [1]. The idea is that individuals can scan the bar codes of items in print and then are automatically linked to assorted Web pages. The problem is that such devices seem to be individually identifiable. Don't use them.

Technical information on how to disable the individually identifiable serial number of these devices is available on-line at http://www.air-soldier.com/~cuecat/.

It is just as easy for a remote entity to retrieve information from one's computer on-line as it is to insert files in it. Given that mere possession of some kinds of material by individuals is strictly illegal in some regimes (e.g., subversive files, bomb-making files, files marked as classified, and even erotic imagery in the case of most regimes), one should be particularly careful about the possibility that incriminating "evidence" may find its way into one's computer under some circumstances. Similarly, defense attorneys must also be aware of this possibility. This incriminating "evidence" can be intentionally inserted by a remote party; it can also be unknowingly received by an innocent user who never solicited it, in the following ways:

- One is accessing an Internet Web site and either mistypes the URL or the correct URL gets one to the wrong site (say, a pornographic one) as a result of domain server name (DNS)[1] problems.

- One is accessing a legitimate Internet site on the Web which is also supported by advertising revenue (as most are today) obtained by flashing unsolicited images and "windows" on the user's screen; those images end up getting saved on the user's computer despite no active "clicking" or other act by the user. An overzealous law enforcer can find this as "evidence of possessing illegal imagery"; unless the defense counsel is well versed on this issue, a nontechnical jury (or judge) will likely convict a totally innocent person.

6.6 Acquisitive Software

Numerous software packages can capture, store, and forward a targeted computer's on-line and off-line activities. A small sampling of such software is provided here.

---

1. DNS servers are the telephone directories of the Internet. When one types in a Web address—http://www.somename.com/—a DNS server is queried to produce the corresponding IP address (e.g., 123.456.789.012) for that name. Time and again, hackers have managed to poison select DNS servers so as to deny access to numerous Web sites.

- **Mom** (http://www.avsweb.com/mom/) tracks a targeted individual's on-line activities.

- **DIRT.** Data Interception by Remote Transmission (DIRT) is a tool that claims to provide remote monitoring of one or more targeted computers without the need for physical access. It is sold by Codex Data Systems (http://www.codexdatasystems.com/menu .html). According to the company's Web site, "All that someone with DIRT needs to know is your e-mail address. Period. All he has to do is send you an e-mail with the imbedded DIRT-Trojan Horse and he is home free, and you are a clueless victim."

- **NoKnock E-Warrant.** Also by Codex Data Systems, this product asserts that it can "execute judicial search warrants by stealth via the Internet" for the purposes of "remotely searching a target hard drive and comparing results with known databases."

- **Investigator.** Put out by WinWhatWhere (http://winwhat-where.com/), this product offers a broad range of capabilities including keystroke monitoring and Internet tracking.

- **SilentRunner.** Offered by Raytheon (Lexington, Massachusetts), this product is intended for network monitoring. The program uses algorithms to analyze communications patterns and turns its analysis into three-dimensional pictures.

- **Silent Guard.** Adavi advertises this product as the "premier surveillance software that allows a single user to monitor keystrokes and Internet traffic for later review." This program can monitor up to 49 computers in real time from a single screen and even provide alarms to the person doing the monitoring "when users reach objectionable Web sites or inappropriate text content based on a dictionary of the user's choice."

6.6.1 Spyware and Adware

Most individuals are unaware of the monetary value of their names and buying habits. Supermarkets in the United States have long been offering substantial discounts to shoppers who agree to fill out a form with their name, address, phone number, and e-mail address. Similarly, the many "free" ISPs are not free at all: Instead of getting paid in cash by users, they get paid in terms of the monetary value of users' names and Web-browsing habits; this information is, in turn, converted into cash by the commercial advertisers to whom it is sold.

A lot of free software (and some commercial for-pay software) makers have also learned the commercial value of software users' names and choices (measured in terms of what other software exists in a user's computer, as well as the user's on-line habits). The moment such software is installed in an unsuspecting user's computer, it starts collecting and relaying this data; this often continues even if that program is never used, and even if it is uninstalled—hence the epithet "spyware."

A current list of software reputed to offer this capability can be found at sites such as http://home.att.net/~willowbrookemill/spylist.pdf, http://www.grc.com/, http://www.alphalink.com.au/~johnf/dspypdf.html, http://www.infoforce.qc.ca/spyware/, and elsewhere. The interested reader is encouraged to check the Usenet forum ALT.PRIVACY.SPYWARE for the latest information on the topic.

TSADBOT, by Conducent, which has since gone out of business, is an example of the type of Trojan horse that can enter an individual's system attached to certain "free" software that the individual has installed. The information is from http://cexx.org/tsadbot.htm. It makes multiple connections to Conducent ad servers, including adsdl.conducent.com and redirects.conducent.com (various ports). Its use of proxy service prevents NETSTAT and similar network tools from disclosing actual addresses that it connects to (they appear in the form of ADS*:portnumber).

TSADBOT is installed as a Windows service when certain software is installed, most notably new versions of PKZip. Several sources actually list this program under "viruses," and it is not difficult to see why. It is secretly loaded onto computer systems when the user installs (or merely attempts to install) completely unrelated software; it makes clandestine network connections without the user's knowledge; it persists even after the software it came with has been uninstalled; and it is very difficult to remove.

Once installed, the TSADBOT program is loaded every time Windows starts and runs invisibly in the background until the computer is shut down. It connects to the Internet and downloads ads, whether the advertising-supported application is running or not, and implements an unauthorized proxy server on the user's system that disguises the adware's network connections. AdGateway (demographic/behavioral) "profiles" are stored in encrypted files on the user's system, and may be transmitted by the TSADBOT software. The TSADBOT software accesses the user's browser cache and history (list of sites one has visited) for purposes unknown, and may use this information in the creation of behavioral profiles or transmit this information.

Once installed, TSADBOT (like many adwares) is very difficult to remove. If deleted, it will often forcibly reinstall itself. In addition, it remains on one's system and continues to monitor one's viewing habits, even after the associated application has been uninstalled. This means that if one installs a "free" version of PKZip or a similar application, runs it once, and finds out that it is powered by adware and immediately uninstalls it, the TSADBOT process remains on one's system and secretly continues to perform its unwanted functions.

The *Risks Digest* (Volume 20, Issue 65) provides information about another "feature" of TSADBOT:

> [A]n even worse fate occurs if the AdBot is thwarted in its attempts to connect to Conducent by a firewall or other controls. It starts to attempt to connect continually, about 10 times/second causing a huge load on local network facilities. If it can't connect even then, it tries to connect using Telnet and other ports with the background AdBot retrying the HTTP connects after several hours.

To a privacy-minded person, the most disturbing aspect of this program is what it does with one's Web browser history. Just as disturbing are the statements made on the Web site responsible for TSADBOT:

> By collecting valuable user data and marketing new and existing soft-ware titles to dedicated users, publishers can drive retail sales of specific titles. Conducent offers Advertisers the unique opportunity to reach specific software users in highly targeted categories.

6.6.1.1 "Fixes" Against Adware and Spyware

One easy "fix" that worked in the past was for the individual to download Steve Gibson's OptOut program from http://grc.com/files/optout.exe. This product is no longer current. A better product, "Ad-aware," is available freely from http://www.lavasoft.de/.

Some programs that install spyware will refuse to run if one removes the spyware functionality; Go!Zilla is one such example. Some will keep reinstalling the spyware function; to get rid of it, one must remove the software that continues to install it.

A user should determine if a new piece of software in his or her computer has any reason to be accessing the Internet; a good firewall (see

Section 12.16) will alert the user most of the time, but not all of the time[2] if a program is trying to access the Internet, at which time a user can permit or not permit that to happen.

One can search one's computer for such telltale file names as "ad.dll," "advert.dll," and so forth. Rename them; if everything still works, delete them. In particular, look for and remove any of the following:

Tsadbot.exe[3] (usually installed as a Windows "service" in software, such as in new versions of PKZip)

Dssagent.exe

Adimage.dll

Amcis.dll

Amcis2.dll

Anadsc.ocx

Anadscb.ocx

Htmdeng.exe

Ipcclient.dll

Msipcsv.exe

Tfde.dll

Tsad.dll

---

2. If a piece of software has installed the capability in one's computer to access the Internet through valid ports and through other valid software (e.g., using port 80 of one's Web browser while that browser is being used by the user anyway), then the user will be oblivious to this, and no firewall will catch it. About the only way to catch such an unauthorized hijacking of one's computer and software is through the use of a "packet sniffer," which actually looks at and displays all data entering and leaving one's computer; WinDump is one such product, and can be obtained, for example, from http://netgroup-serv.polito.it/windump/.

3. TSABOT connects to the Internet without a user's knowledge, downloads ads, sets up a proxy server on one's own system so as to disguise this adware program's network connections, accesses the user's history of Web sites visited and also the Web browser's cache of saved documents, stores profiles in encrypted form in the user's computer, and transmits information to Conducent. TSABOT stays in one's system and continues to function even after the software that installed it, such as PKZip, has been removed. To delete it, one must do so from within DOS, because the file reports as being "in use" if one tries to delete it from inside Windows. Also, Run/REGEDIT and look for any reference to TSABOT and delete it and do not run the program that installed it in the first place (such as PKZip). Finally, if you have a personal firewall that allows you to block access to particular domains, block access to all Conducent domains.

Vcpdll.dll

FlexActv.dll

Look in the Startup folder for any inexplicable entries and remove them. Sometimes, adware/spyware will reinstall entries in the Startup folder; in this case, assuming that one knows what sequence of letters for which to look, one can look in the registry for that sequence and delete those references. *Caution:* Do not edit the registry unless you know what you are doing (see Chapter 4).

6.6.2 Other Unauthorized "Backdoor Santas"

6.6.2.1 Netscape Navigator/Communicator

Do not use Netscape's Smart Update. It has been shown to report to Netscape. Go into Edit/Preferences/Advanced/SmartUpdate and uncheck it.

Unless you are particularly fond of AOL Instant Messenger in Netscape Navigator/Communicator, remove it as follows:

1 Go to C:/Program Files/Netscape/Users/ and remove the shortcut for AOL Instant Messenger ("launch.aim") for each and every profile you have. Do not run Netscape until you complete the additional steps below; otherwise, the program will reinsert the shortcuts just deleted.

2. Go to Search/Find/Folders and enter "AOL" and, separately later, "AIM." Delete any folder identified with either name.

3. Run REGEDIT and search for the string "AOL" and, separately, "AIM." Delete every entry identified that is clearly referring to the AOL Instant Messenger. *Caution:* Ensure that the entry being deleted is indeed referring to AOL's Instant Messenger before deleting it. See Section 4.4 about concerns that must be addressed when editing the registry.

4. Reboot.

5. Double-click on the Netscape icon and make sure that everything is working properly.

6.6.2.2 Registration Wizards

Do not use registration wizards. Time and again, companies—including very reputable ones—have been caught using the on-line registration process to send to the software maker a lot more than the registration information, such as a digest of what is in one's hard disk.

6.6.2.3   Eudora 3.0

All variants of Eudora 3.0, namely the so-called Lite, the fully paid and the ad supported—as well as many other software products today—have an unfortunate feature whereby the software regularly "calls home" (i.e., connects to the Eudora servers without notifying the user). The makers of Eudora (and other software makers) assert that this is done solely to check if a newer version of the software has been released; the fact remains, however, that the Eudora server gets notified on a regular basis whenever a user uses his or her copy of the software, and this happens without the user's knowledge. This feature can be and should be disabled as shown in Section 11.3.3.

6.6.2.4   Microsoft's WebCheck

Microsoft's WebCheck manages subscriptions and user profiles for Internet Explorer versions 4 and 5. (If you don't use subscriptions, you don't need it.) This parasite is run by the registry using the entry

HKEY_LOCAL_MACHINE\SOFTWARE\Microsoft\Windows\CurrentVersion\RunBrowserWebCheck="loadwc.exe"

Caution: Removing this line causes endless subsequent errors.

6.6.2.5   PKWARE

Like Microsoft's WebCheck, PKWARE also installs a parasite, which allows advertisements to be carried inside zip files. It is launched by the registry with the entry

HKEY_LOCAL_MACHINE\SOFTWARE\Microsoft\Windows\CurrentVersion\RunTimeSinkAdClient="C:\ProgramFiles\TimeSink\AdGateway\TSADBOT.EXE

6.6.2.6   HP Registration

HP Registration often installs a registration parasite if one does not register the product. It takes up 6–20 MB and runs remind32.dll, which nags the user to register. Remind32.dll is executed from Start/Programs/Startup.

6.6.2.7   Boreland C++ 5.0

Boreland C++ 5.0 (DOS) also installs a registration parasite that takes up 1 MB of disk space and is invoked by the following line in the win.ini file:

[windows]load C:\BC5\PIPELINE\remind.exe

Clearly, one can remove both the above line and the remind.exe file itself.

6.6.2.8   Microsoft Office 2000 Script Editor

Microsoft's Office 2000 Script Editor allows the user the option of installing the Machine Debug Manager (mdm.exe) through the registry entry

HKEY_LOCAL_MACHINE\SOFTWARE\Microsoft\Windows\CurrentVersion\RunServices

The problem with this feature is that it creates temporary files every time that one boots the computer, and never deletes them, thereby posing a security threat.

6.7   Van Eck Radiation

Information in this section is based entirely and exclusively on the openly available sources identified herein.

6.7.1   General

In 1985, Wim van Eck published a paper called "Electromagnetic Radiation from Video Display Units: An Eavesdropping Risk?" [2]. Electromagnetic radiation as a computer security risk was mentioned in the open literature as early as 1967 [3]. Since then, numerous articles on the subject have appeared on the Internet, such as the ones shown in the Selected Bibliography on Van Eck Radiation at the end of this chapter. Additionally, there are numerous openly available scientific documents on the subject, also shown in the Selected Bibliography.

Because of the obvious security concern with unintended emanations from electronic equipment used in sensitive government activities, standards and procedures have been developed for the purpose of reducing these emanations to sufficiently low levels. These standards and procedures are collectively known as "TEMPEST." TEMPEST is an acronym for Transient Electromagnetic Pulse Emanation Standard.

In the United Kingdom, where TV fees must be paid on a regular basis, vans are routinely deployed that are equipped with means to detect the oscillators of TV sets and compare them against the list of those who have paid for operating a TV. In fact, according to the University of Cambridge's Ross Anderson, unpaid TV fees are a main reason that women in the United Kingdom end up in prison if they cannot pay the £1,000 fine when caught for this offense.

"Data Security by Design," an article by George R. Wilson (http://jya.com/datasec.htm), asserts that such emissions can be picked up "as far away as half a mile" using "a broad band radio scanner, a good antenna and a TV set—all available at electronic stores such as Radio Shack for a few hundred dollars."

According to Kuhn and Anderson [4]:

- "[P]ower and ground connections can also leak high frequency information."

- "Yet another risk comes from 'active attacks' [5].... an attacker who knows the resonant frequency of (say) a PC's keyboard cable can irradiate it with this frequency and then detect keypress codes in the retransmitted signal."

- "A reader of an early version of this paper reported that he was able to get data signals out of a U.S. Tempest certified equipment by directing a 10 GHz microwave beam at it."

- "Smulders showed that even shielded RS-232 cables can often be eavesdropped at a distance" [6].

This same paper by Kuhn and Anderson [4] depicts test equipment alleged to be capable of doing such an interception, the DataSafe/ESL Model 400, by DataSafe Ltd. of Cheltenham, England, shown in Figure 6.7.

The tests performed by Kuhn and Anderson proved the feasibility of such interception, as evidenced from the two images in Figures 6.8 and 6.9, which depict the original screen of the computer being intercepted and the display at the eavesdropping site. It is noteworthy that the targeted computer is a laptop, which had long been considered safe from Van Eck radiation, in comparison to desktop computers.

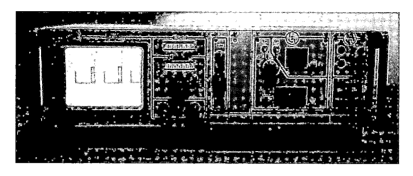

Figure 6.7 DataSafe/ESL Model 400 laboratory equipment. (*Source:* Markus Kuhn, Computer Laboratory, University of Cambridge.)

Figure 6.8 Screen display of encryption key setup on targeted computer. (*Source:* Markus Kuhn, Computer Laboratory, University of Cambridge.)

In the conclusion of [4], Kuhn and Anderson state that "[t]hings will be made much worse by the arrival of cheap software radios...[which] will allow low-budget attackers to implement sophisticated TEMPEST attacks which were previously only possible with very expensive dedicated equipment." An image of the equipment used is provided in Figure 6.10.

See [4] for a list of openly available references on this topic.

More to the point, there are numerous commercial entities that sell equipment for this purpose. In October 1996, the Discovery Channel's *Cyberlife* show aired an interview with the CEO of a company called Codex

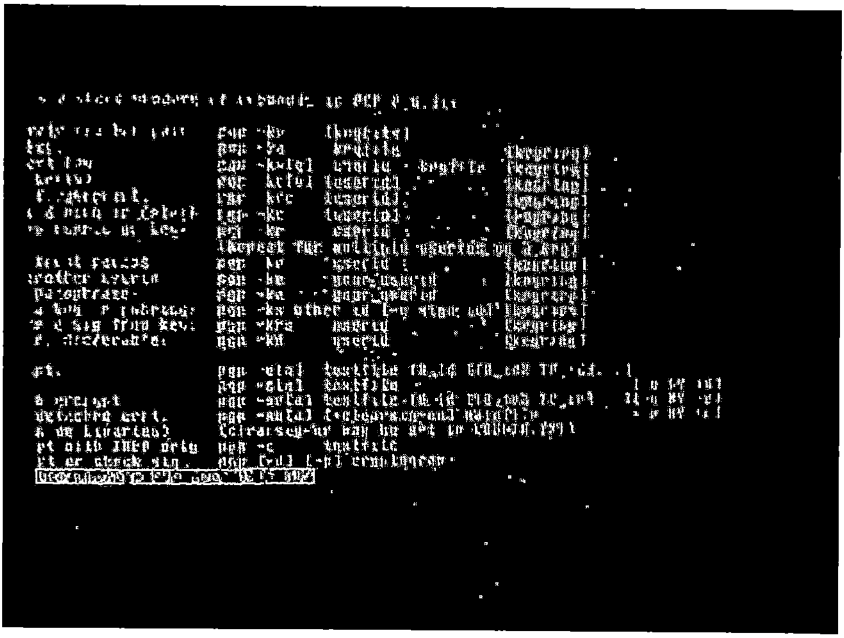

Figure 6.9 Intercepted image of encryption keys using Van Eck radiation. (*Source:*
Markus Kuhn, Computer Laboratory, University of Cambridge.)

in which a demonstration was given of such interception. The Web site for
Codex Data Systems (http://codexdatasystems.com/tempeav.html) depicts
the system demonstrated.

A portable device sold by Codex (http://www.codexdatasystems.com/
datascan.html) is claimed to be usable for ranges exceeding 1,000 yards.
(According to Codex, "The DataScan manufactured by Codex captures the
dominant video signal generated by any computer CRT screen and recon-
structs it via a sophisticated antenna system and special receiver off-premises.
Range has exceeded 1,000 yards under optimum conditions. The unit is
entirely passive in nature. It does not allow the user to access the target computer but rather to monitor via radio wave what is displayed on the target
computer's CRT screen every time the computer is operational.")

6.7.2   Protective Measures

A U.S. patent (US5297201) offers "A system for preventing remote detection
of computer data from tempest signal emanations" (http://patent.wom-
plex.ibm.com/details?patent_number=5297201). According to "Data Security

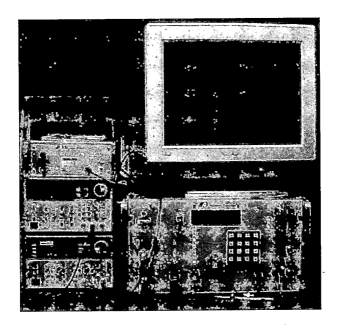

Figure 6.10 Standard laboratory equipment used for Van Eck interception by Kuhn and Anderson. (*Source:* Markus Kuhn, Computer Laboratory, University of Cambridge.)

by Design," by George R. Wilson (http://jya.com/datasec.htm), shielding from electromagnetic emanations is the protective measure one can deploy to thwart this threat to privacy. To this effect, there are numerous companies (such as TeckNit, http://www.tecknit.com/) that offer assorted EMI shielding products.

Similarly, "The TEMPEST Solution" (http://www.ionet.net/~everett/solution.html) suggests numerous steps one should take, such as reducing the length of cables, "using ferrite toroids and split beads on cables," and so on. The interested reader is referred to that article for the specifics. A publicly accessible document (http://www.cryptome.org/af-hb202d.htm) gives an allegedly official perspective on the topic.

An interesting protective scheme is, in fact, built into some openly available versions of the popular encryption software PGP: It offers one the option of using a fuzzy font that is claimed to be difficult to intercept through emanations. Similarly, ScramDisk (see Section 14.4) offers a "red screen mode" for one to enter the password in a manner that is claimed to defeat a TEMPEST attach; this only works for U.S. QWERTY keyboards and not for European and Asian nonstandard keyboards (unless one uses only figures and numbers for the password). Similarly, one can download a "zero emission pad" freeware from DEMCOM, which makes the Steganos Security Suite software, at http://www.steganos.com/english/steganos/zep.htm. The example shown by that company's Web site of how it modifies the fonts that get displayed on the screen is shown in Figure 6.11.

An excellent reference for fonts that ostensibly defeat TEMPEST is at http://www.infowar.com/resource/99/resource_040599b_j.shtml, which also contains downloadable fonts at http://www.cl.cam.ac.uk/~mgk25/st-fonts.zip, which contains Soft TEMPEST filtered and anti-aliased versions of the Courier font, produced using the public domain X11 pixel font –adobe-courier-*-r-normal—40-386-75-75-m-0-iso8859-1. The two available fixed glyph cell sizes are 13×24 pixels and 8×13 pixels, in both medium (m) and bold (b) weight.

According to http://www.infowar.com/resource/99/resource_040599 b_j.shtml, "Since filtered fonts require successful eavesdroppers to come much closer to the target machine, they reduce the probability of a successful interception of confidential text considerably. They are therefore a valuable additional precaution that can be applied easily to maintain a reasonable level of communication and computer security. TEMPEST protection by filtered fonts and related techniques are in the process of being patented internationally."

The reader interested in preventing compromises of his or her privacy through this technology should read the patent description by Kuhn and Anderson, "Low Cost Countermeasures Against Compromising Computer Emanations," U.K. patent application no. 9801745.2, January 28, 1998.

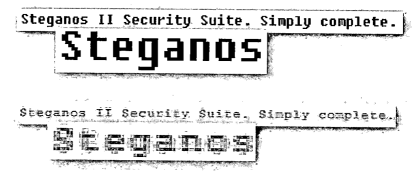

Figure 6.11 Freeware fonts for protection from emanations interception. (Courtesy of DECOM GmbH.)

References

[1] Oslen, S., "Privacy Group Slams Web Tracking 'Cat'," CNET News.com, September 22, 2000, http://news.cnet.com/news/0-1005-200-2841044.html.

[2] Available at http://www.shmoo.com/tempest/emr.pdf, 1985.

[3] Highland, H. J., "Electromagnetic Radiation Revisited," *Computers and Security*, Vol. 5, 1986, pp. 85–93; 181–184.

[4] Anderson, R., and M. Kuhn, "Soft Tempest: Hidden Data Transmission Using Electromagnetic Emanations," University of Cambridge Computer Laboratory, p. 126, full document at http://www.cl.cam.ac.uk/~mgk25/ih98-tempest.pdf.

[5] "Schutzmassnamen gegen Launschangriffe" (Protection Against Eavesdropping Attacks), Faltblaetter des BSI 5, Bonn: German Information Security Agency, 1996.

[6] Smulders, P., "The Threat of Information Theft by Reception of Electromagnetic Radiation from RS-232 Cable," *Computers and Security*, Vol. 9, 1990, pp. 53–58.

Selected Bibliography on Van Eck Radiation

Complete Unofficial TEMPEST Information Page, http://www.eskimo.com/~joelm/tempest .html.

"Electronic Eavesdropping Is Becoming Mere Child's Play," *New Scientist*, http://www.new-scientist.com/ns/19991106/newsstory6.html.

"Electromagnetic Eavesdropping Machines for Christmas?" *Computers and Security*, Vol. 7, No. 4, 1988.

Jones, Frank, "Nowhere to Run...Nowhere to Hide: The Vulnerability of CRT's, CPU's and Peripherals to TEMPEST Monitoring in the Real World," CodexDataSystems, http://www.codexdatasystems.com/, 1996.

McLellan, V., *PC Week*, Vol. 4, March 10, 1987, p. 35(2).

Phrak44, http://www.shmoo.com/tempest/PHRACK44-11.

Russell, D., and G. T. Gangemi, Sr., *Computer Security Basics*, Sebastopol, CA: O'Reilly and Associates, 1991. (See specifically Chapter 10 on TEMPEST.)

Smulders, P., "The Threat of Information Theft by Reception of Electromagnetic Radiation from RS-232 Cables," Department of Electronic Engineering, Eindhoven University of Technology, 1990.

"The Tempest Solution," http://www.ionet.net/~everett/solution.html.

7

Fallacies of Protection

7.1   CMOS Passwords

Any computer user has the option of installing a CMOS password, which when installed is required in order for the computer to proceed with normal tasks. It is useless as a protective measure, except against a nontechnical person who has momentary (as in "less than a minute") access to a computer. It can be readily defeated by removing the CMOS battery from a computer, which erases the CMOS password along with all other CMOS data. Even more quickly, the CMOS password can be defeated in many computer models by entering a default password.

A CMOS password is only useful as a deterrent to a casual snoop with very little time to act unobserved.

7.2   Commercial Software Password Protection

Password protection of files (e.g., those created by Microsoft Word or by Wordperfect) also provides protection only from the totally nontechnical casual snoop. One can purchase software (built by, for example, Access Data Corporation in Utah) for only about $150, which breaks this password protection in very short order.

7.3   Hiding Files from View

Hiding files from view by, for example, in DOS typing

>   attrib [filename] +h

or from within Windows by right-clicking on a file, selecting Properties, and enabling the Hide option, also does not prevent anyone from seeing that file. All a snoop has to do is undo this hiding process; this does not even have to be done for each file; in Windows one can set the properties of the Windows Explorer to display all files, whether "hidden" or not.

7.4   Hiding Data in the Slack

Placing a file intentionally in the slack—that is, in the space between the end-of-file and end-of-cluster (see Section 4.2.1)—or "deleting" it (but not overwriting it) so that it can be retrieved by one later does not offer protection in the course of a forensic examination, when a routine check is made of all data in the slack and free space.

7.5   Placing Data in Normally Unused Disk Locations

Placing data in tracks and sectors of a disk that are normally unused by an operating system is an old trick that goes back to the days of the Apple II computer; it was used by software games ostensibly to prevent users from copying the disks; these disks used their own disk operating systems to read those normally unused tracks; it did not take long before users did, too, in order to copy the disks.

Most any determined forensic examination of a disk will access the data "hidden" this way, too.

7.6   Password-Protected Disk Access

Software programs that claim to password-protect one's computer at bootup time or when it is left unattended (e.g., screen blankers) are also ineffective. In the simplest case, unless a user has disabled the option of booting from a floppy disk (a dangerous proposition if one's hard disk crashes), any person could bypass all these passwords and boot from a floppy disk. But even in the case when a user seems to have taken all the password-related precautions to prevent "unauthorized access," these are ineffective against a forensic examination; a forensics examiner removes the disk from the targeted computer, makes a copy of it (track by track and sector by sector), and looks for data, without ever having to go through any of the protective "barriers" inserted by a user.

7.7 Booby-Trapped Software

Booby-trapping software such as Don't Touch by Cybertech Group typically expects the authorized user to enter a sequence of keystrokes (without any prompting) when a computer is turned on; if that sequence is not entered, then the software destroys a specified file in which the authorized user is understood to have stored the sensitive files, and then erases itself as well. This scheme, too, may protect one from a nosy spouse or coworker, but not from a forensic examination, since a performer of the latter never activates any software in the suspect disk. Such schemes could also backfire, causing an otherwise innocent computer user to end up with an obstruction of justice charge.

7.8 File Overwriting

A file is only a part of the information stored in a computer concerning that file. Also present are:

- *The file name* (stored elsewhere). *Hint:* Do not use revealing file names, just in case you forget to get rid of the file name, which, as shown earlier, is also stored at a location that is different from the file's location.

- *Information about the file.* Depending on which software was used, this information can include who created it, when, when it was modified, and so on.

- *"Temporary" copies of the file* created by the software in case the computer crashed while the file was being worked on. Since the computer is not clairvoyant with respect to if or when a crash will occur, some software always creates a temporary file. Even if it is "deleted," it is still very much available on the hard disk until the space it occupied happens to be overwritten (or is deliberately overwritten).

7.9   Encryption

Encryption, in and of itself, refers merely to the conversion of a readable file to one that, at best, is unreadable by all others than the intended recipient(s). Encryption says nothing about such key issues as:

- Is the unencrypted document, or references to it, also left behind on the disk?
- Is the encryption "key" that is used protected from unauthorized individuals?
- Are there additional decryption keys (ADK) in existence that the originator does not know about? (This was the case in the August 1999 Advisory Circular by the highly respected CERT in connection with PGP. See Section 14.3.8.)

The reader is referred to Chapters 13 and 14 for a thorough discussion of commercial encryption.

7.10   Other Protection Fallacies

Beyond the above classic illusions of protecting sensitive documents, there is a vast collection of "tricks" intended to protect sensitive files. Don't depend on them.

Unless a file is truly encrypted (see Chapters 13 and 14) and/or is hidden using good steganography, *and* all evidence of the unencrypted and unsteganographied (see Section 14.5) file is totally eliminated, or unless the magnetic media in question are out of harm's way (e.g., safe from access by, for example, an oppressive regime or hostile forensics examiner), such measures would deter only a nontechnical casual snoop. Worse yet, they make the individual using such techniques that much more likely to receive a thorough forensic analysis of his or her computer. Also, such measures are totally ineffective against a forensic analysis of a targeted computer's magnetic storage media. Ineffective tricks, which can be used in assorted combinations, include (but are not limited to):

- Renaming a file (e.g., from supersecret.doc to virtue.exe);
- Compressing a file (using the standard zip software) and then renaming it;

- Appending a sensitive file to a different, innocuous file (e.g., appending a document or image to an executable file after the latter's end of file);

- Placing a sensitive file in a normally innocuous subdirectory (e.g., inside Windows/System) and calling it "something.dll" or some other plausible name.

The reason that all such schemes do not protect one from a forensic examination is that such an examination looks at the entire data in a disk, regardless of each file's name, location, degree of compression, compliance with an operating system or disk filing system or lack thereof, with what else it is merged, and so on.

Part II
Computer Privacy and Security

8

Protecting Against Unauthorized Snooping and Hostile Computer Forensics

If some among you fear taking a stand because you are afraid of reprisals
from customers, clients, or even government, recognize that you are just feed-
ing the crocodile hoping he will eat you last.

—Ronald Reagan

Quis custodiet ipsos custodies? (Who watches the watchmen?)

—Juvenal

"Countering computer forensics? But aren't you helping the bad people?"
No! Quite the contrary; countermeasures help the good people ward off the
bad people. They also help reduce crime, by making it much harder for
criminals to engage in identity theft and for thieves to violate the law by
stealing intellectual property and legally privileged information such as medical records and attorney-client communications.

Computer forensics is not practiced only by or for law enforcement;
more often than not, it is practiced by anyone with the means to do it, and
for illegal purposes such as stealing intellectual property and passwords. Just
as there are legitimate uses for knives and for matches, there are many legitimate uses for countering illegal computer forensics, such as:

- Preventing the theft of intellectual property;
- Preventing the theft of proprietary business documents by competitors;
- Preventing the compromise or outright theft of legally privileged information, such as medical records and attorney-client privileged communication;
- Protecting freedom fighters in patently oppressive totalitarian regimes;
- Protecting an individual from having information planted in his or her computer that can be subsequently "discovered" and used against him or her;
- Helping lawyers defend their clients from frivolous accusations supported by contaminated "evidence."

The wide availability of free and commercial software packages that promise to protect the individual from assorted types of unauthorized snooping in his or her computer(s) are, in fact, doing most users a disservice, because they lull the buyer into a false sense of security that is worse than no security at all: Someone who knows that he or she is unprotected will be much more careful with what is entrusted to a computer than someone who thinks that there is no security threat. This cannot be overemphasized.

Then there is the philosophical issue implicit in most civilized societies, as expressed in the following scenarios:

If a man on a deserted island whispers sweet nothings into his girl-friend's ear, what was said is nobody else's business. The privacy these two share should not be contingent upon the distance between the two, nor upon the medium used to communicate, whether that be two paper cups and a string or some technologically advanced alternative.

Similarly, if an individual on a deserted island wants to record private musings in a diary, he or she does so with assurance that no unwanted person will be privy to those thoughts. Civilized society has traditionally bestowed the right of privacy to one's own thoughts. That privacy should not be contingent upon the medium used to write one's thoughts, be that paper and pencil or a personal computer.

But, as members of societies, we don't live on deserted islands. Being part of a society brings in numerous limitations of individual freedoms so that each society can function. Indeed, a society has the self-evident right to protect itself from individual conduct that is out-and-out harmful, such as murder, arson, and the like. Part of the implementation of such societal protection is to have early warning of a planned major crime so that such a crime can be prevented; at a minimum, any society needs to have the means to prevent the recurrence of a major crime by positively identifying the perpetrator. Just as ballistics tests can show which gun fired a bullet found in a dead body or whose DNA was at the scene of a major crime, computer forensics can and should be used if it can show conclusively who planned or executed a major crime.

In this sense, this book is highly supportive of the law enforcer who is trying to prevent a major crime, hence the lengthy chapters on effective computer forensics.

The definition of a "crime" is in the mind of the beholder, however. A totalitarian regime often criminalizes everything that those in power don't like, whether it is the expression of a dissenting political or religious thought, or even a joke that treats the ruler unfavorably. Also, what is a crime one day may not be the next, and vice versa, as laws constantly change in all societies. One cannot conveniently define as a "criminal" anyone that any country's court has branded as one; in recent history, some regimes have made it a crime to talk about freedom, to listen to music by this or that composer, or to whistle this or that tune. If a criminal is simplistically defined to be anyone convicted by any court of a locally defined crime, then Christ and Gandhi would have to be included, along with Bertrand Russell, Galileo, Luther, and most other key intellectuals.

One should not forget Montesquieu's words: "There is no greater tyranny than that which is perpetrated under the shield of law and in the name of justice." Nor the words of William Pitt the Younger: "Necessity is the plea for every infringement of human freedom."

Last but not least, there is theft. According to the FBI, some 319,000 laptops were stolen in 1999.[1] Most of these laptops must have undoubtedly included data not intended for others' eyes, such as corporate proprietary information, personal medical and financial information, and the like. The value of the loss of such data to unauthorized eyes is incalculable and usually far exceeds the value of the hardware lost. It would be nothing short of irresponsible for one to allow this to happen to oneself.

---

1. Most such thefts occur at airport security gates: The laptop is placed by its owner on the X-ray machine's conveyor belt; a seemingly rushed traveler cuts in front of the line to get through the magnetometer but has difficulties because of keys and related items on his or her person; while that traveler is being taken care of, his or her accomplice on the other end of the security gate absconds with the laptop owner's computer, which has already passed the X-ray machine.

One should also not forget that the mere proliferation of information technology has made wholesale surveillance not only possible but also economically cost-effective.

Even time-honored institutions that used to respect privacy may well not do so anymore; for example, the U.S. Census, whose data was advertised as being "protected," may not be so. According to the *New York Times,* the Congressional Budget Office, with the supporting help of some members of Congress, has been angling to get its hands on the Census data to create "linked data sets" on individuals using information from the Internal Revenue Service, the Social Security Administration, and the Census Bureau surveys to help it evaluate proposed reforms in Medicare and Social Security (see http://www.nytimes.com/2000/10/23/opinion/23MONK.html).

An often repeated adage is that if one consults a lawyer and wants "justice," many a lawyer will ask, "How much justice can you afford?" A similar situation exists with privacy and security: How much privacy and security can you afford?

8.1   Anonymity

While encryption protects the content of a file, message, or communication, it does not protect the identity of who communicates with whom.

Unlike encryption, which protects the content of a file from forensic discovery, either on-line or off-line, anonymity by its nature—in the present context—relates to the transmittal of a document from the source to its intended destination. What is to be hidden is not the content but the author. Far from being disreputable, anonymity is at the heart of civilized society, as evidenced in the following quotes by world-renown U.S. Supreme Court justices.

Justice Hugo Black, in *Talley v. California* (1960), wrote:

> Anonymous pamphlets, leaflets, brochures and even books have played an important role in the progress of mankind. Persecuted groups and sects from time to time throughout history have been able to criticize oppressive practices and laws either anonymously or not at all.

According to Justice Stevens, in *McIntyre v. Ohio Elections Commission* (1996):

> Anonymity is a shield from the tyranny of the majority.... It thus exemplifies the purpose behind the Bill of Rights, and of the First Amendment in

particular: to protect unpopular individuals from retaliation—and their ideas from suppression—at the hand of an intolerant society.

Commenting also in the McIntyre case was Justice Thomas:

> After reviewing the weight of the historical evidence, it seems that the Framers understood the First Amendment to protect an author's right to express his thoughts on political candidates or issues in an anonymous fashion.

Indeed, the use of anonymous and pseudonymous speech played a vital role in the founding of the United States. When Thomas Paine's *Common Sense* was first released, it was signed "An Englishman." Similarly, James Madison, Alexander Hamilton, John Jay, Samuel Adams, and others carried out the debate between Federalists and Anti-Federalists using pseudonyms. President Harry S. Truman signed his influential 1947 essay "The Sources of Soviet Power" as "X." Finally, the use of a pseudonym, or nom de plume, in literature has a time-honored history (Mark Twain, George Sand, etc.).

There are many flavors of anonymity, such as using a pseudonym, assuming another identity, and so on. For the purposes of this discussion we interpret anonymity to be any technique that prevents a third party from finding the true identity of an Internet user.

Anonymity is an obvious irritant to law enforcement and is criticized as prima facie evidence of criminal intent. For a different perspective, consider the following view by Julf Helsingius, expressed in an interview with *Wired* magazine's Joshua Quittner, coauthor of the high-tech thriller *Mother's Day*. Mr. Helsingius ran the world's most popular remailer in Finland until he retired in 1996.

> Living in Finland, I got a pretty close view of how things were in the former Soviet Union. If you actually owned a photocopier or even a typewriter there you would have to register it and they would take samples.... so that they could identify it later.... The fact that you have to register every means of providing information to the public sort of parallels it, like saying you have to sign everything on the Internet. [Law enforcers] always want to track you down.

Quite often, anonymity actually furthers the cause of law enforcement. For example, a whistle-blower may need to tip off law enforcement of a serious ongoing or planned illegal activity by his or her employer; a suicidal or homicidal individual may wish to obtain help and counseling that he or she would not seek without anonymity; or a drug-addicted mother of a young child may seek anonymous counseling to help her from using all of her financial resources to support her habit. Even some police departments are experimenting with establishing Web sites for anonymous tips about crimes; this is nothing more than an on-line version of the time-honored practice of anonymous "crime solvers" phone lines.

Less dramatic situations justifying anonymity include: seeking employment through the Internet without jeopardizing one's current job, expressing religious opinions in a community that is strongly opposed to them, and placing a personal ad. Doctors who are members of the on-line community often encourage their patients to connect with others and form support groups on issues about which they do not feel comfortable speaking publicly; it is essential to be able to express certain opinions without revealing one's identity. There is a multitude of situations in which anonymity serves a legitimate social function. Conversely, as with anything else, anonymity can be abused by sociopaths who are attracted by the notion of avoiding responsibility and accountability for their actions.

Many everyday activities that were anonymous in the past leave electronic paper trails behind today. Using the lure of discounts or other benefits, the common "preferred customer" card of supermarkets, bookstores, and other vendors allows those vendors to track one's purchasing and renting preferences even if they are made with cash. The same applies to the use of frequent flyer accounts—to frequent-anything accounts—and to the ever-increasing use of credit cards in place of cash.

With the ubiquitous spread of Signaling System 7 in telephony, caller ID information is available to the called party about the calling party. Blocking caller ID does nothing, in the United States, to toll-free calls to 800 area code numbers; since the called party pays for the incoming call, the phone companies use Automatic Number Identification (ANI) to automatically allow the called party to know who is calling, even if the calling party has disabled the outgoing caller ID feature.

E-mail records are now routinely subpoenaed by prosecutors and by attorneys in both criminal and civil cases as evidence.

And the list of examples goes on. As a matter of principle, many individuals have therefore resorted to technology to protect their privacy, often for privacy's own sake.

Additionally, anonymity is a matter of life and death in many societies in the case of responsible individuals expressing views that are unpopular, or that are perceived as a threat by the ruling party, or that question the status quo, or that debate religious or other topics.

8.1.1   Practical Anonymity

There is a vast amount of resources on practical anonymity on the Internet. Some of the most useful Web sites are listed at http://www.privacy-resources.org/anonymity.htm.

It is important to decide up front from whom one wants to remain anonymous:

- The recipient of e-mail that one is about to send?
- The readers of Usenet posts to which one has elected to post?
- The Web sites that one visits on the Internet?
- Someone in a repressive regime who is tapping one's telephone line?
- One's ISP?
- Someone else in one's local network, if one is in use?
- A forensics investigator who gets hold of one's computer?

Each of these requires a different set of procedures and/or software. They are discussed, among other topics of equal relevance and concern, in separate sections in Chapters 10 through 14.

8.2   Privacy

Civilization is the process toward a society of privacy. The savage's whole existence is public, ruled by the laws of the tribe. Civilization is the process of setting man free from men.

—Ayn Rand

Privacy is the right of individuals to control the collection and use of information about themselves.

8.2.1   Can We Trust TRUSTe?

TRUSTe (http://www.truste.com/) is a commercial organization that has set itself up as the grantor of a sort of "seal of approval" for on-line commercial entities that appear to meet some criteria on respecting the confidentiality of customer-provided information.

Can one place one's trust in this? In a word, no! One of the main failings of this scheme is that it cannot handle the cases of companies that go bankrupt and sell their assets to meet their financial obligations; those assets often include the databases of customer information that the bankrupt company had assured its customers would "never" be sold to anyone; the company receiving those databases does not feel bound under any commitments made by the bankrupt company. A typical example is the news item reported on the Internet on October 27, 2000, to the effect that HealthCentral.com had reportedly signed an agreement to purchase the assets of the floundering on-line drugstore more.com *including its customer list,* and its subsidiary ComfortLiving.com, for approximately $6 million.

8.2.2   Is Privacy a "Right"?

8.2.2.1   In the United States

In the United States, there is no explicit constitutional protection for privacy. According to one interpretation, this is the case because the framers of the U.S. Constitution never thought that privacy would be withheld as a self-evident individual right in the first place.

Another interpretation is that such protection conflicts with other constitutional guarantees, such as the First Amendment's protection of the freedom of expression; that amendment limits privacy, in that it blocks the government from taking action to restrict expression that might compromise the privacy of others. There is also some implicit protection in select private activities, such as the practice of one's religion.

At the federal level, "rights" relate only to protection from the government and not from any private party, with the exception of the Thirteenth Amendment, which prohibits slavery. In general, constitutional rights do not require the government to "do" anything; only "not to do" some things.

There is *some* protection of privacy, but from the government only, in the Bill of Rights. The Fourth Amendment's prohibition of "unreasonable search and seizure" implies some privacy; of course, what is "unreasonable" is in the mind of the beholder, and the guidelines are often revised by the U.S. Supreme Court. In 1928 the Court decreed that federal wiretapping did not amount to an unreasonable search because it did not involve a physical trespass (*Olmstead vs. the U.S.*). This has since changed.

The Fifth Amendment prevents the government from taking private property for public use without due process and compensation. In 1984 the Supreme Court decreed that this protection extends to data, too. Even so, the protection is minimal at best, since it only requires due process and compensation; it is not an outright prohibition and, like anything else in the

Constitution, it applies to government actions and not to actions by private parties.

When it comes to data held by the government, the Federal Privacy Act stipulates that government agencies can only store "relevant and necessary" personal information; this stipulation is clearly quite vague and subject to abuse by unscrupulous officials. In the latest twist, it has been disclosed that the government simply allows private companies, such as CBD Infotek of Santa Ana, California, to collect and store all data possible, and then buys that data as needed. This way, the government can assert that it is not itself "storing" data that is not "relevant and necessary," by paying someone else to do it.

So, in essence, what little there is of federal protection of individual privacy relates to procedures rather than substance.

Basically, if the federal government tries to protect privacy, it often ends up at odds with the First Amendment; privacy rights almost never win over the First Amendment right of freedom of expression. As such, collection and dissemination of information, especially about government officials, are hardly ever restricted by the Supreme Court.

A case in point is the August 18, 1999, decision by a federal appeals court in Denver, Colorado, to reverse Federal Communications Commission rules that had been designed to protect telephone consumers from having the numbers they call and the services to which they subscribe used by the phone companies without the subscribers' permission. The court felt that this protection interfered with the phone companies' First Amendment rights to free speech.

With the foregoing as a background, a list of assorted U.S. federal laws that strive to protect select aspects of privacy is provided here:

Fair Credit Reporting Act (1970)

Privacy Act (1974)

Freedom of Information Act (1974)

Family Educational Rights and Privacy Act (1974)

Right to Financial Privacy Act (1978)

Privacy Protection Act (1980)

Cable Communications Policy Act (1984)

Electronic Communications Privacy Act (1986)

Video Privacy Protection Act (1988)

Employee Polygraph Protection Act (1988)

Telephone Consumer Protection Act (1991)

Driver's Privacy Protection Act (1994)

Telecommunications Act (1996) [Excerpt]

Children's On-Line Privacy Protection Act (1999)

Financial Modernization Services Act (1999) [Excerpts]

Federal Trade Commission Act

Privacy laws in the United States—as in most countries—have not kept up with the extremely rapid pace of technology developments in the last decade in the realm of data communications and storage. The Constitution is of minimal help in this regard, so a number of states have stepped in with an assortment of state laws. These laws are often vague and end up being tested in state courts time and again.

Hawaii and Louisiana make it illegal to "invade privacy," but Hawaii permits the invasion of privacy if there is a "compelling State interest." Arizona, likewise, makes it illegal for one to be "disturbed in his private affairs EXCEPT under authority of law." Alaska's 1972 Constitution provides for the "right of people to privacy"; California, in 1974, deemed privacy an "inalienable right," yet in 1994 it permitted mandatory drug testing of college athletes as being an act that does not violate the students' privacy rights.

Private individuals have almost never won lawsuits brought against private parties for "privacy violations." In general, claims against nongovernment entities for loss of privacy must be worded in terms of loss of property and use laws protecting the rights of ownership of property.

One key issue is "who owns the information" about one's person. Is medical information about one owned by that person or by the medical doctor or hospital or insurance company? U.S. courts have often stated that the information is owned by whoever went to a lot of trouble and expense to collect and store it. Even the Supreme Court has stated that any expectations of privacy must derive their legitimacy from laws governing real or personal property.

It follows that the only substantive means that an individual in the United States can use to protect the privacy of his or her data is to encrypt it in a secure manner.

8.2.2.2   In Europe

Western European countries have strong legal protection of individual privacy. Ironically, this protection is possible precisely because Western European governments have fewer legal limitations placed upon them by their respective constitutions than the U.S. government has; for example, the same First Amendment which prohibits the U.S. federal government from placing individual privacy ahead of the right of free expression prevents the U.S. federal government from enacting broad laws protecting one individual's privacy from another individual's effort to collect and disseminate information.

The European press has often been muzzled by individual governments appealing to "higher" principles. As a result, it has been possible in Europe to enact laws prohibiting the broadcasting of any "harmful programming." This very same broad European authority to intervene in the area of communications and information makes it legally possible for European governments to legislate the privacy of individual communications and information.

European laws have explicit provisions for the protection of data and information about individuals. Such protection varies significantly from country to country in Europe, and this has already become a major contentious issue: One article in the 1992 "Common Position ... of the European Parliament ... on the Protection of Individuals with regard to the processing of Personal Data" (formally approved on October 24, 1995, and implemented in October 1998) prohibits member European countries to give that data to nonmembers (e.g., to the United States) which "fail to ensure an adequate level of protection." This has caused European countries to refuse to provide a lot of data to the United States and to U.S. companies.

Article 1 of this same document clearly states that there is a "fundamental right to privacy with respect to the processing of personal data." The fact that the European Union classifies privacy as a human right means that it will be extremely hard for it to be challenged by other conflicting laws (e.g., commercial codes).

While individual European countries' laws related to privacy vary today, the trend is toward a uniform set of standards.

In the United Kingdom there is no written constitution, but in 1998 the Parliament approved the Human Rights Act, which will incorporate a variation of the European Convention of Human Rights into domestic law, a process that will establish an enforceable right of privacy. Even so, on November 23, 1999, a British cryptographer, Brian Gladman, was quoted in publications stating that a component of the U.K. government may resort to covertly implanting Trojan horse software in targeted individuals' computers as a means of circumventing any encryption being used by them, in possible contravention of the 1990 Computer Misuse Act, but in possible compliance with the 1994 Intelligence Services Act. Indeed, plans to intercept e-mail and Internet calls, let alone to covertly tamper with private citizens' computers, contravene the European Convention on Human Rights (ECHR), which is the United Kingdom's version of the European human rights rules.

A list of international (mostly European) laws and "guidelines" intended to protect privacy is provided here:

Universal Declaration of Human Rights (1948)

Council of Europe Convention for the Protection of Human Rights and Fundamental Freedoms (1950)

OECD Privacy Guidelines (1980)

Council of Europe Convention on Privacy (1981)

U.N. Guidelines for the Regulation of Computerized Personal Files (1990)

European Union Data Protection Directive (1995)

European Union Directive for the Protection of Privacy in the Tele-communications Sector (1997)

OECD Cryptography Guidelines

Italian Data Protection Act

Guidelines for the Protection of Individuals with Regard to the Collection and Processing of Personal Data on Information Highways (Council of Europe, 1999)

Law for the Protection of Private Life (Chile, 1999)

The Personal Information Protection and Electronic Documents Act (Canada, 2000)

8.2.2.3 Elsewhere

The extent of legal protection of privacy from the government in other nations varies considerably. Even regimes with a long history of democracy tend to interpret their obligation to ensure domestic tranquility as superseding any individual citizen's right to privacy; this has the obvious potential for self-righteous abuse. As such, many countries have legislated protection of the privacy of a citizen from other citizens but not from the government itself through its law enforcement arms. Interestingly, some languages (e.g., Greek) do not even have a word for "privacy," even though its essence may be ingrained into the culture.

Most other countries, with the notable exception of totalitarian states, have some form of a legally protected privacy of both personal records and communications; most of these protection rights have some carefully worded exclusions in the cases of suspected but nebulously defined "crimes."

Amusingly, most totalitarian states do have laws in the books that ostensibly safeguard their respective citizens' "rights." The catch is that such laws inevitably include a provision that has some variation of the phrase "except as legally authorized by the government or its lawful representatives." This, in essence, amounts to saying that individual citizens have rights until the moment that any government person with power feels like taking them away. This affords individuals about as much protection as a "lifetime warranty" where the lifetime is that of the warranted product: It is protected until it fails.

8.2.3 The Impact of Technology on Privacy

"The right to be left alone" is how a U.S. justice of the Supreme Court, Louis Brandeis, viewed privacy in 1890. What had alarmed him in the first place was technological change, which in those days amounted to the popularization of photography and of inexpensive printing; these were nothing compared with the electronic means openly available today to collect, sift through, and disseminate data about anyone, not to mention technologies for tracking, detecting, and identifying.

The law enforcement agencies of any country assert something to the effect that "we are here to protect you; to do this we need all the tools possible to know as much as possible about everything and everyone; we want a society with domestic tranquility, free from crime [defined to be whatever conduct a State does not like]," and so on. But this is precisely what a secret police unit of any totalitarian nation claims.

The commercial sector asserts sanctimoniously that it is only trying to reduce costs through such practices as knowing everyone's preferences so that it can send customized advertising most likely to generate revenue. The libertarian side takes the position that amounts to, in essence, "we trust neither the government nor profit-minded strangers."

The law enforcement argument can be soothingly sweet to swallow; after all, nobody can credibly take a position against law and order, as doing so evokes images of unshaved savages roaming through the neighborhoods, killing, raping, setting fires, and the like.

The real issue is different altogether. It is a philosophical issue: In an ideal world, governments and their law enforcement arms have impeccable integrity, act always and without exception in good faith, have impeccable records of having done so, and are inherently trustworthy. In such an ideal world, it would be indeed very hard to support any objection to law enforcement omnipotence because, by definition, law enforcement would never do anything inappropriate or abusive. But the world is not ideal. Furthermore, there is ample documented evidence of abuse of authority in every country in the world that goes back many, many years. And such abuse of authority has always transcended the limitations of any one sick individual: It has, historically, been institutionalized. It is human nature. It is a very bad sign when a government and its law enforcement arms make the huge mental leap of confusing their own survival in power with the survival of the nation they are supposed to serve.

There is a lot of internal peace and lack of crime in most totalitarian regimes. The assorted secret police units see to that. Is that really what we want for ourselves? Sure, everybody wants to prevent crime, but at what cost?

To a reasonable person, crime is murder, theft, arson, and other such offenses. To most any government, crime is whatever conduct it does not like. In many countries, it is a crime to say something negative about the respective leaders. In other countries, it is a crime for a teenager to have a copy of *Playboy* magazine under the mattress. In still other countries, crime is doing anything in opposition to the ideology of the state. As such, it is a very slippery slope when any law enforcement organization makes the claim that it is "only preventing crime" or "only enforcing the law"; it sounds legitimate, but is it? Civilized societies today say, "but we are different; we have laws and courts" and due process. Indeed we do; but so does any totalitarian regime. The catch is that totalitarian regimes and even their respective constitutions, if they have any, guarantee all sorts of individual rights "except as authorized by a legal authority," which means that all such rights are granted at the discretion of the government representative, who may take them away as he or she sees fit.

The point being made is that there is no inherent guarantee of civil liberties in the existence of assorted institutions unless there are also built-in means to minimize the likelihood that abuses of power can masquerade under the banner of "legal authority."

It comes down to the philosophical and societal decision of where the line between law enforcement and privacy should be drawn. Is the solution to have more jails and more surveillance and less privacy? Or does the solution reside in sociological measures (such as tighter-knit families, instilling in children a societal sense of shame to prevent unacceptable conduct, and so on)? One should not delegate such fundamental decisions to politicians and certainly not to law enforcement officials but to the philosophers and ethicists of our societies.

Technology that makes surveillance extremely easy is here, and there is a lot more coming:

- A GPS (geopositioning satellite) receiver in every car and in every watch; soon in a chip that could be implanted on one;
- A camera at every key location, which scans passersby and positively identifies every individual in a database;
- Computer and network forensics allowing a regime to be able to identify the individual who typed every word typed on a keyboard;
- DNA profiling, made possible by the human Genome Project, which will anticipate which newborn is likely to become antisocial (whatever that means) and surveil him or her even more, or even exile him or her in advance of any transgression, "for the good of society."

All for the "public good," of course. But then, from which genetic pool will the new Beethovens and Van Goghs and Nietzsches and Bertrand Russells and Gandhis of the future come from if everyone is prefiltered to be "good"?

One might even argue from an evolutionary science viewpoint that this is a recipe for the suicide of the human species, because humankind has survived as a result of the discoveries of restless minds and not as a result of having docile and content-free humanoids.

Selected Bibliography

Diffie, W., and S. Landau, *Privacy on the Line: The Politics of Wiretapping and Encryption,* Cambridge, MA: MIT Press, 1998.

Lash, A., "Is Your Credit Report Online?" Digital Debtors: Part Deux," http://www.news.com/News/Item/0,4,13604,00.html.

Rothfeder, J., *Privacy for Sale,* New York: Simon and Schuster, 1992.

Wacks, R., *Privacy and Press Freedom,* London: Blackstone Press, 1995. This has a U.K. focus.

Selected Bibliography of Internet Sources on Privacy

http://www.privacy.net/ demonstrates what Web sites get from your browser.

http://www.fipr.org/ for U.K. perspective on privacy.

http://www.privacyware.com/ for privacy-related software.

http://www.cdt.org/action/doubleclick.shtml (U.S. Center for Democracy and Technology).

http://www.users.globalnet.co.uk/~firstcut/privacy.html for technical countermeasures.

http://www.privacytimes.com/ for privacy-related news.

http://www.users.globalnet.co.uk/~firstcut/dload.html for privacy-related software.

http://www.townonline.com/privacyjournal/ for privacy-related guidelines.

http://www.vortex.com/privarch.html for archive postings on the Usenet "Privacy" forum.

http://www.privacyrights.org/ for information about privacy.

http://www.privacyrights.org/links.htm for numerous additional links on privacy.

http://www.andrebacard.com/privacy.html for software and links about privacy.

http://www.privacyplace.com/ for privacy-related news.

http://www.stealthyguest.com/ for information and software for private Web browsing.

http://www.privacy.org/pi/ focuses on international trends in privacy.

http://www.stack.nl/~galactus/remailers/index-anon.html provides tutorials in anonymity and remailers.

http://www.anonymizer.com is one of the many Web sites offering anonymity.

http://www.cs.berkeley.edu/~daw/papers/privacy-compcon97-www/privacy-html.html is a University of California Web site with numerous articles about privacy.

Selected Bibliography of Privacy Organizations

http://www.eff.org/—Electronic Printer Foundation

http://www.epic.org/—Electronic Privacy Information Center

http://www.efga.org/—Electronic Frontier, Georgia

http://www.privacyrights.org/—Privacy Rights Clearinghouse

http://www.aclu.org/—American Civil Liberties Union

http://www.ipc.org/—Interconnecting and Packaging Electronic Circuits Association

http://www.rightoprivacy.com/—Right to Privacy (private organization)

http://www.privacy.org/ipc/—Internet Privacy Coalition

http://www.computerprivacy.org/—Americans for Computer Privacy

http://www.bigbrotherinside.org/—A private group that wants to boycott Intel's Pentium III

http://www.aaas.org/spp/anon/links.htm—American Association for the Advancement of Science

9

Protecting Proprietary and Other Confidential Information

9.1   Installing Secure Windows

"Secure Windows" is a contradiction in terms; Windows was never designed as a secure operating system, with the possible exception of Windows NT, and that only under rigidly controlled conditions that no individual user abides by.

Even so, one can do a lot to remove a large number of security threats to one's setup.

9.1.1   General Measures for Windows Users

1. Disable the built-in microphone (present in most laptops); the easiest way is to connect a plug into the "external microphone" receptacle; this will disable the internal microphone and, since it is just a plug with no microphone, will not allow any sound to get picked up and either recorded in digitized form on the hard disk or transmitted via a modem.

2. Start with a newly purchased hard disk. Even huge capacity hard disks (e.g., 30–40 GB or more) can be purchased for just a couple of hundred dollars these days, and starting from a known clean disk

is the only way of ensuring that one's hard disk is free of anything inappropriate.

3. After partitioning the disk for your needs and formatting it, use a DOS-based free-space wipe utility from a floppy disk (such as Zapempty from http://www.sky.net/~voyageur/wipeutil.htm) and overwrite it a few times for good measure.

4. Install Windows (Windows NT or 2000 is recommended over 95/98), but enter some nondescript name other than your true name during the personalization step; it is much harder to remove one's true name after the fact because the Windows registration name is saved in the registry and is subsequently copied and used by most software installed on the computer.

5. Obtain and use SecureOffice from http://www.mach5.com/sof/. This software allows you to do drafts for Microsoft Office (Word, PowerPoint, etc.) without leaving the massive amount of electronics trash that Microsoft sprinkles all over one's hard disk. Its user interface is very convenient, as is apparent in Figure 9.1.

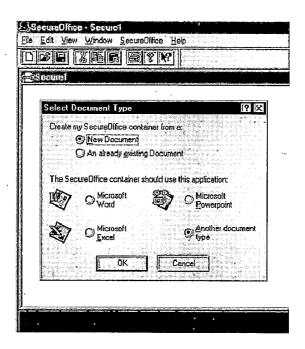

Figure 9.1 Creating a Microsoft Office document securely. (Box shot reprint from Microsoft Corporation.)

6. Go to Recycle Bin/Properties and select "one setting for all drives" and "remove files immediately when discarded" as shown in Figure 9.2, but do *not* put any files in there because it is harder to "wipe" a "deleted" file (meaning one whose name has been forgotten and/or is not readily visible). Instead, obtain and use any of the many utilities for secure wiping of sensitive files, such as those that come with McAfee and Norton utilities. Better yet, periodically wipe your entire hard disk using Secure Clean from Access Data Company and another wiping utility (e.g., Evidence Eliminator if using Windows 95/98 and 2000).

Caution: Do not trust any single disk-cleaning software. It may or may not do the cleaning that it claims it does. There have been unproven allegations about one other file-wiping utility to the effect that it may be a law-enforcement-sponsored effort with a back door. For peace of mind, use two or more different disk-wiping software programs in sequence (e.g., Evidence Eliminator and Window Washer), followed by a disk-defragmenting and a disk-wiping utility such as Secure Clean. And to be sure, use a commercial or freely available disk-snooping utility (such as Directory Snoop, http://www.briggsoft.com/dsnoop.htm), or Encase (which is reportedly used by most law enforcement organizations at the state and local levels in the United States) to ensure that what should not be in the disk is not there at the end.

7. (*a*) Do not allow others to use your personal computer, and certainly not to install any files, games, or such. Last year's computer models are dirt-cheap nowadays, and one can buy one of them for

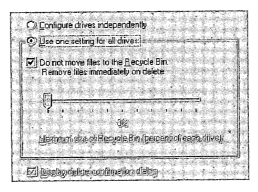

Figure 9.2 Setting the recycle bin so as not to store deleted files. (Box shot reprint from Microsoft Corporation.)

less than a hundred dollars if other family members want to have a computer of their own. The risks of not doing so (having a Trojan or adware/spyware unintentionally installed by a well-meaning family member in a computer that stores sensitive personal information) are just too high.

(*b*) Install and use InstallWatch by Epsilon Squared (http://www. epsilonsquared.com/installwatch.htm) or a comparable program that will inform you what files are placed where during any software installation (e.g., registry changes, and DLLs); this is the ultimate protection against inadvertent installation of Trojans if you have the time and inclination to monitor each installation of software in your computer.

8. Do not connect your personal computer to the Internet, *ever;* the risks are just too high. Instead, get an inexpensive second computer on which is stored nothing even remotely sensitive or identifying, and use that to connect to the Internet. (See Chapters 10–14 on preparing a computer for secure on-line access.)

9. Obtain, install, use, and periodically update (at least weekly) a good virus detection program. Ideally, use two such programs, as no one of them is known to catch all viruses, Trojans, and worms. Recommended ones include:

- **Norton Antivirus.** *Caution:* Its 2000 version is alleged to contain a "call home" feature that you do not want.

- **The Cleaner,** from http://www.moosoft.com/. It is claimed to have superior Trojan detection as compared with mainstream virus detection software packages. It is a bit quirky on Windows 98 and there have been problems with its on-line update.

- **TDS-2** from http://tds.diamondcs.com.au (quirky on Win98 but OK on Windows NT) or similar packages from many other reputable vendors. It, too, does "home calling" (to automatically check for new updates) that individual users may wish to disable.

10. Disable SMARTDRV in Windows 3.1x, and VCACHE in Win95 and Windows for Workgroups (WFW). *Caution:* Doing so will likely result in a performance hit; the computer will slow down. These "write-behind" caches defeat many commercial software programs that claim to "wipe" or "sanitize" disks. In the case of

Windows 3.1x this is done with SMARTDRV, a "terminate and stay resident" program that caches recently used data in memory and also performs "read ahead" caching so as to minimize disk accessing. Win95 and WFW3.11 use VCACHE. The problem is that both can do write-behind caching. Remember that 16-bit programs (such as the superb 16-bit version of PGP) running under Windows 95 cannot sanitize a disk.

11. Do not print decrypted documents, unless you are prepared to go through extra security steps. The problem is that anything sent to the printer is "temporarily" stored on disk and then "deleted" (meaning, made invisible to you but very visible to any forensics investigator).

12. Be very concerned about system crashes. Sure, computers crash with sickening regularity, but this is much more than a nuisance: If your computer crashes during a sensitive operation (encrypting, decrypting, typing, or viewing), there is a good chance that a temporary file will be left behind that one would wish had not been left behind for the benefit of forensics analysis. If the computer crashes, you must go through a full process of securely cleaning it up, meaning:

- Deleting all temporary files;
- Wiping the slack;
- Wiping all free space;
- Wiping the swap file;
- Wiping disingenuously chosen file names.

13. Download, install, and use Tweak UI's "paranoia" option (see Figure 9.3). This is a handy collection of utilities put together by Microsoft that includes the option of cleaning up after the long list of electronics trails left behind by using Windows. Keep in mind that a separate version exists that works best for Win95/98, WinNT, and Win2000. The main source is http://www.microsoft.com/ntworkstation/downloads/PowerToys/Networking/NTTweakULasp; another source is http://twocows.apollo.lv/shellnt.html. All options under "paranoia" should be checked, as shown in Figure 9.3. At the same time it must be remembered that this utility "deletes" rather than "wipes," which

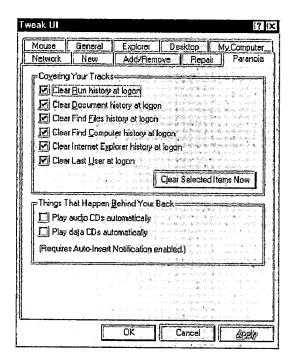

Figure 9.3 Tweak UI "paranoia" option. (Box shot reprint from Microsoft Corporation.)

means that everything is still left behind for a forensics investigator unless one actually wipes the empty space of the hard disk.

9.1.2   Measures Specific to Windows 95/98

Follow measures 1 through 13 in Section 9.1.1 and continue as follows.

14. Create a RAM disk by including the line

DEVICE=C:\WINDOWS\RAMDRIVE.SYS 1024 /2

at the end of the config.sys file in your C: drive, using any text editor. This will create a 1-MB RAM drive whose letter designation will most likely end up being D:\. *Caution:* Your CD-ROM drive will become F:\, and you will want to know that when your software asks you where to look for the CD-ROM.

After installing software, use a text editor and open the Auto-exec.bat file and look for any lines that set a temporary directory. Change them all to point to your RAM drive. Some software programs (e.g., PGP) require that you specify their temporary directory from within the software; do so, and specify your RAM drive above.

15. Consider purchasing and installing an inexpensive program called VRAMDIR (see Figure 9.4) from Virtual Software Corporation (http://www.virtusoft.com/). It works independently from the RAM disk and allows you to automatically intercept data that would have been written onto your hard disk and place it in dynamically allocated RAM. This little program is worth its weight in gold. One should specify the full directory path of all sensitive files, such as all Netscape "user profile" files (see Section 11.1) as shown in Figure 9.4, in addition to Windows temporary files and printer spool files.

16. Assuming that you have at least 256 MB of RAM (as you should), opt for zero virtual memory. The procedure is similar—although not identical—in all versions of Windows. For Windows 98, for example, go to Control Panel/System/Performance/Virtual Memory and

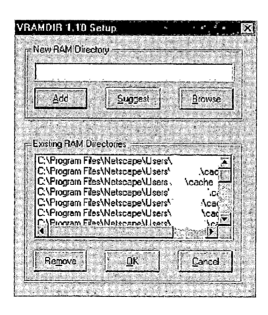

Figure 9.4 VRAMDIR file specifications. (Box shot reprint from Microsoft Corporation.)

deselect the default that allows Windows to pick whatever size of virtual memory it wants; select "Disable Virtual Memory." In Windows NT, go to Control Panel/System/Performance/Virtual-Memory and select "Change" as shown in Figure 9.5.

· If you have less than 256 MB and you do not want the massive security benefit of not having to worry about the swap file, then you can at least set your own virtual memory (or swap) size by specifying the same amount for minimum and maximum; a good starting number is 128 MB. This makes it possible for swap file overwriters to clean the swap file without you having to wipe the entire free portion of your hard disk every time. Ignore Windows protestations. See Figure 9.6.

17. Consider getting a small program called WinPatrol from http://www.winpatrol.com/, which will inform you any time some software elects to run without your knowledge, and ask your approval before this is allowed to happen. Periodically, run it to see which programs are "running" on your computer, and ensure that

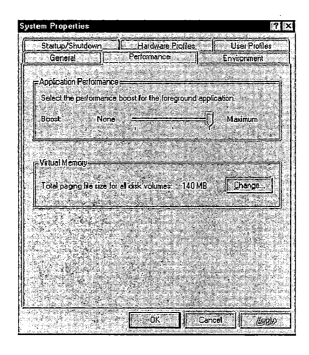

Figure 9.5 Setting virtual memory in Windows NT4. (Box shot reprint from Microsoft Corporation.)

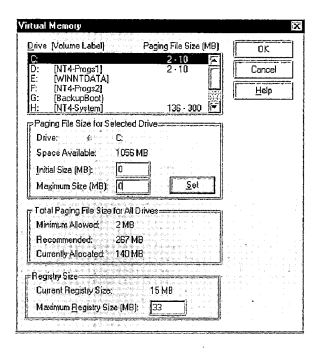

Figure 9.6 Virtual memory disabling. (Box shot reprint from Microsoft Corporation.)

each one that does, has a legitimate reason for running in the background; this can be tricky, as some of them have nondescript names (such as deskcp16.dll), and malicious programs could be intentionally using innocuous-sounding names (such as sysfile.dll).

18. It is extremely important to ensure that "sharing" of files/folders and of printers has been disabled in one's computer. Go to Control Panel/Network/Configuration/File and Print Sharing/ and disable any and all sharing. This is particularly important if one goes online.

19. Consider getting the following security-related software programs, installing them, learning how to use them, and using them:

- **Eraser** from http://www.tolvanen.com/eraser/. Free software that wipes one's disk clean.

- **Evidence Eliminator** from http://www.evidenceeleminiator.com/. Does a thorough job of cleaning practically all traces that one does not want to leave behind.

- ScramDisk (version 3; do not use earlier versions) from http://www.scramdisk.clara.net/. Free software to create fully encrypted partitions in your hard drive. (See Section 14.4.)

- **PGP version 6.02 CKT Build 7.** Obtain from http://www.ipgpp .com/ and follow the recommendations in Section 14.3. Its main claim to fame is that it supports much longer keys than the "mainstream" PGP and is backwards compatible.

- SecureClean. From Access Data Corporation (http://www.access-data.com/). This is an excellent additional file- and swap-wiping utility; you don't want to be at the mercy of the weaknesses of any one wiping utility, so use this in addition to Eraser, listed above.

- **Window Washer** (and free attachments for various software packages) from http://www.webroot.com/.

- Surf Secret. For use by the "cheap" computer that will go on-line for Internet access. Get Surf Secret from http://www.surfse-cret.com/.

9.1.3 Measures Specific to Windows NT

The use of Windows NT is highly recommended. If using this package, fol-low measures 1–13 in Section 9.1.1 and continue as follows.

14. Create a RAM disk by using either the Microsoft-made RAM disk for NT software or the commercial software shown in Section 9.1.4.

15. Convert to NTFS using the simple Windows NT command to do so, and, if possible, select 512-byte cluster size.

16. Disable Print- and File-Sharing as shown in Section 9.1.2.

17. Set up the Windows NT registry to automatically wipe the swap file every time you power off by doing the following:

    a. Run REGEDT32.exe.

    b. Go to HKEY_LOCAL_MACHINE\SYSTEM/CurrentCon-trolSet/Control/Session Manager/Memory Management, as shown in Figure 9.7.

    c. Change the value of "ClearPageFileAtShutdown" to 1. If this parameter does not exist, add it as follows:

       1. Value Name: ClearPageFileAtShutdown

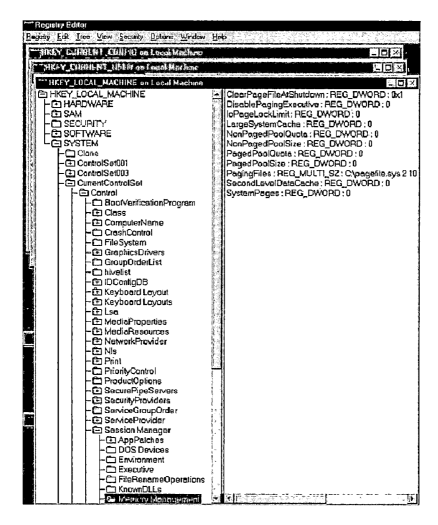

Figure 9.7 Registry editing with REGEDIT. (Box shot reprint from Microsoft Corporation.)

2. Value Type: REG_DWORD
3. Value: 1

This will become effective only after the computer is restarted.

This "recipe" works for Windows NT and Windows 2000 as well.

Caution: There is no information from Microsoft as to just exactly how the data is overwritten; it may or may not be adequately

secure; one would be well advised to (also) wipe the registry using
standalone independent software (such as SecureClean and
SCORCH).

18. Consider getting the following security-related software programs,
installing them, learning how to use them, and using them:

- **BestCrypt.** From http://www.jetico.com/, to create fully
encrypted partitions on your hard drive. See also Section 14.4.

- **Eraser.** From http://www.tolvanen.com/eraser/. Free software
that wipes one's disk clean.

- **PGP version 6.02 CKT Build 7.** Follow the recommendations
in Section 14.3. Its claim to fame is that it supports far longer
key lengths than the "mainstream" PGP and is backward compatible. Do not use the "pgp disk" option on Windows NT, as
it is faulty for all versions of PGP.

- **SecureClean.** From Access Data Corporation (http://www.access-
data.com/). It is an excellent additional file- and swap-wiping
utility; you don't want to be at the mercy of the weaknesses of
any one wiping utility, so use this in addition to Eraser, listed
above. Unlike many of its competitors, it seems to have no difficulty finding the swap file after automatically switching to DOS
(as it should, to clear the swap file). It works with all versions of
Windows, but Windows NT and 2000 do not need a swap-file
cleaning as it can be done from within Windows if set properly.
It is very configurable, as shown in Figure 9.8.

9.1.4   Measures Specific to Windows 2000

Follow measures 1–13 in Section 9.1.1 and continue as follows.

14. First and foremost, dissociate yourself from the notion that Windows 2000 is more secure than NT; it is not. Its "encryption"
option conveys a false sense of security; it is simply not secure with
respect to any competent forensics analysis. The reasons are as
follows:

a. The swap file is not allowed by that system to be encrypted;
given what was stated in Chapter 4 about the swap file and the
fact that it usually contains a lot of what one does with the

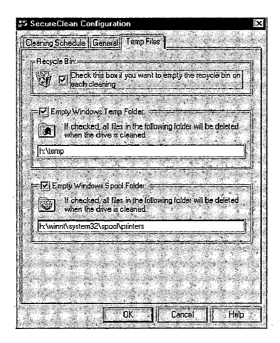

Figure 9.8   SecureClean setup to wipe data. (Courtesy of AccessData Corp.)

computer, encrypting a file or folder but not the swap file is like locking your front door and leaving the back door wide open.

b. System files (e.g., registry) are also not allowed to be encrypted. Given what was said in Chapter 4 about the wealth of sensitive personal data placed by Windows into the registry, leaving that encrypted is like leaving all of one's windows in the house wide open (in addition to leaving the back door open as per (a).

c. There is no encryption of the slack in the disk; given what was discussed in Section 4.2.1 about what can exist in the slack to delight the forensics investigator, this is like leaving a floor plan for the convenience of the burglar of one's house.

d. While one can (and should, but often does not think of doing) specify that the "temporary" folder is to be encrypted as well, the fact is that different software have the bad habit of using their own temporary storage locations in one's disk. As such, there is no one temporary folder to protect. This is like locking one piece of jewelry in the safe but leaving the rest for a burglar to take.

e. Even though a folder can be specified to be encrypted and files created in or copied into it become encrypted, the folder itself is not encrypted at all and anyone with the right access permissions can see the names of the encrypted files in it.

In view of the foregoing, the much heralded "encryption" option of the Windows 2000 operating system is a useless gimmick; in fact, it is worse than useless because it will tend to instill a false sense of security in the minds of those that use it in the mistaken belief that it protects their sensitive data from forensics analysis. It does not.

15. Unlike Windows NT, Windows 2000 has a very convoluted way of renaming the administrator account to a name that is hard for an unauthorized person to guess.

16. Do not display the last user's name in the logon sequence screen, which you must manually enable; do not accept the automatic logon. To disable the last user display, go to the "Local Security Policy" and make the change. The reason for doing this is that there is no reason that an unauthorized person should know half of your login magic words (user name) and only have to guess the other half (password).

17. Convert to NTFS5 with the command-line command:

    convert C: /fs:ntfs

    (if converting a drive other than C:, use the appropriate letter).

18. Once Windows has been set up, do not log in for day-to-day usage with the administrator account or with any other that has administrator privileges; use, instead, one created for your use that has simple user privileges; this is so that surreptitious access to your system files (that require administrator privileges) cannot be made while you are using some software that has a dual, malicious, function.

19. Beware of Windows 2000's "MFT" (master file table). It has at least one entry for each and every file in an NTFS volume in your computer, along with extended information about each such file (date/time stamps, data content, etc.). Worse yet, in the interest of speed, Microsoft does not edit and compact that MFT "super file" but merely appends to it. Because of this, it can contain a list of files that goes back to the day when you installed Windows 2000, long after you think that you deleted all references to them. Also, if you have a huge number of files on your disk after a year or two and

Windows runs out of the preallocated MFT space, you will get no warning and the directory table for the volume will crash. To prevent that, you need to "hack" the registry as follows:

Run "regedt32"

Go to HKEY_LOCAL_MACHINE\System\CurrentControlSet \Control\FileSystem

Select "Add" from the Edit menu

In the dialog box, enter:

Value Name: NtfsMftZoneReservation

Data Type: REG_DWORD

Data: (enter 3 or 4; 4 is the maximum)

Close regedt32

This hack will only fix the possibility of a volume directory crash and not the security problem, which is unfixable. About the only fix for the security problem is to use file names that are nonincriminating and nondescript.

20. If you elect to avail yourself of the encryption option in Windows 2000 (and there is really no benefit as per above other than some protection from a totally unsophisticated person that might take an interest in your computer), then at least realize that even then, someone can easily spoof your computer into revealing those encrypted files by logging in as an administrator through a back door as follows:

To encrypt a folder from the command line, type:

CIPHER [/E| /D] [/S:dir] [/I] [/F] [/Q] [pattern or directory]

Where:

/E   Causes the encryption of the specified directories.

/D   Decrypts the folder and stops any further encryption.

/S   Encrypts all files and subfolders in that directory.

/I   Forces the encryption to continue even if an error occurs. (Normally encryption stops if an error occurs.)

/F   Forces encryption on all directories specified. (Already encrypted directories will not be encrypted again.)

/Q   Reports minimal information about the status of the encryption of a file or folder being encrypted.

If individuals want to hack into your encrypted files without your knowledge, all they have to do is restart your computer from the emergency repair disk (ERD), reinstall the Windows 2000 operating system (e.g., from the distribution CD-ROM), set themselves up as the administrator, and use the default file recovery certificate that you will most likely have left in the computer.

To preclude that, export the default recovery certificate to a floppy by:

a. Logging in as administrator.

b. Start/Run mmc.

c. Select Console, Add/Remove.

d. Select Add.

e. Highlight the "Certificates" option and click Add.

f. Select "My User Account."

g. Click "Finish."

h. Close and click "OK."

i. Open Certificates—Current User, Personal, Certificates in the left panel. On the right side, you will see a certificate listed. Right-click on it and select "All tasks," Export. This will start the "Certificate Wizard."

j. Choose "Yes," "Export the private key." Click on "next."

k. Select "Personal Information Exchange" and then remove the check on "Enable strong protection" and also on "Delete the private key if effort is successful." Select "Next."

l. Enter a good password. Make sure you write it down somewhere so that it is not forgotten. Select "Next."

m. Make up a file name to save that key. Put a floppy disk in the computer and type A:RECOVERY.PFX.

n. Select "Next" and "Finish."

o. Now you must delete the certificate on the hard disk. Right-click on the entry for the certificate and select "Delete."

p. To verify that the certificate has indeed been deleted, reboot the computer, log in as administrator, and try to read any file on the disk that has been encrypted as any user other than administrator; it should fail.

21. Install and use a RAM disk, such as the one depicted in Figure 9.9, from http://www.jlajoie.com/ramdiskNT. A free trial version is available from that source.

Caution: Do *not* enable the option, shown in Figure 9.9, whereby the RAM disk is saved onto the physical hard disk just before shutting down; doing so would negate the security benefit of having a RAM disk in the first place.

Caution: This admonition applies to all computer users, regardless of which operating system is being used and whether or not the computer in question is ever connected to any network: If you plan to have your computer serviced or repaired by someone else, make sure that the hard disk is removed first. The reasons should be self-evident by now.

An alternate source for a RAM disk function is Hurricane 98's Dynamic RAM drive (see http://www.musicgraveyard.com/hurricane98.html).

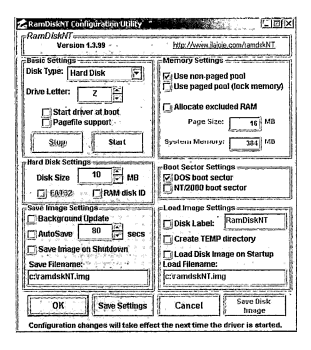

Figure 9.9 RAM disk for Windows 2000. Do not enable any of the "Save image" settings. (Courtesy of John Lajoie Consulting, Inc.)

9.1.5   Heroic Protective Measures for All Windows Versions

The following is a list of heroic protective measures for all Windows versions.

1. If using a laptop, consider removing the hard disk and either taking it with you or storing it in a physically safe place when you cannot exercise physical control over the laptop. Most laptops' hard disks are easily removable and are inconspicuous to carry even in a shirt pocket.

2. Consider using either of the two "full disk encryption" packages discussed in Section 14.2, but realize that they do not protect from anything while one is legitimately using the computer (e.g., no protection from viruses/Trojans/worms coming from installed software or from connectivity to a network). They do protect from anyone, however, when the computer is off, but not from keyboard and other commercial cable taps discussed in Sections 6.3 and 6.4.

3. If you are mostly concerned about a relatively unsophisticated intruder—that is, one who will try to turn your computer on, rather than remove and copy your hard disk—you may want to consider using Don't Touch. This is a Russian software program (e-mail is cyteg@mail.ru) that wipes any folder you designate (and all of its contents as well as the Don't Touch software itself) if the intruder does not push a particular sequence of keys (which is not solicited) during bootup. Frankly, it is better to encrypt the files you are trying to protect.

4. Do whatever you feel would indicate to you if your computer has been physically accessed in your absence; this includes not only electrical access but also physical access to its disk(s) inside.

5. There is no sense protecting the computer if the backups (in the form of tapes or disks) are not protected equally well. If you have backups, as you should as it is only a matter of time until your computer will crash for any one of many reasons, keep those backups out of reach of whoever you are (or should be) concerned can get them and cause you harm. To prevent the total loss of your data if there should be a fire in your premises, make a habit of hand carrying your backups to a friend's house on a regular basis.

6. Use the TEMPEST-resistant fonts openly available through the Internet, as per Section 6.7.2, when composing anything sensitive, specifically password entries.

7. Purchase a keyboard as well as the keyboard cable, monitor cable, and printer cables from a store yourself. Mark them in a way that would indicate to you if they are ever changed.

8. Look for any new "adapters" that may appear in line with any of these cables (Section 6.3 on the commercially available keyboard taps).

9. This measure is tedious but well worth it if the situation warrants. Obtain a simple "hash signature" program, such as CRC.COM, HASH.EXE, or MD5.ZIP. The intent of any of these programs is to "fingerprint" whichever file(s) you want to ensure have not been doctored without your knowledge. The ritual for using any of these programs is:

   a. You "apply" any of these programs to the file you want to protect. All this does is generate a few bytes on the screen that you should copy down and store securely, because they represent the "signature" of the file at a time when you trust that file to have been unmodified by anyone. Applying these programs to a file, such as "stuff.doc" is as simple as typing (from DOS)

   CRC [path]stuff.doc

   in the case of crc.exe.

   b. Whenever you suspect that someone may have doctored any such protected file, reapply the same program to that file and compare the new "signature" to the old, securely stored, one; if they differ, it means that the protected file has been changed. This should be done for all sensitive files, such as encryption-related files (keys, executables, etc.) and all major system files, such as DLLs in C:\Windows\System\.

9.1.6 Last But Not Least

No cookbook of technical countermeasures and steps can ever take the place of common sense and sound practices [which is what operational security (OPSEC) is all about].

Such self-evident blunders that can never be prevented by any technical countermeasure include but are not limited to:

- Poorly chosen passwords, or passwords written on scraps of paper that others can find;

- Overused and infrequently changed passwords;
- Having a computer monitor facing an open window;
- Leaving a computer unattended while it is "on";
- Allowing one's computer to be used promiscuously by others;
- Storing sensitive papers or magnetic media (such as backups, "recover" disks, or encryption software) in locations easily accessible to others;
- Dismissing important security recommendations such as those described in this book;
- Leaving a computer's hard disk physically unprotected.

9.2   The Pentium III Serial Number Threat

Most Pentium III Intel chips, as well as some mobile Pentium II chips and Celeron microprocessors (http://www.infoworld.com/cgi-bin/displayStory.pl?990310.wcpsn.htm) have been endowed with a serial number that is different for each and every such microprocessor and can therefore be used to identify the computer it is in and, by extension, the user.

Intel viewed this initially as a "security" feature to help reduce on-line fraud, because this serial number can be retrieved on-line by the remote Web site. As a result of widespread condemnation of this feature and calls for boycotting all Intel products, Intel backtracked and agreed to ship newer versions that still have this feature but have it "software disabled" in the default state—but still enable-able by a user.

It has been demonstrated by ZeroKnowledge (http://www.zks.org/), a Canadian firm, and reported on the Internet (http://www.infoworld.com/cgi-bin/displayStory.pl?990310.wcpsn.htm) as well as by others (e.g., http://www.heise.de/ct/english/99/05/news1/) that the software provided by Intel for disabling this feature can be hacked and that this feature could be enabled without a user's knowledge; furthermore, the chip ID can be doctored by a knowledgeable user so that the chip ID reported would be faked, according to noted cryptographer Bruce Schneier in his article "Why Intel's ID Tracker Won't Work" at http://www.zdnet.com/zdnn/stories/comment/0,5859,2194863,00.html.

Interestingly, the Chinese government has restricted the sale of Pentium III chips because of national security concerns; it has ordered domestic manufacturers to turn off the serial number and has also ordered its government agencies not to connect Pentium IIIs to the Internet (http://jya.com/

cn-p3-peril.htm). Intel has, reportedly, decided not to include this "feature" in its next generation of microprocessors.

In practical terms, a security-conscious user would be well advised not to use computers that have the Pentium III chips in them, and certainly not to connect them to a network. Internet-related functions do not require the computational speed and capability of a Pentium III chip and are more than adequately served by Pentium II and earlier microprocessors.

9.3 Additional Privacy Protection Measures

9.3.1 Individually Serial-Numbered Documents

Some popular software (e.g., versions of Microsoft Office) have the privacy-compromising feature whereby any document saved also includes the serial number of the individual software copy that created it; this information is not displayed to the user when viewing the document but is saved nonetheless. This is known as the "globally unique identifier" (see http://www.nytimes .com/library/tech/99/04/circuits/articles/08pete.html). It was reportedly used to identify the perpetrator of the Melissa virus.

The problem with this is that a savvy recipient of an electronic copy of a document (e.g., an e-mailed one or one handed in a floppy disk) or a computer forensics investigator will be able to infer additional information about the creator of the document who may have wanted to have remained anonymous. To protect from this, a user who wishes to remain anonymous should not provide electronic copies of documents created, but printed ones on paper.

9.3.2 Adobe's New "Web Buy" Feature

"Web Buy" allows users to buy, download, and view documents produced and sold by publishers using the Adobe PDF Merchant.

Users should know that this feature will transmit unencrypted information, possibly including storage device ID, logon name, and so on when contacting the provider's server.

9.3.3 Microsoft Documents That "Call Home"

In a nutshell, a Microsoft document (Word, PowerPoint, Excel 2000) can contain an invisible Web "bug" that, when opened, can access the Internet (when one is on-line) and send the host name of the computer and related identifying information. (See http://www.privacyfoundation.org/advisories/advWordBugs.html.) As the Word file is given or e-mailed to others, those recipients become vulnerable to the same privacy-violating situation.

On the positive side, such a Web bug can be used by a company to help track leaked confidential documents and even the edit/copy/paste of sensitive paragraphs (that contain the Web bug) to other documents. What makes this possible is the ability of Microsoft Word documents to link to an image file that resides at some remote Web server. Every time the Word document is opened, the Internet-enabled computer will try to get the image from the remote site; this, in turn, allows the remote site to know who is accessing the document, when, and from where. The Web bug image need not be any larger than a single pixel.

Inserting a Web bug is simple:

1. Use the Insert/Picture/From File option.

2. In the file name of the "insert picture" dialog box, enter the URL of the Web bug.

3. Opt for the "Link to File" option of the "Insert" button.

A demo of this is available at http://www.privacycenter.du.edu/demos/bugged.doc, /bugged.xls, and /bugged.ppt for Word, Excel, and PowerPoint, respectively. This is done through Microsoft's Internet Explorer.

The countermeasure is to disable cookies in the browser, and to use a firewall that alerts a user to any unexpected attempt by the computer to access the Internet. This threat is not unique to Microsoft. The generic threat can become part of practically every file format, such as MP3 music files (hotly contested by the music industry), images, and so on.

9.3.4 NetBIOS and Other Threats from Unneeded Network Services

Most individuals use a computer that is either standalone or connected to the Internet. For those people, there is absolutely no need to accept the default network setups that come with Windows, because they include services that can only cause security-related grief.

Go to Network and Dial Up Connections. (In the case of Windows 95/98 it is under "My Computer"; in the case of Windows 2000 it is under Settings/Control Panel.) Under Properties/Networking, disable all options except for TCP/IP (which is needed for Internet access). Specifically disable NetBIOS and any Microsoft Networking.

This will take care of one of the "10 most critical Internet security threats" identified by the respected SANS Institute (http://www.sans.org/topten.htm).

9.3.5   Vulnerability of Backups

All hard disks will, sooner or later, crash for any one of many reasons; it is totally reckless on the part of the individual not to make regular backups. These backups, however, should be viewed as every bit as vulnerable to unauthorized viewing and analysis as the originals; in fact, they are more vulnerable because:

- They are almost always portable and easily removed from one's premises.
- They are rarely "wiped" by users; instead, users either overwrite on top of the previous backup or—worse yet—simply append the changes since the last backup using any one of many backup-making software programs.
- They can provide an adversary with a chronological record of changes and events.
- In those cases when encrypted partitions are not amenable to routine backup software, one has to first decrypt those partitions, and the backups therefore often include files that are encrypted in the original.

The process of making a backup is almost always viewed as a "chore" (until one's disk crashes, at which point one is elated for having had the foresight to make one). Because of this, users do not usually apply security considerations to the task.

The following list of security-motivated steps is recommended for backups:

1. Wipe each previous backup *before* proceeding with the next one.
2. Use full backups and never incremental ones.
3. Be aware that some disk-encryption software programs have the quirky requirement that they can only back up the encrypted portion after it has first been decrypted; this means that the backup will be extremely vulnerable. Do not use such encryption software.

4. Use a password to protect the contents of the backup. This provides no protection against a forensic attack, but does protect from casual perusal. Also, use compression, which is usually offered as an option in the backup process, to make it just a bit more difficult for one to glance at the contents.

5. Store the backups away from the computer that was backed up, preferably at some location not accessible by a potential adversary (business or personal).

6. Do not acknowledge the existence of backups to unauthorized others.

7. Protect the backups as if they contained the family jewels. They often do.

10

Basic On-Line Computer Forensics

A few years ago, TV viewers in Germany were shown how an unsuspecting Internet user who had accessed a seemingly innocuous Web site had his hard disk modified by that site. In particular, the innocent-looking Web site had searched the unsuspecting Internet user's hard disk, found that he was using a particular software for on-line banking, and remotely modified its "to do" list; the next time the unsuspecting user connected to his bank for his regular on-line banking session, he unwittingly directed his bank to make a payment to the account of the hackers running the Web site he had browsed a few days earlier.

If one's browser supports JavaScript (a default setting), one may elect to connect to certain sites that enable the computer's hard drive to display one's C: drive directory to oneself. While this information is not, in fact, seen by the remote site, who is to say that the remote site that enabled this to happen does not have access to it as well? In those cases that the remote site gets this information, it is most unlikely that it will alert the victimized user to the fact.

In short, there is a multitude of ways whereby the files in one's computer can be viewed by a remote third party if one is connected to the Internet:

- Some exploit the security weakness of a targeted person's Web browser, such as when JavaScript is allowed to remain enabled (the default position).

- Others use security weaknesses in HTML.

- Others use weaknesses in popular e-mail software.

- Others use the security weaknesses of Microsoft's ActiveX in its Internet Explorer.

- Others use security weaknesses in plug-ins (add-on software that one can download—typically at no cost—and merge with a particular family of software) for Netscape Navigator/Communicator.

- Others use adware (or "spyware") installed by unsuspecting users of freeware downloaded from the Internet, which "call (their) home" and report on a user's hard disk contents. (See Section 6.6.1.)

- Still others use commercial keystroke-capturing software or hardware that also "calls home" and reports on a user's keyboard activity. (See Sections 6.3 and 6.4.)

And the list goes on. Unless one has guarded against each and every possible way that information can be remotely accessed from one's computer, one's computer can be remotely analyzed and, as the example at the beginning of this chapter showed, files can be added to one's computer—perhaps to be "found" by unscrupulous forensics investigators (e.g., in an oppressive regime) at a later time.

"But I am using a firewall; this cannot happen to me," one might say. Not true in most cases! Despite its name, a firewall is not an impenetrable barrier; depending on just exactly what it does and how it is configured, its protection could range from "none" to merely "some." (See Section 12.16 for more information on firewalls.) As an example, some firewalls (such as inexpensive hardware or software implementations widely available today) merely filter out incoming probes from the Internet and do not filter any outgoing data streams (such as a complete dump of one's computer directory of all files in it). Even those that alert the user to outgoing data through unusual "ports" (see Section 12.17 for more information on ports), do not usually take any action if such data is going out through the normal ports used by Web browsers (e.g., Port 80 for HTML) because the alternative would be to overwhelm the user with approval requests for innocuous legitimate traffic as well; yet this is precisely the "trick" used by some adware that call home and report on a user's activities without the user's knowledge.

This section will list the most common ways whereby one's privacy can be compromised while on-line, and ways of defeating them. The reader must appreciate, however, that different ways of compromising one's privacy on-line can be easily developed and that there is really no foolproof way of ensuring that one's files are not browsed by unauthorized others remotely. The best that one can do is minimize the likelihood, not eliminate the possibility.

It is for this reason that a security-minded user is advised to use two different computers: The "good" one, for all activities, should never be connected on-line. The "other" one can be an inexpensive one to be used only for on-line (or network or cable or xDSL) connection, and it should contain no identifying information and certainly nothing sensitive.

Both computers should be subjected to the same security-related procedures detailed in this book to ensure confidentiality of private information; the computer allowed to be connected on-line should be subjected to *additional* precautions (detailed later in this chapter) since it is vulnerable not only to physical forensics but also to on-line unauthorized access of its contents. As an example, encrypting the entire hard disk (an option recommended in Section 14.2) is totally ineffective for an on-line computer, because the disk has to be functioning in its decrypted state while one is on-line.

Any data to be transferred between these two computers (e.g., a recently downloaded file intended for the off-line computer) could easily be transferred through a removable disk (such as a floppy or Zip).

Adding security-related protective measures always results in varying degrees of inconvenience, just like the process of having a lock for one's front door results in the inconvenience of having to carry a key and having to unlock the door each time one wants to enter. Each user will have to decide for himself or herself whether the security benefits derived from each of the detailed steps recommended in the rest of this chapter are worth the associated inconvenience they introduce. Such a decision can only be personal because each individual has different security needs: A freedom fighter in a repressive regime has security needs that are different from a teenager in a free society who uses his or her computer mostly to play computer games and who never connects it on-line.

10.1   Assessing Your On-Line Threats

The importance of answering the question of which of the many on-line threats one needs protection from cannot be overemphasized. In normal life, too, one takes different protective measures outdoors to protect one's self from, say, malaria-carrying mosquitoes than to protect one's self from pickpockets and heavy rain.

The threats to one's privacy that one is exposed to when on-line are:

- Malicious remote Web sites that attempt to read (or write on) one's hard disk from afar;
- Adware installed by an individual in his or her computer that "calls home";
- Commercial keystroke-capturing software or hardware that "calls home";
- Remote attempts to hack into one's computer from afar;
- A nosy Internet service provider;
- A tap on one's telephone by a private detective or other entity;
- Hostile viruses, Trojans, and worms.

Each threat requires a different set of protective measures. Most protective measures can work in conjunction with each other.

It must also be appreciated that some protective measures may raise one's profile and, in essence, invite even more intrusiveness and inquisitiveness into one's affairs. An individual who prances around a disreputable part of town with a briefcase visibly handcuffed to his hand is inviting far more unwanted attention and trouble than the same person dressed in clothes that match the environment and carrying personal belongings in a concealed pocket. Similarly, an on-line computer user in a totalitarian regime would be unwise to connect with a fully encrypted connection as a matter of principle just to browse the latest posting of antique furniture on eBay. Each security-conscious user will have to use good judgment and common sense in deciding what technical security, if any, to use.

10.2   Installation of Windows for Secure On-Line Operation

When "personalizing" Windows during installation, use a nondescript made-up name rather than an actual name. Numerous remote threats can readily view the name and other personalized information entered by one when installing Windows; this personalized information gets saved in the registry (see Chapter 4) and is very hard to remove in some cases (as, for example, in the case of Microsoft Office). Many other application software programs read Windows personalizing information and copy it into their own personalization sections. However, please note the following:

- *Caution:* In an effort to reduce software piracy, Microsoft has shifted to a system of software distribution that requires one to register it on-line. If one does not, the software stops functioning after 50 uses. This "registration" has to be done from each computer in which the software is installed, as it entails an abstract of that computer's configuration.

- *Caution:* Up until (and including) Office 97, Microsoft embedded the individual serial number of a user's copy of Microsoft Office on many documents created by the software. The electronic copy of such documents (i.e., a software copy on a disk or even the file sent by e-mail to a recipient) would therefore include a serial number that could be traceable to the purchaser, regardless of what alias was used during installation. A means for disabling this annoying "feature" was made available—amusingly, by Microsoft. The feature has been reportedly discontinued as of Office 2000, whose latest releases, however, have introduced the more dangerous requirement that one "register" the software on-line; otherwise, it stops functioning after 50 uses.

Intel's notion was to help facilitate e-commerce by preventing fraud. It was an implementation doomed to fail, because it is easy to hack and alter: The software that reads this serial number and relays it via the Internet could readily be "doctored" to show a fake serial number.

When installing application software, too, there is no reason why one must enter an actual name to be saved on one's disk that remote unauthorized individuals can retrieve.

- *Caution:* A small percentage of shareware that gets "enabled" by sending the vendor a credit card number utilize a scheme whereby the enabling code that an on-line buyer is provided is derived from that user's credit card name and works only if the user enters that exact name in addition to the enabling code.

- *Caution:* Any software that requires a serial number or other code to be entered to validate it is traceable to its point of sale. If a credit card was used to buy it, it is linked to that credit card as well. Putting aside the serious legal issues involved, an individual in a totalitarian regime whose software bears a serial number that is traceable to a freedom-related foundation or to a buyer in an opposing regime could easily find himself or herself in serious political trouble.

10.3   Software to Enhance On-Line Security

10.3.1   Junkbuster

Junkbuster (http://www.junkbuster.com/) is a highly recommended free software that can be merged with both Netscape's Communicator/Navigator and Microsoft's Internet Explorer. It blocks banner ads that match its frequently updated block file, it deletes unauthorized cookies and other unwanted header information (such as from which Web site one was referred, which browser one is using,[1] and so on) that is exchanged between Web servers and browsers, and so on. Proxomitron is a similar free software package.

10.3.2   SurfSecret

SurfSecret (http://www.surfsecret.com/) helps enhance anonymous Web browsing by periodically destroying cached files and information that a Web browser collects in the user's disk while the user is browsing the Web; if not periodically destroyed, these cached files mirror a user's on-line browsing. This is shown in Figure 10.1. Notice the need to configure it.

10.3.3   Assorted Browser Cleaners

At the end of any on-line browsing session, browsing software has collected a considerable amount of stored tidbits of information, such as sites visited, cookies collected, and so on. Software such as NSClean and IEClean (for Netscape and Internet Explorer browsers, respectively) by Privacy Software Corporation, and ComClear, a freeware package by Luke Reeves (see http://www.neuro-tech.net/), remove those electronic paper trails left behind.

10.3.4   Evidence Eliminator

The function of cleaning the electronic trails left on one's computer by on-line activities is a part of what some software programs that clean up non-on-line electronic trails do. Most notable among them is the disingenuously named Evidence Eliminator (http://www.evidenceeliminator.com/) from the United Kingdom.

---

1. Since an attacker benefits considerably from knowing which software and version thereof one is using, a JunkBuster user has the option of having his or her browser masquerade as a different browser from what is actually in use. Also, the "referring Web site" can be changed to a nondescript one of the user's choice.

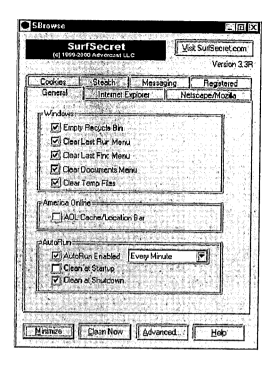

Figure 10.1 SurfSecret configuration. (Courtesy of Jon Oringer, SurfSecret Software.)

10.3.5 Window Washer

Window Washer, by Webroot Software Inc. (www.webroot.com), goes beyond cleaning up the electronic traces left behind from on-line activities, and cleans up the electronic trails left by many (though not all) of a computer user's activities, whether on-line or off-line. The user can download free add-on files—one for each software package that a user may have installed—which instruct Window Washer exactly how to clean the electronic trails from the use of each such installed software package.

10.4 Basic Do's and Don'ts

Do's

• Use a good virus protection software package and update it at least weekly.

- Use a good firewall software.

- Periodically (meaning at least once per month, and certainly imme- diately after any computer-related activity that might be frowned upon by a regime), defragment your disk(s) and "wipe" the disk(s) as per Chapter 9.

- Consider migrating away from Windows 95/98 to Windows NT or 2000. The sooner, the better.

- Depending on your situation, consider deploying the means described in the next two chapters for intermediate-level and advanced protection.

- Do get in the habit of using only encrypted e-mail for those with whom you routinely communicate. There are numerous simple ways of doing this, described in this book. When you do, compose your plaintext e-mail in RAM-disk, then encrypt, and store on hard disk only the encrypted version; the reverse holds for incoming encrypted e-mail.

- If traveling with your laptop, remove the hard disk and have it car- ried separately, preferably by another person with whom you may be traveling and who should clear customs ahead of you. This will dras- tically reduce the damage from theft as well as the motivation to a country you are traveling in to spend much time sifting through what may be your company's proprietary data.

Don'ts

- Do not give anyone else access to any computer that gets connected on-line.

- Do not allow software of suspect origin to be tried out on or installed in your computer.

- Do not download and install software of suspect origin (such as soft- ware e-mailed to you by others, unless the sender is well known to you and you have confirmed that it has not been e-mailed by some- one impersonating them).

- Do not open any e-mail sent to you by someone you do not know, and most certainly do not open any attachments to such e-mail.

- Do not register on-line or allow any software to be registered on-line.

- Protect your e-mail address almost as carefully as you protect your Social Security number; do not give it out except to individuals you know well.

- Do not register with any on-line service or group that wants to list you or your interests in any directory.

- Do not post to Usenet groups using your true name or your true e-mail address.

- Do not—ever—leave your hard disk in the computer if you have your computer serviced or repaired.

- Do not leave your computer "on" and "on-line" unless you are sitting in front of it, even if (especially if) you have a high-speed connection (xDSL or cable modem).

- Do not store your e-mail (especially copies of outgoing e-mail) for long. Thin it out to the minimum that you absolutely must keep and convert that into an encrypted form for storage in a removable disk that you can keep in a nonobvious place that will be known only to yourself.

- Keep in mind that, for all practical purposes, whenever you do something with your computer, someone is sitting right behind you and is dutifully noting everything you see or do. As such, do not "see or do" things with your computer that can land you in jail in your particular country. If you are a freedom fighter, religious activist, or otherwise liable to be singled out for scrutiny, and you *must* use a computer, learn all the security-related issues first (all of them spelled out in this book), before you risk life and limb.

11

Intermediate On-Line Privacy

All Web browsers, in their default settings, engage in the annoying practice of volunteering far more information than they need to Web sites that are visited. This information includes the type and version number of the browser in use, information which makes it that much easier for a malicious remote Web site to know exactly how to exploit a browser's unique security weaknesses. Moreover, it makes it possible for a Web site to make a political or marketing statement by refusing to deal with this or that Web browser.

The browser also reveals the "referring page," the Web site that was visited prior to the site currently in use. Additionally, a Web browser gives away the user's current IP address, which remote sites record. This is in part a necessary evil, because the remote site must know where to send the information asked for. Web browsers also have a long history of security "bugs" that allow hostile remote Web sites to take full control of an individual's computer from afar, depending on how the user has set up the Web browser.

Specific security suggestions applicable to all browsers and e-mail software are as follows:

- Disable all "autocomplete" features, such as autocompletion of Web addresses and especially of passwords. In Internet Explorer 5, for example, an enabled autocomplete feature allows IE5 to remember user names and passwords one enters for Web sites that require them.

- If you use Web browsers for e-mail or Usenet reading, disable HTML-enabled e-mail and Usenet message reading in addition to cookies (see below). This is because HTML-enabled e-mail and newsgroup readers can be exploited to tie a "cookie" to a specific e-mail address; Web sites and third-party advertising entities can then collect information about the sites one frequents (e.g., insurance sites, adult sites, and cosmetics sites), and sell one's e-mail address to others.

- Avoid using Web-based e-mail accounts, even if they are pseudonymous. E-mail targeted by a company to a person using HTML can contain a standard image tag that, when read, calls a Web server to fetch the invisible image and this, in turn, leaves an electronic trail of the individual's true IP address.

- Visit one of the many Web sites that do an on-line security analysis of your setup and tell you what can be obtained from your computer. One such site is http://www.privacy.net/analyze/.

Measures related to specific browsers are outlined in the next sections.

11.1   Netscape Navigator/Communicator

Use a 128-bit version.   Until recently, when U.S. export regulations on encryption were relaxed, users outside the United States had to be content with a lower-grade encryption version. This is no longer the case. Even for those who, for whatever reason, do not want to get a late-vintage 128-bit version of Netscape, one can still have 128-bit encryption by availing oneself of a patch available to anyone on-line from http://www.fortify.net/. Figure 11.1 depicts the various options in a graphical form.

Create (at least) two different "user profiles."   Both a public and a private user profile should be created.[1] For the public one, get a "security certificate" from any one of the many companies that make them. Thawtee Company is recommended for this because it is free and every bit as good as the "for pay"

---

1. If one's situation is such that one needs to prevent others from finding out that two (or more) profiles are, in fact, one and the same person, then one should not have more than a single profile in a single computer, because the two (or more) profiles can be discovered during computer forensics (off-line or on-line).

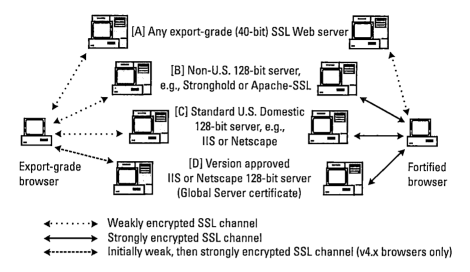

Figure 11.1 Web browser encryption security options.

ones. The procedure is self-explanatory; simply click on the lock icon on the top line of the Netscape browser.

Also, there is an easy way to "copy over" the security certificate(s) you have created for one profile to another. Go to Program Files/Netscape/Users and open the folder containing the profile for which you already obtained the security certificate. Copy the following three files to the "other" user folder(s):

cert7.db

key3.db

secmod.db

The same procedure can be used to copy the security certificates you obtained using one computer to another one using Netscape as well. Keep in mind that one cannot use the same certificate for both Netscape and Internet Explorer (the use of which is strongly discouraged due to its numerous security flaws, anyway).

Install and use Junkbuster. For more information on Junkbuster, see Section 10.3.1. For the "private" user profile, select the following preferences (under Edit/Preferences):

1. Home page: http://internet.junkbuster.com/cgi-bin/show/proxy-args (see Figure 11.2).

2. Set Navigator to start with "home page."

3. Under "proxies," select "manual proxy configuration"; under "view" enter the word "localhost" (without the quotes) in both the HTTP and the Security windows, and the number 8,000 under both ports for these two. This is shown in Figures 11.3 and 11.4.

Make anonymous and clean up the configuration. From a security perspective it is preferable not to use the Web browsers (especially Internet Explorer) for e-mail. Use a dedicated e-mail program instead (see Section 11.3). This is so because integrating the e-mail function into a Web browser exposes the e-mail functionality to many of the security weaknesses of the Web browser.

1. Under Mail Identity, leave all spaces blank or fictitious.

2. Likewise with mail servers and news servers. Under "Advanced," disable Java, disable JavaScript, disable "style sheets," and disable cookies. Enable only the "automatically load images."

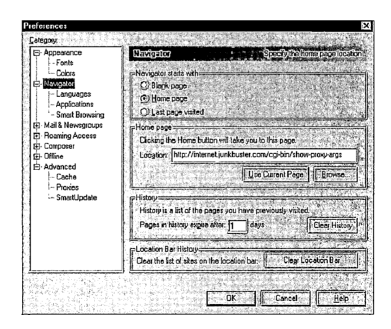

Figure 11.2   Proxy settings for Netscape. (Courtesy of Netscape Communications.)

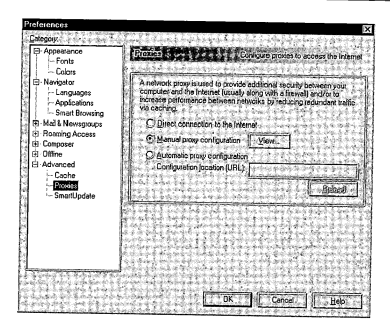

Figure 11.3 Navigator proxy settings in detail. (Courtesy of Netscape Communications.)

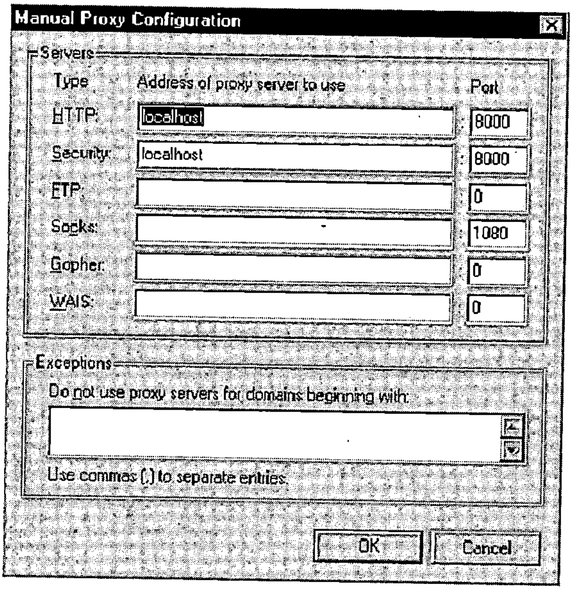

Figure 11.4 Navigator proxy settings in further detail. (Courtesy of Netscape Communications.)

3. Under Advanced/Cache, set Disk Cache to zero and memory cache to not much more than 1,024 KB. Clear both.

4. Double-click on the "cache" folder. Delete all files in it. Remember that this is useless until you "wipe" the disk as per Section 4.3.

Remove the instant messaging capability. Unless you use AOL as your ISP or AOL Instant Messenger (AIM) for instant messaging (any instant messaging service is a bad idea from a security perspective, because instant messaging works by broadcasting your being on-line every time you go on-line), get rid of that feature. Since Netscape is now owned by AOL, AOL is pretty tightly integrated with Netscape; one must take a few steps to get rid of it.

1. Find the location where Netscape keeps its user-related files. It is usually in C:\ProgramFiles\Netscape\Users\. Click on the folder for whatever you have named your private profile.

2. Remove AOL/AIM altogether as follows:

   a. Go to Program Files/Netscape/Communicator/Program and delete any folder titled AIM.

   b. Remove all references to AOL and AIM from the registry, because some registries install the AIM software and icons on Netscape every time you boot, even if you removed the shortcuts. Be *very* careful when editing the registry; any carelessness or error can render the computer unbootable. It is best to make a backup copy of the registry (see Chapter 4) before editing it, especially if you have not been editing it on a routine basis. Again, proceed slowly and carefully.

   c. Run REGEDIT.

   d. Edit/Find for the string "AOL" (without the quotes). For each occurrence that is obviously referring to America Online, delete that entry. Make sure you do not inadvertently delete any entry where the "aol" has nothing to do with America Online.

   e. Repeat this Edit/Find and deletion for the string "AIM." Here you must be even more careful not to delete strings having nothing to do with America Online's AIM, such as "Application X-aim" or "EudoraImport" or "AphaImageLoader" or "DataImport," and so on, because all of these entries are needed by other software and should not be removed.

f. Repeat this Edit/Find and delete for the string "America Online."

g. Go to Program Files/Netscape/Users. For each user profile you have (if you don't have more than one, then go to the "Default" folder), find and remove all occurrences of the AIM icon named "launch.aim." Reboot, double-click on the Netscape icon (or however else you run the Netscape software), and exit from it. Now go to the same location(s) where you deleted the "launch.aim" file and make sure it is not there; if it has miraculously been recreated, it means that your cleanup of the registry to remove all references to AOL and AIM and America Online was incomplete and you must redo it.

Wipe (overwrite and delete) the "netscape.hst" and the "fat.db" files. These are two files created by Netscape that have no socially redeeming value; from the moment that Netscape is installed, Netscape keeps a record of the user's on-line and off-line activities that involve using the browser.

The surfing log is "netscape.hst." It is in the ProgramFiles/Netscape/Users/Default/ subdirectory; if the user has more than one Netscape "personality," the "default" word should be substituted for the name of each such personality. See Figure 11.5.

The file "fat.db" identifies the files in the browser "cache," and this is usually a huge collection of HTML pages that image files. These files are mildly encrypted and may appear "essential" to the uninitiated, but can and should be securely deleted; even more importantly, to prevent Netscape from creating new files after the old ones are securely deleted, one should take the following steps:

Figure 11.5 A useless and potentially troublesome Netscape-created file. (Courtesy of Netscape Communications.)

1. Find "netscape.hst" and "fat.db" and wipe them. They sit in each and every user profile folder (Program Files/Netscape/Users/...).

2. Create new text files (File/New/Text) in the exact locations where the old ones were deleted, and call them "netscape.hst" and "fat.db," respectively; save them.

3. Right-click on each of those two files, select Properties, and make each a "read-only" file. This will prevent any records about your Netscape usage from being stored on disk.

4. Periodically recheck those files to make sure that they continue to have a size of zero and are "read-only" files, because Netscape updates, and some well-meaning software programs that "clean up" Netscape's trails often remove the "read-only" feature.

Get rid of "cookies" for good.

1. Search for, find, and wipe "cookies.txt"; there is one in each user profile, just like netscape.hst. Just because Netscape admonishes one with a "Do Not Edit" warning, this does not mean that the file cannot or should not be edited. Edit it despite the warning.

2. Right-click on the file "cookies.txt," select Properties, and make it "read-only" as well. This will prevent any cookies from being written; this is an additional layer of protection beyond what is provided by Junkbuster. (*Note:* Since "cookies" are stored in RAM memory during an on-line session and are only written to disk at the end of each such session, this scheme will prevent the writing of cookies to disk but will not prevent the incoming and outgoing of cookies during the on-line session; Junkbuster and the configuration of Netscape will do that.)

Wipe some other hidden threats.   Go to Program Files/Netscape/Users. For each user profile you have (if you don't have more than one then you merely have to open the Default folder):

1. Right-click on the file "pab.na2," select "open with," and open with any text editor such as Notepad. Look at whatever is in ASCII text. If you feel that it contains too much information about your system or your past usage of Netscape (these .na2 files often contain such

sensitive information as verbatim copies of e-mail sent long ago and lists of Usenet newsgroups visited), then proceed with Step 2.

2. Edit/Select All/ and delete everything.

3. Save the empty file.

4. Right-click on the saved empty file, select "Properties," set it to "read-only" status (so that Netscape will not add to it later on) and click on "apply."

Also, if you have the Shockwave plug-in for Netscape, get rid of it. If not, don't get it. It has been associated with numerous security compromises. Most importantly, when done, defragment the disk and go through a secure "wiping" as per Chapter 9 so as to truly remove what was, essentially, merely marked for deletion in following the steps above.

11.2 Microsoft Explorer

The use of Microsoft Internet Explorer (IE) is not recommended, because of a seemingly never ending litany of security-related weaknesses that even Microsoft has acknowledged in the numerous security-related "patches" that the company has made available. Still, you may want to keep it for specific tasks such as "Windows updates" that Microsoft refuses to allow through other browsers.

There is a fundamental security problem when a Web browser is integrated with the operating system; this is the position of the author of the security software products NSClean and IEClean at http://www.nsclean.com/ (which remove the electronics trails left behind on one's disk by Netscape and Internet Explorer, respectively), who wrote the following in 1996:

> The greatest risk of all to personal on the Internet however comes from the integration browsers into the operating system itself. At one time, browsers were external applications which did not have hooks directly into the computer's operating system. Java JavaScript applets were kept isolated from the operating system entirely which meant that the only risks to privacy were those voluntarily or unwittingly given up by the user.... Now we are faced with the Internet Explorer product [going] directly into the operating system where no walls of separation will exist which will serve to protect the user against unauthorized rummaging through the most personal and private parts of their computers.

This is above and beyond the cookies[2] issue. Since 1996, there has been, on the average, one security alert per month issued by Microsoft regarding security weaknesses involving IE and/or Outlook or Outlook Express.

If you absolutely insist on using Internet Explorer, then at least take the following precautions:

1. Get the latest version of the browser.

2. Disable cookies from session to session. Unlike Netscape, which saves all cookies in one file (cookies.txt), Explorer saves each in a separate file but in the same folder. As long as you have only a single profile, you can make that folder a read-only. As with Netscape, this will only protect against cookies being remembered from one on-line session to the next, and not within any one session. If you have multiple profiles, you will have to do this for each such profile.

3. Go to Start/Settings/Control Panel and select the Internet Options icon.

   a. Under Address, enter http://www.internet.junkbuster.com/cgi-bin/show-proxy-args, as shown in Figure 11.6.

   b. Under History, set the days to zero, and clear history.

   c. Under Internet Options/Content/Personal Information/Auto-complete, disable all autocomplete options. This stops IE5 from gathering this information but does not delete information already gathered; to delete such preexisting information, use Clear Forms/Clear Passwords and General/Clear History. Then wipe the disk clean using the procedures shown in Chapter 9.

   d. Under Security/Internet, select Custom level and disable everything except "file downloads" (enable) and "font downloads" (enable). In particular, make sure that you disable all "scripting" and all "ActiveX" options. See Figures 11.7 to 11.9.

   e. Under Connections, find the profile you access your Internet service provider as, select it, and click on "LAN Settings." Under "proxy server," enter the word "localhost" in the address field and

---

2. Cookies are files that remote Web sites can put in Web browser users' computers that allow those Web sites to know which individuals have visited which Web sites and when. Most versions of Web browsers allow users to reject cookies, but doing so incurs the wrath of many Web sites, which then refuse to deal with those users. One is better off "pretending" to accept cookies, and then to unceremoniously trash them automatically after each on-line session, or, better yet, after a few seconds during an on-line session.

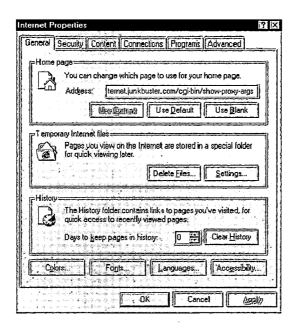

Figure 11.6 Setting Junkbuster filter in IE. (Box shot reprint from Microsoft Corporation.)

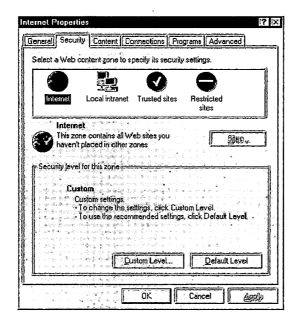

Figure 11.7 Improving IE security. (Box shot reprint from Microsoft Corporation.)

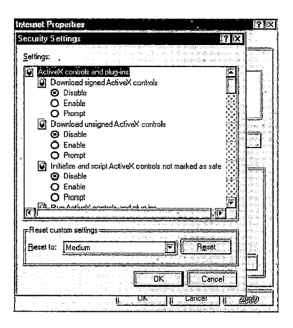

Figure 11.8 Enhancing IE security. (Box shot reprint from Microsoft Corporation.)

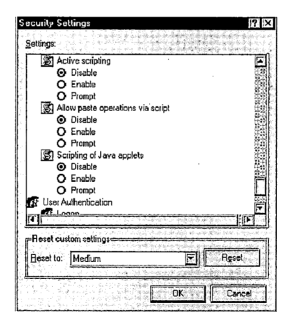

Figure 11.9 Disabling mobile code and scripts in IE. (Box shot reprint from Microsoft Corporation.)

e. Under Connections, find the profile you access your Internet service provider as, select it, and click on "LAN Settings." Under "proxy server," enter the word "localhost" in the address field and the number "8000" in the port field (both without quotes). Then click "advanced" and make sure that this shows up under both the HTTP and the secure "type"; click the "use the same proxy for all protocols" option. See Figures 11.10 and 11.11.

f. Under Programs select an HTML editor other than IE, such as Netscape, because IE has been found to have serious security problems when hostile HTML code tries to execute command in your computer.

4. Click on the Security tab. Disable JavaScript.

5. Click on the Advanced tab. Double-click on JavaVM and uncheck all three options.

6. Consider using Secure2Surf from http://www.netmenders.com/secure2surf/. Microsoft's IE uses Microsoft's Virtual Machine software to enforce more Internet accountability, which is precisely contrary to on-line privacy. It places all Internet traffic in the region between "restricted sites" and "trusted sites"; what a security-conscious user needs is to put them all, instead, in the "not trusted" bin, and this software does that.

7. If you are using the Shockwave plug-in for IE, get rid of it. If not, don't install it. It has been associated with numerous security problems.

8. If you use software, such as SCORCH, to wipe specific files from your computer on shut-down (or on power-up, which is not

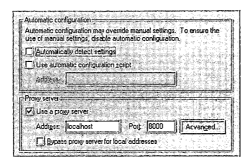

Figure 11.10 Setting up a local proxy to filter hostile content. (Box shot reprint from Microsoft Corporation.)

Figure 11.11 Further settings for the local proxy. (Box shot reprint from Microsoft Corporation.)

C:\WINDOWS\cookies*.*
C:\WINDOWS\history*.*
C:\WINDOWS\Temporary Internet Files\
C:\WINDOWS\Recent\
C:\WINDOWS\TMP\
C:\WINDOWS\TEMPOR~1*.*

11.3 Desirable E-Mail Software Configuration and Modifications

11.3.1 Threats Posed by Web-Based E-Mail

In August 2000, a major security flaw was discovered in Web-based e-mail that affects well over 100 million users. Users cannot defeat it by merely changing passwords. The problem is based on a well-known Web browser vulnerability that allows stealing a "session cookie" from a Web mail user; this can be done by sending an HTML message to the intended victim with an embedded image file containing some JavaScript code. While users could protect themselves by disabling JavaScript in their browsers (see Section 11.2), many Web mail systems refuse to function if a user has done so; for this reason alone, users should avoid any Web-based service that requires one to have enabled JavaScript, Java, or ActiveX.

Messages sent through Yahoo!, Hotmail, or other such popular accounts, including instant messaging software such as ICQ and AOL's Instant Messenger (AIM) are just as accessible to employers and government as conventional e-mails (see http://news.cnet.com/news/0-1007-200-2924 978.html).

Even Web sites that sanctimoniously promote privacy are not to be trusted. HushMail, for example, hosted two tracking networks on its Web site, doubleclick.net and valueclick.net. One can fix this by creating a firewall "rule set" that denies access to doubleclick.net, valueclick.net, and value-net.com, and by abiding by the rest of the recommended security-related procedures in Chapters 9 through 14.

Ultimate Anonymity, another site that pontificates about the virtues of anonymity, is a division of Cyber Solutions that is reported to be a bulk e-mail provider. If one follows the links from http://www.cyber-so.nu/ to http://www.cyber-so.com/, one finds the following offer: "Broadcast your ad and even include an image if you desire to as many as 200 newsgroups at a time, twice a week using methods to ensure your ads remain intact and undisturbed by Usenet cancelbots for a full month."

11.3.2   Outlook and Outlook Express

Outlook and Outlook Express are not recommended, due to numerous security problems acknowledged regularly by Microsoft's own security alerts. Outlook Express does have an interesting use in conjunction with PrivacyX (www.privacyx.com) which is an anonymizing e-mail server that, when used with Outlook Express, allows one to have a fully encrypted connection between one's computer and the PrivacyX server, thereby keeping a nosy local ISP in the blind. On balance, readers are advised for security reasons not to use either Outlook or Outlook Express for e-mail.

11.3.3   Eudora E-Mail Software

Go to Tools/Options and perform the following:

1. Under "attachments," change setting to anything other than the default, after having created such a folder (e.g., C:\junk\suspect). This prevents a Eudora security weakness from being exploitable. See Figure 11.12.

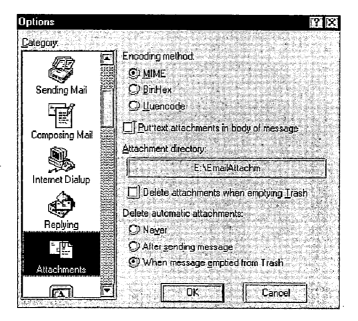

Figure 11.12 Eudora e-mail attachments setting vulnerability. (Courtesy of QUALCOMM Incorporated.)

2. Under "viewing mail," uncheck the "use Microsoft viewer" option, so as to prevent another known security weakness in Eudora, as shown in Figure 11.13.

3. Under "viewing mail," disable the option that allows executables in HTML content; see Figure 11.13.

4. You may elect to opt for having all incoming and outgoing e-mail copies stored in a fully encrypted volume rather than being in the open for the world to see. To do this you must first create such a volume (see Section 14.4, for example, on ScramDisk, which uses encrypted volumes).

Caution: Users of the latest (as of late 2000) Eudora versions, 4.3 and 5, should be advised that they "call home" (call the Eudora server) every so often and without a user's knowledge; the manufacturer claims that this is done merely to check for a new version of the program available. Regardless, users would be well advised to disable this dubious feature; the Eudora Web site has instructions on how to do so. To disable it, copy and paste the following text into the message window of a new message in Eudora 4.3:

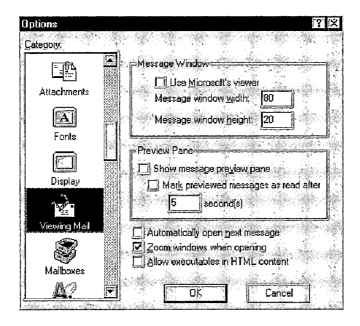

Figure 11.13 Eudora message viewer vulnerability. (Courtesy of QUALCOMM Incorporated.)

<x-eudora-option:DontShowUpdates=1>

This text will show up in blue as a URL. Hold down the Alt key and click on the URL; a window will appear asking the user to click "OK." Click "OK."

Caution: Users of PGP encryption should *not* use the PGP plug-ins for either Eudora or Outlook and Outlook Express; instead, encrypt the clipboard and cut and paste the ciphertext into the e-mail software program's window. The danger is that the "Out" mailbox saves on the hard disk—under some conditions—both the plaintext and the ciphertext; this is about the worst scenario from a security perspective.

11.4   Secure E-Mail Conduct On-Line

The following is a list of recommendations to save you grief in connection with the use of e-mail.

11.4   Secure E-Mail Conduct On-Line

The following is a list of recommendations to save you grief in connection with the use of e-mail.

1. Get in the habit of using encryption for *all* of your e-mail; it is really not onerous anymore. You have numerous choices:

   • If you really are allergic to encryption because you think it is "complicated" (it is not), consider using Zix Mail, which is free, very simple to use, and quite effective (http://www.zix-mail.com/). However, as with all "simple to use" encryption that is proprietary, it requires that one places one's full faith in the software maker and the operator of the sites that cater to it. See Sections 11.5.2 and 12.15 for more on such software and services.

   • If your situation is such that you are primarily concerned about interception by (or at) your local ISP (or if you live in a country where wiretapping is commonplace), you may have considered using PrivacyX, which no longer exists as a company but whose servers were still operational as of July 2001, and was free and provided anonymity (http://www.privacyx.com/), in addition to using Outlook Express, configured in accordance to the instructions provided on-line by PrivacyX so that your connection to Privacy X is fully encrypted. The advantage of PrivacyX used this way was that it hid not only the content of the message but also the "from whom" and "to whom" information from any such interceptor. If you did not trust PrivacyX's encryption (which was really a 128-bit SSL encryption that you have no reason mistrusting), you could also preencrypt your messages (e.g., using PGP; see Section 14.3) over and above the encryption provided by PrivacyX. To prevent recovery of your e-mail through physical forensics on your computer, you must overwrite your e-mail, both sent and received (using the techniques discussed in Chapter 9), by wiping the entire hard disk after you delete such e-mail (make sure that you also delete it from the "trash" folder in Outlook Express before such disk wiping).

   • By far the most effective e-mail encryption available to anyone worldwide is PGP. Download PGP 6.02 CKT Build 7 from

editor, never save them to disk, edit/copy them onto the clipboard, invoke PGP to encrypt the clipboard, and edit/paste them into the message window of whichever e-mail software you are using (even a Web-based free e-mail account such as those provided by Yahoo!, Netscape, and Hotmail).

2. Get rid of the bad habit of storing old e-mail forever, especially outgoing mail (you are not as culpable for what others e-mail to you as for what you send others). Large corporations that have taken notice of how some companies have been stung by the content of employee e-mail are now professing "hard disk storage limitations" as a legitimate-sounding excuse to have policies whereby all e-mail is permanently removed from corporate records after rather short lengths of time. ("Getting rid of," of course, means more than merely "deleting"—which does nothing. It is necessary to wipe the disk clean, as per Chapter 9.)

3. If you absolutely must keep some old e-mail, then move it to a folder for that purpose and encrypt that entire folder's content, realizing that in most countries you can be compelled by law enforcement to decrypt it. Consider hiding the fact that such a folder exists by using steganography (see Section 14.5), or even physically shipping it (encrypted, of course) to a trusted friend in another country for storage on your behalf. See Chapters 13 and 14 on encryption for the numerous options available to one.

4. Have at least two e-mail accounts—a public one (where you will inevitably receive junk mail), which can be obtained freely from numerous providers, and a jealously guarded personal one that you only give to trusted correspondents. Even the personal one should not have your true name as part of the e-mail address. Do not cross-contaminate the two.

5. For your personal e-mail account, sign up with any one of the many e-mail–forwarding entities, such as:

   http://www.privacyx.com/;

   http://www.IEEE.org/ (for IEEE members only);

   http://www.mail.org/;

   http://www.gmx.co.uk/ (for UK-based individuals).[3]

   These services will forward your incoming e-mail to your "real" one. Give out only this "go-between's" e-mail address so that when

http://www.mail.org/;

http://www.gmx.co.uk/ (for UK-based individuals).[3]

These services will forward your incoming e-mail to your "real" one. Give out only this "go-between's" e-mail address so that when you do change your ISP for whatever reason, you don't have to notify any of your correspondents (but only that go-between e-mail-forwarding service). In addition, you get an extra layer of insulation from assorted on-line crackpots.

6. If you do use encryption for your e-mail, as is highly recommended, do not use software that enables you to read the messages that you yourself have composed and sent [this means do not use browsers' S/MIME, because the locally saved copy of your outgoing e-mail is also decryptable by the sender, and do not use any symmetric encryption, such as DES; use PGP instead (see Section 14.3)]; this is so that you cannot possibly comply with any demand to decrypt outgoing e-mail, and to limit your alleged culpability to incoming e-mail (which you should overwrite soon after reading and not keep for posterity as it can only cause you grief). If you are concerned (as you should be, because you really do lose all control of your e-mail after you have sent it) about what an intended recipient may do with your e-mail (e.g., print it out, edit/copy/paste it to another e-mail that goes out unencrypted to third parties, and so forth), then you should consider using one of the handful of new commercial schemes that control (with varying degrees of success) your e-mail's fate even after it has left your hands on its way to the intended recipients. See Section 11.4.1 on this topic.

7. Never reply to unsolicited junk mail that offers to remove your name from its distribution list, as this will confirm that your e-mail address is valid and will subject you to more junk e-mail. If it becomes too bothersome, consider forwarding the offending e-mail to "abuse@ . . ." where ". . ." is the name of your ISP and, if you can find it, of the sender's ISP, but don't expect much to happen as a result. You will have more luck by configuring your e-mail software (such as Eudora) to filter out incoming e-mail that has telltale junk

---

3. *Caution:* Since the passage of the RIP Act in the United Kingdom, any and all Internet traffic transiting the United Kingdom is amenable to being intercepted and stored.

such an attachment from the sender. Most e-mail–propagated viruses/Trojans/worms come as e-mails that have hijacked the e-mail address of a sender you trust. If all of the above conditions are met, use safe software for opening some kinds of attachments, such as Word Viewer in the case of Microsoft Word files. If the e-mail does not meet those qualifications, delete it without opening the attachment, and then go and overwrite the attached file (which usually stays in your disk even after you delete the e-mail that brought it).

9. If you use Eudora for e-Mail, perform the bug-fixing steps shown in Section 11.3.3.

10. Always keep in mind that, unless you encrypt your e-mail and also hide the "from whom" and "to whom" information from whoever may be intercepting your e-mail (now or through forensics in the future), do not compose e-mail that you would not want used against you in a court of law. Even if you encrypt your e-mail, you still have no control over what the intended recipient does with it, and it could haunt you in the future.

11. If, for whatever reason (such as by virtue of being the publisher of the newspaper of the political opposition in your country), you are the likely target of extensive surveillance by those with the means to do so, then:

- Forget about using e-mail for your sensitive communications needs.

- Consider establishing an account with an out-of-country ISP and establishing an encrypted (128-bit SSL; see Section 12.7.1) connection with that ISP before anything else. Alternately, you can use a local ISP and simply connect to the Web site of an out-of-country commercial entity that offers end-to-end SSL encryption between that site and your computer, such as https://anon.xg.nu/ and https://www.rewebber.com/.[4]

- The user interface to such anonymizers is straightforward, as shown in the example in Figure 11.14.

4. Although anyone can access the non-SSL version of Rewebber, that company requires one to "register" first before using the SSL version which includes providing a real e-mail address to receive the required login password; thus, anonymity is problematic at best.

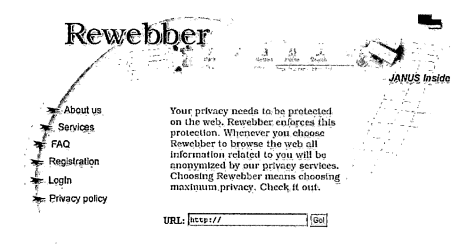

Figure 11.14 Easy user interface for Rewebber anonymizer. (Courtesy of ISL Internet Sicherheitslösungen GmbH.)

Caution: Most so-called anonymous remailers, such as http://www. anonymizer.com/, are not recommended at all, because they have one or more of the following security shortcomings:

- They do not remove your IP address from what is sent; even though the e-mail received by one may appear to be coming from god@heaven, the IP address and the rest of the information in the detailed header (see Section 11.5) of the message pretty much gives away where it came from.

- They are not establishing an encrypted connection between your computer and theirs, leaving you vulnerable to local interception and to snooping by your local ISP.

- They keep a copy of all traffic going through them, which can be subpoenaed by the authorities of the country where that remailer resides. Do not use a remailer in your own country or in a country with which your country has extensive cooperation.

- Pseudonymous remailers (which assign you a pseudonym, in place of your true e-mail address, so that others can respond to you through that remailer), too, are vulnerable to a subpoena from their local judicial system and will reveal who said what to whom and when; this, in fact, happened with a Finnish remailer (anon.penet.fi) a few years ago.

12. Consider the use of encrypted concatenated remailers (such as Mixmaster) through the use of programs like Private Idaho or Jack B. Nymble (JBN), available for free worldwide and discussed in more detail in Section 11.5.2. Keep in mind that the use of such schemes stand out like the proverbial sore thumb if someone is keeping tabs on your on-line activities, but they do protect the content of your messages as well as the "from whom" and "to whom" information.

13. It is sometimes possible to recall and delete an already sent e-mail message before it reaches its destination, *if* it has not left your ISP already on its way to the destination. From Outlook 2000:

    a. Open the message from your "sent folder."

    b. Select "Actions."

    c. Select "Recall this message."

    If the message still resides on your mail-ISP server (and that is a big "if," because e-mail sent to one's ISP tends to be forwarded to its destination almost instantaneously), it will be deleted and this will be confirmed to you.

11.4.1 Self-Protecting E-Mail

Today's e-mail, tomorrow's legal evidence.

—Anonymous lawyer

Getting rid of incoming e-mail, and of locally kept copies of outgoing e-mail, is not easy. E-mail software tends to store e-mail in assorted "proprietary," condensed ways, whereby one cannot simply identify a single file that contains just one piece of e-mail. Instead, one has to depend on the good graces of each such piece of software to respond to a user's request to "delete" an e-mail that one would rather not keep on one's disk. (This usually places that particular e-mail in yet another location on the hard disk, this one corresponding to the "trash folder" of the e-mail software, which one also needs to get rid of.)

If, despite all the vulnerabilities shown in this book, one still persists in not insisting on encryption for all e-mail, one way to work around these security vulnerabilities of e-mail software is to ask correspondents to send e-mail as an attachment, rather than as the text in the body of an e-mail; in that case, the attachment is a file that can be overwritten and wiped clean as needed by the recipient.

For e-mail whose text is in the main body, as is the case with the vast majority of e-mail, about the only effective strategy that one has is to customize one's e-mail software to "store" incoming e-mail and the e-mail software's "trash" folder on a RAM disk (see Chapter 9). This is not easily feasible with most e-mail software programs, which tend to store files within their own subdirectory in "Program Files."

In the case of Eudora Pro, change the "target" line in Properties of the "shortcut" icon for Eudora on one's desktop to the following:

E:\Mailbox\Eudora.ini

where:

1. "E:\" is the drive name of whichever drive name is used for the RAM disk (can be D:\ or whatever else).
2. "Mailbox" is whichever name one wants to give to the folder (which must have been precreated for the occasion).

If that is not possible, then:

1. Delete incoming e-mail.
2. Delete the same e-mail from the e-mail software's "trash" folder.
3. Proceed with a full disk-defragmentation.
4. Follow up with a full disk wiping (slack, free space, and swap file; see Chapter 9).

All this pales in comparison with the potential headaches from *outgoing* e-mail. The reasons are that:

1. Unlike incoming e-mail for which the recipient is not legally liable, outgoing e-mail is the sender's full legal responsibility.
2. Once outgoing e-mail has left, the sender loses all control of it and is at the mercy of the intended recipients.
3. E-mail can end up in the wrong recipient's hands through any one of many possible ways such as:

- The sender inadvertently clicked on a name directly above or below the name of the intended recipient in the sender's local address book.

- The sender mistyped the recipient's e-mail address; this caused the e-mail to be rerouted by the receiving host to an "e-mail postmaster" (this is common in universities), who read it in an attempt to figure out who it is for and forwarded it to numerous possible intended recipients "just in case."

- The Internet erred, as it often does, and misdirected an e-mail to the wrong place.

Even under the best of circumstances, when the e-mail goes only to the intended recipient, the sender has still lost control of that e-mail. The recipient can forward or redirect it to others, can print it and keep or send copies to others, can edit/copy/paste portions of it out of context to others (possibly after having altered something in it), and so on. Think of the example of the priest who stated in a sermon that "The Devil wants you to think that 'God is dead'," but was reported out of context in a newspaper headline, which read "Priest says in sermon that 'God is Dead'."

In more practical terms, a corporation may understandably want to ensure that its internal confidential and proprietary e-mails do not leave the confines of that corporation. There is a need, therefore, for a means whereby e-mail (1) can only be read by the intended recipient, and (2) cannot be printed or electronically copied into anything else.

The first requirement is easily met with public key encryption (see Section 13.2.3), whereby the message is encrypted to the public key of the intended recipient, and then that recipient is the only one who can read it. In addition to the many encryption programs, such as PGP (see Section 14.3), and the many anonymizing programs, such as JBN and Private Idaho (Section 11.5.2), many commercial products allow for this, including ZixMail (http://www.zixit.com/) and 1 on 1 (http://www.1on1mail.com/)—both of them free to the user—and numerous others.

The second requirement is vastly more difficult to meet because it has implications with respect to the receiving computer's unknown capabilities and operating system:

1. To prevent printing, the receiving computer's "PrintScreen" must be disabled.

2. To prevent edit/copy/paste, the receiving computer's e-mail software itself must be changed.

A handful of commercial "solutions" to this conundrum have been marketed:

- **Cryptolopes.** Its name derived from the term "cryptographic envelopes" (http://www.research.ibm.com/people/k/kaplan/cryptolope-docs/crypap.html), Cryptolopes is an IBM effort that was transferred to Lotus in 1997. The initial version, Cryptolope Live server, was to allow Web publishers to both protect and sell data on the Web.

- **Secure Information Management System 2.0.** This product, by TriStrate (http://www.tristrata.com/), is a software solution running on any TCP/IP network intended to provide end-to-end file, e-mail, and virtual private network security; it is integrated with MS Exchange, Outlook, and Lotus 4.1–4.6.

- **Disappearing.** From Disappearing Inc. (http://www.disappearing.com/faq3.html); very perceptively, the company's own description of this product states that it cannot protect from someone defeating the purpose of its product by doing a screen capture, screen print, and so on, but is intended for the situation in which "all parties are interested in a private exchange."

- **Content Guard** by Xerox Corporation (http://www.content-guard.com/productmenu.htm). This converts documents from many popular file formats to encrypted "self-protecting" documents without requiring consumers to install any client-side software to access the protected documents. If this is indeed true, then the product is unlikely to be particularly secure, since protected documents could end up in the swap file or be captured by screen-capture software.

- **SafeMessage** by AbsoluteFuture Company (http://www.safemessage.com/). This software has the interesting twist of facilitating the sending of e-mail as encrypted packets point-to-point that bypass e-mail servers completely. It requires the recipient to have SafeMessage software installed and to have logged onto the server at least once.

- **PageVault** by Authentica Company (http://www.authentica.com/). Like many other systems, this product requires the installation of a full infrastructure that includes a dedicated server for PageVault-protected e-mail.

All of these schemes take one of the following approaches:

1. Requires that e-mail be only in the form of a specific attachment type that uses a particular software (provided by that vendor) to view and that has no edit/copy/paste or print functions in it.
2. Requires that all e-mail be stored in a trusted central server and that access to it be allowed only for individually authenticated users using vendor-controlled software that can neither edit/copy/paste nor print.
3. Requires a separate infrastructure of servers, databases, and so on within an organization that is meant to handle the "self-protecting" e-mail only.

Clearly, none of these approaches is particularly practical to use for e-mailing to the world at large, though they may be tolerable for a closed group such as a tightly knit organization or corporation. Worse yet, if one thinks of the problem above, there really cannot be a technical solution to the problem of preventing an authorized e-mail recipient from copying the e-mail and further disseminating it at will: An e-mail recipient can always snap a photograph of the screen, print it, OCR it (run it through commercial optical character recognition software), and convert it into a plain old e-mail that can be disseminated worldwide on the spot.

The only real "fix" is never to e-mail verbiage from which one would not like to have pieces removed out of context and displayed on the front page of the local newspaper, or show up on the desk of an overzealous law enforcer in a repressive regime, or on the desk of an opposition lawyer in any litigious society.

11.4.2 Accessing E-Mail from Anywhere on Earth

One does not have to dial in to one's own ISP to retrieve one's e-mail. One can dial into any ISP anywhere on Earth and retrieve one's e-mail from any other POP3- or IMAP4-based e-mail server.[5]

To access one's e-mail from anywhere using most any e-mail software (e.g., Eudora and Netscape), all one has to do is to configure that e-mail software with the particulars of one's own ISP, namely:

POP3 e-mail server name (e.g., incomingmailserver.myISP.com);

SMTP e-mail server name (e.g., outgoinge-mailserver.myISP.com);

Login name;

Password.

At that point, one can launch one's e-mail software and it will dutifully retrieve one's e-mail, plus send whatever e-mail one wants to send.

Caution: Doing this allows one's e-mail address and password to be seen not only by the out-of-town ISP being used at the moment but also by anyone along the way from where one is to where one's ISP is.

Caution: If one is using someone else's terminal to do this (e.g., hotel terminal and Internet café), one has no assurance that everything being sent and received (including passwords) is not being captured by the owner of that terminal.

Finally, it is worth mentioning that, in cases when one does not have access to an ISP at whichever location one happens to be (e.g., a foreign country) and if one's home ISP does not have a local access number for that location, one may want to consider subscribing to a handful of services that offer worldwide access to one's ISP. These include http://www.ipass.com and http://www.gric.com/.

11.5   E-Mail Forensics and Traces

Just because an e-mail says that it was sent by God@heaven does not mean that it was. It is extremely simple for a sender to "fudge" the sender's ID merely by temporarily entering any old e-mail address for himself/herself in the configuration of the e-mail software. It is just as easy for the receiving person to use an editor and change the sender's name to anything at all and then save the incoming e-mail.

In addition to the message itself, every e-mail has a header that amounts to a sequential list of how the message came from the originator to you; this header normally complies with the standards set in Internet RFC 822.

True, some parts of that (though not all) could be deliberately modified by a sender who wants to cover his or her identity. In fact, most people do not know how to do this in a way that can escape competent analysis. Of

---

5. All e-mail servers use either the POP3 (Post Office Protocol) or the IMAP4 (Improved Mail Protocol) unless they are of the type that requires a user to access e-mail through the Web; the latter is usually done by the free e-mail accounts only.

course, the recipient can remove the entire header; this would be effective only if the remnants of the original header are also wiped from the disk, and the ISP that delivered the e-mail (over whom a user is unlikely to have any control) has also deleted all audit records about that e-mail.

When the sender's e-mail is sent, the sender's e-mail software (e.g., Eudora or Netscape) adds some information to the header. Specifically:

- A Message ID, which assigns a string of symbols that is unique to that message (e.g., **Message-Id: 678901234.0123@fakedISPname.com**);

- An X-Mailer line, which gives the name of the e-mail software (e.g., **X-Mailer: QUALCOMM Windows Eudora Pro Version 4.2**);

- The date/time when it was created or sent. This can be faked, since anyone can set his or her computer to show any time at all (e.g., **Date: Fri, 18 Sept 2000, 12:10:04 −0400** [the offset (−0400) is the time difference from Universal time in London. A minus sign means west of UTC, or GMT, as it used to be called]).

Next, the e-mail goes to the SMTP server of the sender's ISP, which adds a new line to the header that starts with "Received:" It shows:

- Who the e-mail was received from [you, in this case; e.g., **Received: from fakedISP.com (trueISP.com [3.4.5.6])**]. The real IP address of the sending computer is shown in parentheses, just in case the "from" address was faked by the sender.

- Who it was received by [e.g., **by nameofsmtp.com (3.4.5/3.4.5) with SMTP ID ABC12345**]. Here, "3.4.5/3.4.5" is the version number of the SMTP server's software, and the "with" part shows the protocol used (SMTP in most cases).

- The date and time when this happened (e.g., **Fri, 18 Sept 2000 12:20:02-0400**). This date/time has to be later than the date/time stamp when the message was composed or sent, unless the sending computer's clock was not set correctly; this in and of itself does not imply any misdeed.

Next, the e-mail received by the sender's mail server goes through a few go-between Internet nodes on its way to the mail server of the intended recipient. Each such go-between adds lines to the header showing:

- Who it was received from;

- Who it was received by;

- Date and time.

For example:

> Received: from nameofsmtp.com (nameofsmtp.com [9.8.7.6]) by
> firstgobetween.com (6.7.8/6.7.8) with SMTP id DEF67890 Fri, 18
> Sept 2000 12:25:07 −0400

Eventually the e-mail arrives at the mail server handling the account of the intended recipient, which adds its own lines to the header plus an additional one with the notable difference that the From header does not include a colon after the name of the header. For example:

> From fakedname@fakedISPname.com Fri Aug 18 12:27:43 −0400
> Received: from lastgobetween.com (lastgobetween.com [1.3.5.7])
> by recipientmailserver.com (2.4.5/2.4.5) with SMTP id DEF67890
> for recipient@recipientISP.com; Fri. 18 Aug 2000 12:27:43 −0400

Since most people don't want to be bothered with all of the above detail in their incoming e-mail, it is politely hidden by most e-mail software, but the user can opt to see it; in Eudora Pro, for example, the user simply clicks on the "blah blah" icon.

Of all of these header lines, the only lines one can believe are those added by go-between hosts that one trusts. Worse yet, a savvy sender can cause fake lines to be added to the long header to further obfuscate things. About all one can do is detect the existence of such faked lines (sometimes); this does not, however, help identify who the true sender of an e-mail is.

The clues to look for in identifying faked "Received from" header lines are basically anything that deviates from the standard detailed above, which is an uninterrupted concatenation of:

> Received: from *sending_server* [(*sending_host_name sender's_IP_address*)]
> by *receiving_server* [(software_version)]
> with *mail_protocol* and *id* [for *recipient_name*]; *date*

One needs to:

- Check the dates and times to ensure logic and consistency;
- Check for extraneous information and lines in the above sequence;
- Check for illogical server names and locations for the purported sender's location;
- Check for incorrect syntax (any departure from syntax above);
- Look for any deviation from the norm, as stated above;
- Look for relay sites (see the following).

Relay sites are sites whose SMTP server is used by someone without an ISP account at the site to send e-mail. Most (but not all) ISPs reject outgoing e-mail that does not come from their own account holders. The use of a relay site means nothing in and of itself; it merely suggests the increased likelihood that someone is trying to cover his or her tracks (although there are far more effective ways of so doing, as per Sections 11.5.2, 12.15, and 14.3.11, on anonymity).

Relay sites are shown explicitly on the header, as in the following example:

Received: from relaysitename.com (RELAYSITENAME.COM [123.456.789.12]) by receivingsite.com (1.2.3/1.2.3) with SMTP if ABC12345 for recipientname@hisISP.com; Fri, 18 Aug 2000 12:22:41 −0400

One can at least verify if the relay site referenced is read and indeed relays outgoing e-mail by accessing it and sending a test message to oneself. This can be done, for example, through the TELNET program by accessing port 25 of that site, at which point the response may be:

220 relaysitename.com SMTP Sendmail 1.2.3/1.2.3; Fri, 18 Aug 2000 12:53:31 −0400

Using TELNET, type:

HELO your_own_site.your_own_domain

This should evoke the following response:

250 relaysitename.com Hello your_own_site.your_own_domain [IP address]

At which time you can specify:

MAIL FROM: your_name@your_own_site.your_own_domain

To which you should get a response like:

250 your_name@your_own_site.your_own_domain . . . Sender ok

And then you state that you want to send your name to yourself by entering:

RCPT TO: your_name@your_own_site.your_own_domain

If that site indeed relays mail, it will respond with:

250 your_name@your_own_site.your_own_domain . . . Recipient ok

But if it does not, it will respond with:

250 your_name@your_own_site.your_own_domain . . . We do not relay

Type "quit."

If one's intent is to hide the IP address of the originating computer, using a "relay" as per above is one way to accomplish this. For other ways, see Chapters 8 through 14 for sections on various aspects of anonymity.

More information on learning how to read e-mail headers can be obtained from http://www.stopspam.org/email/headers/headers.html. Also, the interested reader will find a lot of specific information on tracing suspect e-mail at http://www.happyhacker.org/gtmhh/gtmhh2.shtml.

11.5.1   Tracking Suspect E-Mail

There are numerous software packages out—some free and some for pay—that make it extremely easy for one to find all there is to know about any Internet server, either by its name or its IP address.

One excellent free software program is NetLab from http://members.xoom.com/adanil/NetLab/, which offers all the network-search options one would need, such as Finger, WhoIs, Ping, Trace, and PortScan, as shown in Figure 11.15. As one can readily see, it offers numerous functions for

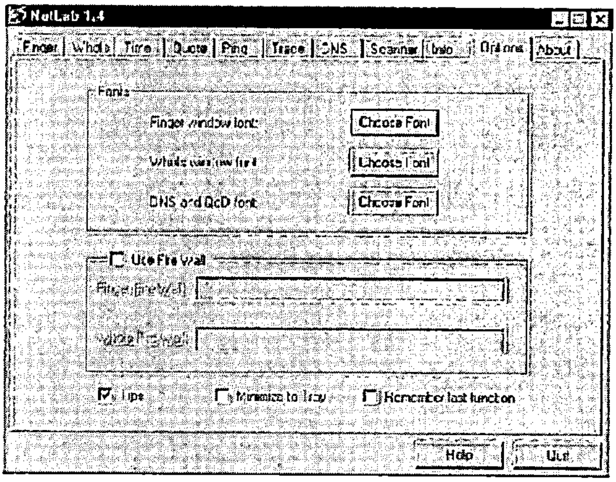

Figure 11.15 NetLab options.

searching Internet-related issues about servers and users. Similar openly available software includes Sam Spade, available at http://www.samspade.org/ ssw/.

Even without special software, to find the domain name of a site through its IP address, one can go to http://wwwnet.princeton.edu/tools/dnslookup .html, http://ipindex.dragonstar.net/, and http://combat.uxn.com/. To get more information one can then go to http://www.networksolutions.com/, http://www.arin.net/intro.html, or http://www.arin.net/whois/index.html. For non-U.S. servers, one can go to http://www.ripe.net/db/whois.html, http://www.ripe.net/cgi-bin/whois (for Europe and Middle East), and http://www.apnic.net/apnic-bin/whois.pl (for Asia/Pacific).

To obtain information on individuals in the United States, two of the most prolific sources of information are http://www.cdbinfotek.com/ in Santa Ana, California, and http://www.digdirt.com/ (both require subscription and a legitimate business reason for requesting such information).

Information that is publicly available can also be obtained on-line from numerous other sites:

http://www.whowhere.com/

http://www.four11.com/

http://www.555-1212.com/

http://www.bigfoot.com/

http://www.switchboard.com/

http://www.infospace.com/

http://www.iaf.net/

http://www.findmemail.com/ (available in four languages)

http://www.phonebook.com/

A set of procedures for finding people's e-mail addresses is also available on-line at http://www.qucis.queensu.ca/FAQs/email/finding.html.

11.5.2   Sending Anonymous E-Mail Via Remailers

Introductory information about forged e-mail addressing can be obtained from http://smithco.net/~divide/index.html and http://happyhacker.com/ gtmhh.

Anonymous and pseudonymous remailers are computers accessible through the Internet which launder one's true identity so that it is concealed from the recipient. They are almost always operated at no cost to the user, and can be found in many countries.

A pseudonymous remailer replaces the sender's true e-mail address with a pseudonymous one affiliated with that remailer and forwards the message to the intended recipient. The recipient can reply to the unknown origina-tor's pseudonymous address which, in turn, forwards it to the true address of the originator.

Anonymous remailers come in three flavors: Cypherpunk remailers, Mixmaster remailers, and Web-based remailers. The header and from infor-mation received by the intended recipient gives no information on how the originator can be contacted. One can concatenate two or more such remailers.

For additional privacy, anonymous remailers support layered public key PGP encryption, wherein the message, including the e-mail address of the intended recipient, is first encrypted with the public key of the last remailer to be used just prior to the intended recipient. This entire encrypted "package," plus the e-mail address of the last remailer above, is then encrypted with the public key of the remailer to be used just prior to the last remailer. This process of layering encryption is repeated for each and every remailer that the originator wants to route the message through. This is depicted in Figure 11.16.

When the end result is sent by the originator to the first remailer, that remailer peels off the outer public key encryption layer (which is all he or she

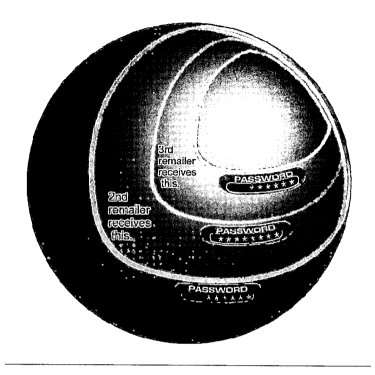

Figure 11.16 The essence of concatenated anonymous remailers.

can decrypt) and finds inside a message encrypted with the "next" remailer's public key and the e-mail address of that "next" remailer to which to forward it. This process is repeated as the message goes from remailer to remailer until the last remailer, which forwards it to the intended recipient.

The implementation of this is automated and is very easy for the origi-nator of a message. Two popular such implementations are in freely available software packages, Private Idaho and Jack B. Nymble, and are available from numerous sources on the Internet; those packages contain current lists of the remailers, and take care of the tedious ritual of placing the various layers of encryption on the message, using the correct public keys and in the right order, and so on.

Jack B. Nymble can be obtained from numerous sources on the Internet, including http://www.skuz.net/potatoware/. Private Idaho can also be obtained from numerous sources, including http://www.skuz.net/Thanatop/contents.htm

(which provides lots of help on setting it up), http://www.eskimo.com/ ~joelm/pi.html, and http://www.itech.net.au/pi/.

An excellent set of detailed instructions on setting up a secure pseudonymous e-mail operation using, for example, Private Idaho (version 2.8 or later is required), is available at http://www.publius.net/n.a.n.help.html. If additional help is needed, one can also see http://www.dnai.com/~wussery/ pgp.html and the Usenet newsgroup alt.privacy.anon-server. Quicksilver can be obtained from http://quicksilver.skuz.net/. It is available for Windows 95/98.

In practice, the process works well as long as a message is not routed through more than a handful of remailers; as that number increases, so does the probability that nothing will emerge out the other end. It has been argued that there is no good technical reason why some remailer traffic is "lost," and that the explanation may be that some "anonymous" remailers are, in fact, operated by governments that have an interest in monitoring such traffic and, perhaps, in deliberately and selectively deleting mail to particular destinations, or causing selective denial of access by flooding the system.

Cypherpunk remailers receive the message to be forwarded, strip away all the headers that describe where the message came from and how it got there, and send it to the intended recipient (which can be an e-mail address or a Usenet newsgroup). Conceivably, someone with access to such a remailer's phone lines could correlate the incoming and outgoing traffic and make inferences.

Mixmaster remailers (also known as Type II remailers) get around some of the security problems of conventional or cypherpunk remailers. They use stronger encryption, as well as numerous procedures to frustrate traffic analysis, such as padding a message to disguise its original length. While extremely secure, even Mixmaster remailers are not foolproof in providing impenetrable anonymity under all conditions. For example, a concerted effort could detect a correlation between sender A, sending an encrypted message through remailers, and receiver B, receiving a message at some variable time afterwards. Problems of this nature can be solved with appropriate procedures and processes and not with technology alone. Also, the fact that most such remailers' encryption keys change very infrequently, due to logistics reasons, makes them more vulnerable than one might otherwise think.

Web-based anonymizers, too, come in different flavors, ranging from a straightforward Web-based version of a conventional anonymizer, to ones where the connection between one's computer and that anonymizer is itself encrypted with 128-bit encryption using the standard Secure Socket Layer encryption built into all late-vintage Web browsers.

A mainstream version of concatenating a string of remailers, each with its own encryption layer, is Naval Research Labs' Onion Routers. This concept has the additional advantage of allowing anonymized and multiple-encrypted Web-browsing in real time. Early development versions ("alpha") are already available and later development versions ("beta") are in the works. Symmetric, rather than public-key, encryption is used, which is much faster but which may run the risk of compromises of the widely disseminated decryption keys.

Internet anonymity can be achieved through a multitude of means other than remailers. These include but are not limited to the use of public Internet terminals (e.g., Internet service providers' sales booths, in public libraries, and Internet cafés).

The reader is strongly urged to read the extensive information available on the subject at http://www.dis.org/erehwon/anonymity.html and at http://www.stack.nl/~galactus/remailers/index-mix.html, before being lulled into a false sense of security through half-measures. Also, the reader is advised to periodically check the following Usenet newsgroups on the subject for any new developments:

alt.anonymous

alt.anonymous.email

alt.anonymous.messages

alt.hackers

alt.security.keydist

alt.security.pgp

comp.security.pgp

comp.security.pgp.announce

comp.security.pgp.discuss

comp.security.pgp.resources

comp.security.pgp.tech

misc.security

sci.crypt

sci.crypt.research

Caution: Some remailers are, allegedly, operated by or for law enforcement or governments. If so, then one should not use a single remailer for anything, but a concatenation of numerous remailers located in different countries. The biggest vulnerability is posed by the very first remailer in the chain (which knows where an e-mail is coming from) and the very last one (which knows where it is going).

Caution: With the recently discovered PGP weakness of Additional Decryption Keys (see Section 14.3.8), one should be even more careful about the choice of the remailers to be used.

Caution: The use of anonymizing remailers for routing encrypted e-mail is an obvious irritant to any local law enforcement. One should balance its privacy benefits against the likelihood of attracting attention from a repressive regime's interceptors.

11.5.2.1 Anonymous or Pseudonymous E-Mail Services

The following sites offer anonymous or pseudonymous e-mail services:

https://www.replay.com/remailer/anon.html

https://www.ziplip.com/sp/send.htm

http://209.67.19.98/lark2k/anonymail.html

http://www.MailAndNews.com/

http://www.graffiti.net/

http://www.privacyx.com/

http://www.ureach.com/ (One of the few big-name e-mail services that hides the sender's IP address from the recipient.)[6]

http://pintur.tripod.com/

http://www.zeroknowledge.com/ (It is recommended that this be purchased with cash, not credit card.)

http://www.cyberpass.net/

http://www.ultimate-anonymity.com/

http://www.surfanon.net/ (For anonymous Web browsing.)

http://www.safeweb.com/ (*Caution:* Requires JavaScript-enabled, which is risky.)

http://www.secure-ibank.com/

---

6. Even so, one should not forget that an Internet service provider can always be compelled by a court order to reveal the true account information of a user of its services.

Caution: Setting up an account with any one of the many Web-based free e-mail services under a pseudonym does not guarantee e-mail anonymity. Such e-mail services keep detailed logs of the IP address from which they were contacted each time, and this can be subpoenaed along with the logs of the ISP whose IP address is identified there to show exactly to whom a pseudonym belongs.

Anyone who needs true anonymity in e-mail is strongly advised to opt for the concatenated remailers with layered encryption described in detail above.

11.5.3   General Network-Tracing Tools

Perhaps the easiest way to find a lot about the identity of IP addresses, information about hosts, and use of such tools as TraceRoute, Finger, and so on, is to use the free services provided by http://www.cotse.com/iptools.html.

Alternately, one can obtain and use one's own software tools, such as NetLab, whose intuitive interface was shown earlier in this chapter.

12

Advanced On-Line Privacy

12.1 Virus/Trojan/Worm Protection

Protection against viruses, Trojans, and worms is an absolute "must have." There are numerous software packages available that provide this protection on a low-cost yearly subscription basis. What is important is to:

- Update the virus-detection signature files at least every week.

- Set up the configuration so that the software checks incoming e-mail in addition to any attachments as they come in on-line, and automatically scans files in inserted floppy disks. This is in addition to periodically scanning one's disk, say, no less often than once a month.

- Subscribe to a "mail list" service, such as the one from Computer Emergency Response Team (CERT) at Carnegie Mellon University, which sends e-mail when a serious new security problem has been discovered, and suggests effective fixes. To be added to that mailing list, send an e-mail to cert-advisory-request@cert.org and include "SUBSCRIBE [your e-mail address]" (without the quotes) in the subject of your message.

12.2   Protection Against Keystroke-Capturing Software

Given the large number of keystroke-capturing software programs, such as KeyKey (discussed in Sections 6.3 and 6.4), that are openly available on the Internet, there is no one easy way for an individual to detect and eliminate all of them from his or her computer. Given the major security threat that such programs represent, however, one would be well justified in taking the time needed to weed such programs out and, better yet, to minimize the likelihood that they get into one's computer in the first place. Adhering to standard security measures such as the following is the only way to accomplish the latter.

- Do not open e-mail attachments unless you know for a fact who sent them and why; the fact that the sender's e-mail address is that of a friend means nothing, as it can be routinely faked; in fact, the most troublesome recent worms (Melissa and "I love you") hijacked personal computers, looked up the list of friends' e-mail addresses in Outlook/Outlook Express, and sent infected e-mails to those addresses, ostensibly from the friendly computer.

- Do not download and install assorted software from the Web from sites with unknown or dubious agendas. Check first with a privacy-minded Usenet forum such as alt.privacy for any postings about unknown sites.

- Do not allow others to insert floppy disks (or CD-ROMs) of unknown origin into your computer.

- Do not allow others to use your computer in your absence.

Some antivirus and anti-Trojan software programs detect some (but not all) of the keystroke-capturing software available. To do this manually, one can simply search the hard disk for any software running in the background that one cannot recognize; this assumes that one performs this task often enough to spot what is unusual, and also that one begins with a computer that is known for a fact not to have any such software running on it.

To detect what software programs are running in the background:

- In Win95/98, type CTRL-ALT-DELETE *once* to see which software are running in the background. Alternately, use WinPatrol from http://www.winpatrol.com/; it will alert you every time a new program wants to run without your knowledge.

- In WinNT, type CTRL-SHIFT-ESC.

12.3 Protection Against Commercial Adware/Spyware

There is an obvious commercial incentive for companies to know as much about an individual as possible, so that customized advertising can be sent to him or her. Since most individuals do not volunteer much information about themselves to total strangers, and since personal computers today contain a fairly accurate image of their respective owner's persona, many companies have taken it upon themselves to acquire as much information as they can about an individual from his or her computer. This unauthorized acquisition—stealing—of information from individual PCs for marketing purposes is made possible when PCs are connected to the Internet; most users have no idea what information is going out.

This is made possible through:

- *On-line software registration.* In an on-line registration process, the user may think that the only information going out is what he or she manually enters, when in fact what often goes out is a digest of one's entire hard disk. Even reputable large companies have been caught red-handed engaging in this practice. *Hint:* Never fill out on-line registration forms or allow software programs to register themselves on-line. If caught acquiring personal information through the registration process, the offending companies have usually professed that the activity resulted from an "unfortunate programming error."

- *ISP collaboration.* A business practice by some marketing companies (such as Predictive Networks, http://www.predictivenetworks.com/), involves participating ISPs providing the marketing companies with individual users' Web browsing habits. This involves not only free ISPs, where tracking of this sort has become the norm, but also subscription ISPs that one pays for by the month. What follows is a statement from Predictive's "privacy policy":

  > Predictive Networks uses Digital Silhouettes to match Internet content and advertising with appropriate subscriber recipients. As a result, subscribers receive information that appeals to their current needs and interests. To develop a Digital Silhouette, the Predictive Network analyzes URL click-stream data, such as web pages visited, and date and time of visit…. To optimize the format of the content delivered to subscribers, the anonymous digital silhouette may include specifications about the subscriber's computer, such as processor type, browser plug-ins and available

memory.... Predictive Networks urges subscribers to consult their ISP before opting out, as doing so may affect their Internet service and/or their Internet service rate.

For more information, see "Start-Up's Tracking Software Sets Off Privacy Alarm," by Jom Hu, CNET News.com, May 1, 2000, http://news.cnet .com/news/0-1005-200-1795712.html.

- *Hidden software.* A large collection of seemingly legitimate software packages that one installs on one's computer after purchasing them either on-line or otherwise contains hidden software. Such programs scout the user's hard disk, collect various kinds of information, and relay it on the sly and without the user's knowledge when the user is on-line on the Internet. This type of software is known as adware or spyware.

What makes this threat particularly bothersome is a new law called the Uniform Computer Information Transactions Act (UCITA), which has already been passed in Maryland and Virginia, and, until the recent massive opposition to it, was likely to pass in many other states as well. This legislation allows companies to spy on a consumer's computer to make sure that all licensing requirements are met; companies have the option of remotely turning off the software, without notifying the user, if they feel that the terms of the license have not been abided; finally, licensers can require that individual users not publicize flaws in their respective software and also prohibit legal action from being taken by the buyer of the software, except in the form of a mediation in the jurisdiction of each such company's choice.

A typical example, according to Steve Gibson of Gibson Research Corporation (http://grc.com/), is Real Networks' Real Download, Netscape/ AOL's Smart Download, and NetZip's Download Demon in their default configurations. In his Web site, Gibson has stated that:

> Every time you use one of these utilities to download any file from anywhere on the Internet, the complete URL address of the file, along with a unique ID tag that has been assigned to your machine and—in the case of Netscape's Smart Download only—your computer's individual Internet IP address, is immediately sent to the program's publisher. This allows a database of your entire personal file download history to be assembled and uniquely associated with your individual computer.... for whatever purpose the program's publisher may have today or tomorrow.

Gibson continues:

Aureate/Radiate and Conducent Technologies [have] advertising, monitoring, and profiling software [that] sneaks into our machines without our knowledge or permission. Comet Cursor secretly tracks our web browsing, GoHip hijacks our web browser and alters our e-mail signatures...and [there are] many other hopeful and exploitive newcomers on the horizon. When confronted with their actions, such companies invariably say "read the fine print, what we're doing is spelled out there and the user agreed."

It must be emphasized that some adware leave the secretly installed utility (that periodically sends out such information) even after the original software that installed the utility has been removed from one's disk.

A list of software programs that, according to Gibson, engage in the practice of installing utilities that periodically send out over the Internet information about users' habits can be found at http://grc.com/oo/spyware.htm and includes the popular CuteFTP utility. This list, current as of the time of this writing, is included in Appendix B.

Perhaps the best protection is to install and use a program that actually observes what gets sent out from one's computer over the Internet. Products with such a capability are known as "network packet sniffers." They are recommended only for those who have—or are willing to invest the time to acquire—a thorough understanding of TCP/IP and IP. (An excellent source of information on this subject is the 738-page "TCP/IP Tutorial and Technical Review" by IBM International Technical Support Organization, which is available freely as a 3.2-MB Adobe Acrobat file that can be downloaded from http://grc.com/oo/packetsniff.htm; it references numerous TCP/IP reference books, such as Richard Stevens's highly regarded three-volume *TCP/IP Illustrated* [1], Douglas Comer's three-volume *Internetworking with TCP/IP* [2], *TCP/IP Blueprints* by Birk and Bligh [3], and numerous others.)

There are numerous packet sniffers available, including the SpyNet Sniffer from eEye (http://www.eeye.com/html/Products/Iris/overview.html) and the CommView v2.0 sniffer from Tamos Software.

- *Hidden HTML code.* A particularly insidious recent threat is the use of invisible images that may be only one pixel ("pixel" is shorthand for "picture element") square on Web pages. They are invisible because they are the same color as the background of the Web page, yet they include malicious HTML code that can be used to gather

information about one's surfing habits. When a Web browser connects to a Web site, the browser normally requests and receives all
images and text and whatever else makes up the page; that "content"
often comes from numerous different computer servers. The image
with the invisible pixels is, therefore, requested from the Web server,
whose job is to collect information from Web surfers. The HTML
code in that image can request additional information from one's
Web browser; depending on how one's browser is configured, it will
most likely provide the requested information. This information is
not limited to what is stored in a Web browser's configuration settings but can extend to anything in one's computer, including the
registry.

The best defense against this security threat is to:

1. Disable graphics in one's browser, at least for all untrusted Web
   sites being visited.

2. Ensure that the security steps outlined in Sections 11.1 and 11.2
   for setting up one's browser in a secure manner are followed.

12.4   Using Virtual Private Networks for Content Protection

The Internet was never designed to be a secure network but rather a surviv-
able network that can automatically route around any nodes and paths that
do not function. Because of its security vulnerabilities, an international
group authorized under the Internet Engineering Task Force (IETF) developed the Internet Protocol Security Protocol Suite (IPsec), which is a set of
extensions to the IP to enhance security at the network level. While individual encryption software does provide security, what was needed was a way to
obtain Internet security regardless of which application software is in use.

   The VPN concept was definitized, and it is really just a concept and
not a set of technical specifications, as evidenced by the fact that there are
numerous mutually incompatible VPN implementations. From a user's perspective, an on-line connection is established with a server, and then the
user's computer and the server establish an encrypted connection over that
same path after some initial back-and-forth electronic "handshaking." From
that moment on, and for the duration of that connection, there is end-to-end
encryption between the user's computer and the host. As with SSL connection, the content of the information between the user and the host is

encrypted and cannot be deciphered by anyone along the way (such as the user's ISP, a telephone tap, or any node in between the two communicating entities).

Caution: As with encryption schemes, all VPNs are not equally secure. Noted crypto expert Bruce Schneier states in a June 1998 announcement (http://www.counterpane.com/pptp-pressrel.html) that "Flaws [have been discovered] in Microsoft's implementation of a communications protocol used in many commercial VPNs. These flaws lead to password compromise, disclosure of private information, and server inoperability in VPNs running under Windows NT and 95." Schneier further states that "Microsoft's implementation is seriously flawed at several levels. It uses weak authentication and poor encryption. For example they use the user's password as an encryption key instead of using any of the well known and more secure alternatives." Another evaluator, Mark Chen, CTO of Veriguard, Inc., of Menlo Park, California, is quoted in that same press release as stating that "[t]he flaws in this implementation are quite amateurish. A competent cryptographic review would have prevented the product from shipping in this form."

Caution: A VPN connection merely protects a user from interception outside of the secure connection to the host. It does not protect the user from malicious content (e.g., a virus) that the user might obtain from another user through that host.

Caution: Some VPN implementations conflict with some firewall implementations. While one could argue that there is no need for a firewall when using a VPN, most users use a VPN only when connecting to a particular host (e.g., the employer's computer) and not at all other times, when a firewall *is* needed.

12.5 Using Proxy Servers for Anonymity

A proxy server is a go-between between one's computer and whichever server one connects to through the Internet. Depending on the specifics of a proxy, it can serve any one or more of numerous needs:

1. To get around slow nonoptional ISP "caching" (meaning "locally stored content"), avoiding having to get such content from the Internet each time; in so doing, one can get speed improvements even if the proxy used is on the other side of the world.

2. As a means of defeating local censorship or local monitoring. This is done by establishing an encrypted connection with an out-of-country proxy (see discussion below about SSL and VPN). Once connected to such a proxy, one can perform all Internet activities in a manner that is not observable by anyone in the path between the user and the proxy. Of course, the fact that one has established an encrypted connection to an out-of-country server will be very much visible to the locals, and this is unlikely to endear one to the local regime.

3. To prevent a Web site that one looks at from knowing who is looking at it. Since Web browsers broadcast a lot of information about a Web surfer, and especially since there are countless ways whereby a hostile Web site can retrieve any and all information from one's browser, the motivation to prevent such security compromises is self-evident.

4. To avoid ending up on advertisers' lists and/or receiving unwanted e-mail. Individuals who feel compelled to post to Usenet forums without the—sadly inevitable—result of being added to advertisers' mailing lists or receiving harassing e-mail by assorted strangers elect to use proxies to post anonymously on Usenet forums.

5. To allow adaptable Internet access. Some proxies serve the visually impaired; ea.ethz.ch:8080 is one notable example. Still others translate Web pages into languages that the user may understand; for example, mte.inteli.net.mx:3128 translates English Web pages into Spanish and zip-translator.dna.affrc.go.jp:30001 translates English Web pages into Spanish. As such, the often-heard assertions by law enforcement that proxies are used only by those with criminal intent are without merit.

Setting up a proxy on one's browser is quite simple. In the case of Netscape, go to Edit/Preferences/Advanced/Proxies, select "Manual proxy configuration," click on "View," and fill in the blanks in accordance with the instructions of the particular proxy you want to use.

In the case of a local proxy (software in one's own computer that assumes a go-between filtering role) such as Junkbuster, for example, one merely needs to enter the word "LOCALHOST" in the Address blank for both the HTTP and the Security field, and the number "8000" (all without quotes) in the blanks for Port.

Web sites that provide a current list of proxy servers of all sorts, or that provide information about a particular proxy, include:

http://www.webveil.com/matrix.html (highly recommended)

http://www.webveil.com/proxies.html

http://www.tools.rosinstrument.com/cgi-bin/fp.pl/showlog

http://www.somebody.net/

http://www.egroups.com/community/proxy-methods-list

http://proxys4all.cgi.net/public.shtml

Internet users from oppressive regimes should utilize out-of-country proxy servers.

Caution: Most of the proxies one can find at proxys4all (http://prox-ys4all.cgi.net/) actually mask very little and give a false sense of security because they reveal to the Web site being visited the IP address of the originator.

Remember that a remote proxy is nothing more than an untrusted go-between. That server will know precisely who you are (because he or she must know your IP address to forward to you whatever it is you are browsing through the proxy) and he or she will also know what you are browsing. Proxy servers usually do keep logs of who did what and when, and such logs can be subpoenaed by the local (to the proxy) authorities, whose interest will be piqued by the mere fact that you are using a proxy, especially one that encrypts its connection with you. Because of this:

1. Try to use a proxy from a suitable country other than your own.

2. Keep in mind that the longevity of a proxy is iffy. Many survive for just one day; others for years. You need a continuously updated list of current ones, which you can get from the sites listed above.

3. Be suspicious of proxy servers, such as http://www.safeweb.com/, that require that you enable JavaScript, because they can then see a lot in your computer that they really have no reason to see.

4. Do not overuse any one proxy; spread your on-line communications over different proxies, preferably located in different countries.

5. If you don't (and you shouldn't) trust any one proxy to protect your privacy, consider chaining proxies. From a posting by Anonymouse (which has since been sold) on February 5, 1999:

- Record your own current IP address; you can get it, for example, by going to http://www.tamos.com/bin/proxy.cgi, or by typing:
  netstat –n

- Go to the Anonymizer form at http://www.anonymizer.com /surf_free.shtml and enter http://www.tamos.com/bin/proxy.cgi into the form's box followed by the "enter" key. This will take you to http://www.tamos.com/bin/proxy.cgi.

- Now look at the URL displayed for the page http://anon-free.anonymizer.com/http://www.tamos.com/bin/proxy.cgi.

- That prefix (http://anon-free.anonymizer/com/) is the prefix that you must write ahead of any URL you want to chain through Anonymizer in the future; for example: http://anon-free.anonymizer.com/http://www.cnn.com/.

- Also notice the IP address shown (209.75.196.2); it is the identity that Anonymizer gives out instead of your real IP address.

Equivalently, you can go through other combinations, such as Anonymicer, as follows:

- Go to the Anonymicer form at http://www.in.tum.de/~pircher/ anonymicer/ and type http://www.tamos.com/bin/proxy.cgi into that form's box (and hit "enter").

- This takes you, again, to http://www.tamos.com/bin/proxy.cgi, yet if you look at the URL shown for that page, you will see http://www.in/tum.de/cgi-bin/ucgi/pircher/anon-www.pl/http:// www.tamos.com/bin/proxy-cgi.

- The prefix http://www.in.tum/de/cgi-bin/ucgi/pircher/anon-www.pl/ is the prefix that you should write in front of whichever URL you want to go to through Anonymicer.

A good current reference of the status of many free Web-based proxies can be found at http://www.webveil.com/matrix.html. It provides about 10 long pages of detailed information on the current status of such proxies.

For additional information about the strengths and weaknesses of proxies, consult the following sites:

http://www.ijs.co.nz/proxies.htm

http://www.ultimate-anonymity.com/ (The name is misleading.)

http://tools.rosinstrument.com/proxy/proxyck.htm

http://proxys4all.cgi.net/

Numerous others can be found by keyword searching on the word "proxy."

12.6 Protection Against Intel's Individually Serial-Numbered Microprocessors

This was an unfortunate blunder by Intel: It was disclosed that Pentium III microprocessors (and some Pentium II microprocessors for portable computers) had individual electronic serial numbers that could be retrieved remotely through a network, such as the Internet, to positively identify a respective computer.

Facing intensive and vocal criticism, Intel backtracked and shipped these microprocessors with the serial numbers "feature" disabled, rather than enabled, in the default mode, but still capable of being enabled at any time through software. Shortly thereafter, privacy groups posted on the Internet ways whereby the disabled feature could be enabled without the knowledge of the computer owner or user.

The threat that the serial number poses is primarily one of privacy rather than security; however, one can easily envision scenarios where security becomes an issue: For example, a businessperson whose laptop computer uses this chip and whose particular serial number is known to a competitor, could be selectively targeted by a Web site based on that businessperson's unique Pentium III serial number.

Indeed, news reports have indicated that China has banned the importation of microprocessors having remotely retrievable electronic serial numbers.

In view of the above, the security-minded individual is advised not to go on-line using a Pentium III computer.

12.7 Using Encrypted Connections to ISPs for Content Protection

The initial connection to one's ISP is never encrypted. What *could* be encrypted is what happens afterwards.

In the simplest case, one can connect to any one of many Web pages that support SSL (see Section 12.7.1) and this will establish an end-to-end encrypted connection between that Web server (which may be on the other side of the Earth) and one's computer; this prevents anyone else from becoming privy to the content of the data flow. Of course, the primary ISP will know where one has connected to, but not the content of any subsequent information flow.

Many corporate computing centers have established a secure means whereby employees can log in to the corporate network from afar; this is useful for traveling employees and those who work from home. It is accomplished through a virtual private network (VPN), discussed in Section 12.4, and it amounts to a connection that is end-to-end encrypted between the individual's computer and the remote server; it shares many of the characteristics of SSL, but the technical details are quite different.

If one is using PrivacyX servers (still operational as of July 2001) and Outlook Express, then an encrypted SSL connection can be established between one's computer and the PrivacyX e-mail servers to upload and download e-mail, including attachments. This keeps the local ISP and any interceptors along the way safely out of one's business.

Encrypted e-mail with or without attachments can always be sent through unencrypted connections. All that is observable to the ISP, or anyone else, is the outer envelope; that is, who is sending something to whom. If anonymous remailing techniques are used (see Section 11.5.2), then that information is not very helpful to an interceptor or ISP, except in a negative sense, because it raises the profile of the sender as someone who may be "up to no good" and hence worthy of more detailed surveillance.

12.7.1   Secure Socket Layer

Secure Socket Layer (SSL) is a protocol developed by Netscape that allows end-to-end encryption between one's browser and the Web site one visits. The encryption level can be weak (40 bits) or strong (128 bits). Since the recent change in U.S. export policy, practically anyone can have legitimate access to the 128-bit key versions of SSL offered by both Netscape and Microsoft (for its Web browser). An SSL connection is verified by looking at the little lock icon on the lower left side of Netscape.

The process of using Web-browser encryption to send and receive encrypted e-mail is quite straightforward from within either Netscape or Microsoft's browser:

1. One connects to any one of a handful of popular "certificate"-issuing organizations, such as Verisign (http://www.verisign.com/), which charges about $10 per year, or Thawte (http://www.thawte.com/), which gives free certificates even though it has been bought out by Verisign.

2. After installing this certificate, one can exchange encrypted e-mail with others who have gone through the same ritual. *Caution:* SSL mail does not encrypt the "from whom" and "to whom" information, or the "subject" line. Also, outgoing SSL-encrypted e-mail is encrypted so that the sender can read it after it has been sent; it follows that a sender can be compelled by local authorities to decrypt that mail; by comparison, a user of PGP (which is highly recommended as a superior alternative for e-mail encryption; see Section 14.3) cannot decrypt outgoing e-mail encrypted for some intended recipient; the recipient is the only one who can decrypt it.

12.7.2 Using PrivacyX for Encrypted E-Mail Connection to E-Mail Servers

PrivacyX is a highly recommended means for exchanging e-mail, but only if it is done "right."

PrivacyX (http://www.privacyX.com/) was a Canadian firm that allowed—nay, *encouraged*—one to log in anonymously and establish an e-mail account with a pseudonym. One can connect to the e-mail server that PrivacyX had over a fully encrypted connection (SSL). This is an end-to-end encryption that defeats interception by anyone else, and hides both the content and the "from whom" and "to whom" information. To the extent that one was willing to trust PrivacyX, one's e-mail privacy was established. The SSL connection can be established either through one's Web browser or, interestingly, through Outlook Express, if (and only if) one followed the precise instructions provided on-line by PrivacyX.

The only advantage of using Outlook Express, which is otherwise not recommended due to its many security vulnerabilities acknowledged by Microsoft, is that, if one has multiple e-mail accounts that one wants to check with a single piece of e-mail software for incoming mail in any one of them, one can do so with Outlook Express and could do so with full SSL encryption for PrivacyX accounts (Eudora does not offer SSL encryption); checking through Netscape, by comparison, requires setting up a different "Profile" for each and launching Netscape "from scratch" for each.

The disadvantage is that Outlook and Outlook Express have had an unenviable list of security flaws that allowed a hostile remote hacker to cause an unsuspecting user's e-mail list to send virus-containing e-mails to all addresses on the list, and make it appear as if they came from the unsuspecting user.

12.8 Secure Shell

Secure Shell (SSH) is simply a piece of software that allows one to connect to another computer over a network, and do so securely over inherently unsecured channels such as the Internet. As such, it is a secure replacement to Telnet "rsh," "rlogin," and "rcp," familiar to old-timers in the Internet world. There are over 2 million SSH users around the world.

There are two mutually incompatible versions: SSH1 and SSH2. The interested user is referred to a thorough reference of frequently asked questions (FAQs) on SSH at any of the sites below:

http://www.employees.org/~satch/fq/ssh-faq.html

http://www.tigerlair.com/ssh/faq/ssh-faq.html

http://www.onsight.com/faq/ssh-faq.html

http://www.ayahuasca.net/ssh/ssh-faq.html (in the United Kingdom)

http://member.ctinets.com/~dhackler/ssh/faq/ssh-faq.html (in Hong Kong)

http://www.cs.univ-paris8.fr/ssh/faq/ssh-faq.html (in France)

12.9 Caller ID Traps

Most countries of the world have leapfrogged interim technology and have migrated from the mechanical Stromberg Carlson routers of telephone calls to the latest implementation of what is known as Signaling System 7. This all-electronic system allows one to offer such popular features as caller ID, selective call rejection, call forwarding, and so on. What may not be as evident is that identification of the origin of a telephone call is instantaneous in all cases. Caller ID blocking—that is, when a subscriber thinks that he or she blocks his or her own phone number from being forwarded downstream—is an illusion; the number is still forwarded all the way, except that—in some cases—it is not seen by the called party; in many cases (such as when calling a toll-free number—where the called party pays for the call and is presumed to be entitled to know for whose call he or she is paying[1]—or when calling emergency numbers or some government offices), caller-ID blocking does absolutely nothing.

The bottom line is that the initiator of an Internet dial-up connection, whether the call is local or international, is immediately identifiable and there is nothing that the caller can do about it other than using someone else's telephone.[2] This applies to cellular calls as well.

12.10   Cellular Phone Traps

A visitor from a democratic country to a totalitarian state might mistakenly think that an Internet connection through a cellular phone will provide anonymity and not be traceable. Nothing could be further from the truth.

As stated previously, a cellular phone enjoys no more protection against being identified than any landline telephone. With the increasing interest in offering position-location services for emergency purposes (and any country's law enforcement's insatiable appetite to know everything about everyone), cellular phones cannot only be listened to with the same (or greater) technical ease as regular landline telephones, but can be geolocated with an accuracy of a few hundred feet using commercial technology being implemented by the cellular telephone companies, which are now required to comply with the U.S. CALEA[3] requirements.

In the case of GSM cellular telephones, the identity of the subscriber is not so much in the telephone instrument itself but in the subscriber-identification module (the "SIM card"), which is a small "smart card" that can be used with any GSM phone anywhere in the world. If the SIM card corresponds to a user registered within the country where the phone is being used, that country can know everything about that user; if it corresponds to a user registered with some other GSM country, the country where the GSM phone is being used will know only the issuing country; even then, however, the location of the GSM phone can be pinpointed within a few hundred feet using commercial technology.

---

1. This is known as Automatic Number Identification (ANI) and is separate from caller ID.

2. Some bill-collection agencies that are faced with the obvious problem of having their calls ignored by those they are trying to reach have been reported to be using equipment that allows them to cause a different number to be displayed on the called party's caller-ID box.

3. Communications Assistance for Law Enforcement Act, passed by the U.S. Congress in October 1994.

About the only anonymity one can have with cellular phones is through the vastly popular business model whereby a buyer purchases a phone (usually a GSM phone) with a prepaid amount of "air minutes"; such purchases are usually anonymous or pseudonymous, as the selling vendor and GSM service providers are protected from unpaid charges since the phone will stop functioning when the prepaid limit is used up. Such accounts are almost always usable only within the country that sold them.

12.11   FTP Traps

File Transfer Protocol (FTP) is the standard way of downloading files from the Internet. It is also an option for any two individuals for sending and receiving such files by interjecting a go-between: The sender FTPs the file to some interim "parking space" such as an ISP or a Web site; the intended recipient is then notified and retrieves that file from its designated parking space. This two-step process provides some insulation between the sender and the recipient; a freedom fighter in a repressive regime could, for example, use this to avoid being associated with the "other" party to the communication. The danger is that this file now sits in some third site (the parking space); unless it is protected by encryption, which may be alerting in and by itself, there are security risks from this process. FTP software can be obtained freely from many sites, such as http://www.cuteftp.com/.

   Caution: CuteFTP is one of a number of software packages that have been identified as adware or spyware, in the sense that they also install a file in personal computers that, unbeknownst to the user, periodically contacts the maker of the software through the Internet. See Section 6.6.1.

12.12   Threats Posed by ICQ

ICQ (the acronym is derived from the phrase "I seek you") is a very popular software application that allows on-line users to be notified right away if anyone on their list of designated friends or associates is on-line, and allows one-on-one (or many-with-many) textual communications between them. It is very convenient.

   It is also a security disaster. There are easy ways whereby one's ICQ identity can be hijacked by someone else. Also, anything typed becomes a matter of record for a long time to come. Finally, one may well not wish to advertise to the world when one is or is not on-line.

The same goes for all other "instant messaging" software, such as AOL's Instant Messenger, the Yahoo! messenger, and the MSN messenger, according to CERT. Depending on the version used, many are vulnerable to crashing and even running a program on your computer if they receive a malicious "buffer overflow" message.

Also, regardless of the message, one never really knows who is on the other end of the line. Finally, since all messages typed back and forth are unencrypted, they are eminently interceptable.

12.13   Pitfalls of On-Line Banking

The example at the beginning of Chapter 10 showed how a popular on-line banking program was "doctored" remotely by a malicious Web site to cause it to direct the user's bank to send a payment to a hacker's account. This underscores the fact that when a computer goes on-line to the Internet, unless the user has taken the many protective measures spelled out in this book, it is potentially vulnerable to having any of its files read, stolen, or modified.

To that extent, on-line banking is vulnerable by merely having its files exist in a vulnerable computer.

In addition, one should ensure that the encryption used uses key lengths that are:

- No shorter than 1,024 bits if public-key encryption is used (as is likely the case);
- No shorter than 128 bits if symmetric encryption is used or if a symmetric "session key" is used.

Since this level of technical detail is unlikely to be shown in software intended for nontechnical users, one may wish to ask before using such software; even if the encryption uses acceptably long keys, there is no assurance that it is implemented properly.

If the same on-line banking software was made available outside of the United States prior to the recent liberalization of the U.S. encryption exportation laws, one should be concerned that the encryption used is weak (and hence exportable at that time). Please note that, since U.S. export laws on encryption were drastically liberalized about a year ago, encryption software that is "exportable" is not necessarily using weak encryption anymore.

Caution: Some banks use on-line customers' Social Security numbers as those customers' ID for all Web-based banking. This is an outrageous violation of privacy and a practical nuisance because, for example, it precludes a customer from having more than one on-line account with that bank.

In the final analysis, the on-line banking user's only real protection can be a clause that indemnifies and protects the user in case of a problem caused by unauthorized use of the on-line banking software; since banks have no control over that, however, it is unlikely that a user will get such legal protection. The best a user can do is to secure his or her computer using the methods discussed in this book.

12.14   XML

XML (extensible Markup Language) is the forthcoming replacement of and enhancement to HTML (HyperText Markup Language). We are all familiar with the words and icons on a Web page or document that one can click on and get more information on that topic; HTML is basically an access and display mechanism.

In contrast, XML is designed to transport data; whereas HTML tags are finite in number and are predefined, XML tags are infinite in number and are defined by the author, in addition to containing data.

One might say, "So what?" What is significant from a security perspective here is that XML allows the transfer of data in both directions. Intercepting an XML document that contains sensitive data from one banking application to another is likely to entice enterprising hackers.

Since XML has not been popularized yet, the advice to individual users is not to use it when it does become part of Web browsers until enough time has passed and its security weaknesses have been identified and—to the extent possible—patched.

12.15   Secure Usenet Usage

Where are Usenet messages stored? They are *not* stored in any one big computer. As one (anyone) posts a message to any of the more than 100,000 different Usenet forums, that message goes out right then and there to the world; hundreds of thousands of computers that "listen" to Usenet postings will capture it and store it for varying lengths of time if they are set up to capture messages to that particular forum.

It is generally not a good idea to use one's true name to post to Usenet forums, for the following reasons:

1. Unless the topic has absolutely no political, religious, cultural, or other implications and unless the prose used has absolutely no "barbs," it is inevitable that some person(s) reading it may take exception to its contents. Given how easy it is to "e-mail-bomb" someone (i.e., to subscribe the victim to a few thousand "mail lists," each of which generates some 100 messages a day that are then e-mailed to list members, thereby clogging one's e-mail beyond belief and rendering one's account unusable), one should not post messages that could offend anyone.

2. Even if the topic is totally "clean" (e.g., posting a technical question on how to deal with a technical problem in Windows), one will end up on the list of "spammers" (e-mail advertisers), whereupon one's e-mail box will be clogged with messages offering instant wealth, sex, miracle cures, and the like.

It follows that, since Usenet can provide an extremely useful source of quick technical advice (e.g., when some popular software or hardware misbehaves and one is at a loss as to the cause), the only way to post a question (e.g., "My xyz software seems to crash the computer under such-and-so conditions; does anyone know of a fix?") and avail oneself of this vast resource is to post anonymously or pseudonymously.

But even looking at what others have posted on this or that Usenet newsgroup can incur the wrath of select law enforcement zealots in one country or another. As with anything that is a network activity (such as the Internet), there is no such thing as a "passive" act. "Merely browsing" is a very active endeavor, in that it amounts to asking one's ISP to fetch and send to the subscriber the specific documents that the subscriber wants to see. Even in browsing through Usenet postings, therefore, a user must be anonymous.

Here again one must ask oneself: Anonymous with respect to whom?

- Usenet readers around the world?

- The in-country ISP that may be in collusion with local law enforcers? (If so, it is unwise to read—let alone write to—Usenet forums that deal with topics that are taboo in that country for religious, political, or other reasons.)

- Someone who might get physical access to one's computer for hostile forensics purposes?

12.15.1   Anonymity with Respect to Usenet Readers

Anonymity with respect to other Usenet readers is easy to take care of in an amateurish fashion but not so easy to handle in a professional fashion. Merely altering the user ID and e-mail address in one's Usenet software before composing and sending a Usenet message will cause the message to be posted with the assumed name; this is only a fig leaf, however, because the IP address of the sending entity is not disguised.

It is far better to post through any of the many anonymizing remailers that accept postings to newsgroups, such as:

http://www.MailAndNews.com/

http://www.zedz.net/

http://209.67.19.98/lark2k/anonymail.html (hides the IP address of the sender)

This is in addition, of course, to using Private Idaho and other such services.

Alternately, one can use services that allow Usenet posting from e-mail, such as Mail2News (http://canal3.hypermart.net/mail2news.htm). Of course, unless one is willing to place full faith in such services' discretion, it is best to combine this with e-mail from a reasonably untraceable source, such as from a public library or Internet café. Mail2News gateways come in numerous flavors, such as Web-to-News and E-mail-to-News.

12.15.2   Anonymity with Respect to In-Country ISPs

Concealing one's identity from the in-country ISP is more difficult to accomplish. Certainly one's Internet service provider—unless end-to-end encryption is used—can see everything that the subscriber types and sees on his or her screen. The issue is whether the ISP would bother to monitor subscribers' Usenet usage. The answer is an emphatic yes under any of the following common conditions:

1. If the ISP is served with a court order to log a user's on-line activities, an ISP will always comply. Unless a user is running his or her

own news server (not common, but quite possible), an ISP will have the ability to record all of user's Usenet activities.

2. If the subscriber has been giving an ISP a very hard time in terms of complaints, it is human nature to expect that individuals at the ISP can spy on that user out of curiosity or even vengeance. If that user's Usenet activities then turn out to be ones that local law prohibits, then the ISP can tip off local law enforcement by stating that a "routine" or "preventive" maintenance uncovered that conduct (so as to preclude appearing to have violated any applicable privacy acts and have the evidence thrown out of court). Software for doing such "routine maintenance" does exist; for small ISPs that may not have it, it is a simple matter to write a few lines of code to end up with the same selective data collection; most ISPs that offer access to Usenet require individual authentication of users before such access is granted, anyway.

3. *Posting to* (as opposed to browsing of) Usenet messages is almost always monitored and recorded by ISPs.

If one merely wants to minimize (as opposed to eliminate) the likelihood that the local ISP will monitor a subscriber's Usenet access, then the subscriber can use Usenet service offered by servers other than his or her own ISP—preferably in a different country. Such servers include, for example:

http://www.newsfeeds.com/

http://www.altopia.com/

http://www.ctservice.de/taker/cgi-bin/anon-www.cgi/http://ctservice.de/taker/news

http://www.uncensored-news.com/

http://liberty.banhof.se/

http://www.GUBA.com/

http://www.newshog.com/

http://www.newsnerds.com/

http://www.nuthingbutnews.com/

http://www.vip-news.com/

http://www.supernews.net/

http://www.randori.com/

Most of the above servers require a fee, and some offer anonymous access. The user is cautioned, however, that one should not depend on the "anonymity" promises of a for-fee news-server because:

- Any server must comply with the in-country court orders to retain logs (such as the IP address showing where it is being accessed from and any other identifying information).
- Unless the communication is end-to-end encrypted (using SSL, for example), a user's on-line activities are still perfectly visible to that user's local ISP.

Since one's ISP sees everything that goes in and out of a subscriber's computer, the only "fix" is to establish an SSL connection (see Section 12.7.1) with a remote Web site (preferably out of the country and hence out of reach of the local constabulary) that will accept posting to an ISP; once the SSL connection has been established, the in-country monitors are left with nothing to read other than the fact that a user being monitored has connected to an out-of-country Web site with an encrypted connection. This will protect the content of the ensuing communication, but is guaranteed to raise the user's profile that much higher in the eyes of the frustrated local investigator.

Remote Web sites that accept SSL connections include:

http://www.privacyx.com/

https://anon.xg.nu/post.html

https://www.rewebber.com/

An excellent list of URL sites for anonymous posting can be found at http://www.fen.baynet.de/~na1723/links/links10.html.

12.15.3   Anonymity with Respect to Hostile Computer Forensics

Concealing oneself from the hostile forensics examiner falls within the category of general counterforensics discussed throughout this book. An easy-to-follow step-by-step set of instructions on "nym" (pseudonym) creation that allows one anonymity in Usenet postings as well as in e-mail can be found at http://www.stack.nl/%7Egalactus/remailers/nym.html ("Nym Creation for Mere Mortals").

If one was unwise enough to post something on Usenet in the heat of the moment and using one's true e-mail address, there is a chance that it could be *partially* removed by going to http://www.deja.com/forms/ nuke.shtml. However, it must be realized that the Usenet is not any one big computer sitting somewhere but hundreds of thousands of individual computers that capture Usenet postings "as they are posted"; expecting all of them to delete a posting just because the originator had a change of heart is unrealistic.

Finally, there is the commonsense approach to posting anonymously to Usenet: sitting in front of the keyboard of some publicly accessible computer, such as that at a public library, at a university, at an Internet café, at a computer trade show where there are terminals on-line, and so on.

Caution: Surprising as it may seem, there is a lot of material available on-line for free downloading that is positively illegal to download and view in most countries. This applies to Web sites and especially to the Usenet forums, many of which are on topics that strain credibility, are positively distasteful to even the most broad-minded person, and test one's level of tolerance. It is always best to browse Usenet forums and Web sites through an SSL connection to an out-of-country go-between proxy server, so as to avoid incurring the wrath of local enforcers of local morality and political correctness.

12.16   Firewalls

A firewall, despite its name, is a semipermeable membrane that, depending on how good the particular implementation is, prevents most undesired data to cross it, whether coming into one's computer (such as through malicious attacks on one's computer) or going out of one's computer (such as via adware programs that call home and report on a user's activities).

The need for even an imperfect firewall is quite apparent to anyone who has monitored intrusion attempts from random Internet users. The most common such attempts are:

- "Port-scanning" of one's ports (see Section 12.17). Would-be intruders with Sub7 typically scan port 27374, while others scan just about any port they hope to find open. If one has used ICQ, Napster, or other such software programs that essentially broadcast one's IP address to others, one's computer could be routinely port-scanned to find (and exploit) vulnerabilities.

- Unauthorized outgoing messages sent via adware/spyware (see Section 6.6.1) that has been surreptitiously installed on an unsuspecting user's computer.

There is no standard as to what a firewall must do or how well; as a result, numerous products that have quite different capabilities go by this name. A firewall can be a standalone piece of hardware, such as a full-blown computer or a dedicated "box," or it can be software in one's computer, or both. Information on firewalls beyond what is provided in this section can be found at an archive maintained at http://lists/gnac.net/firewalls/. FAQs about firewalls can be downloaded from http://www.interhack.com/pubs/fwfaq. An excellent technical overview of firewalls can be downloaded from http://www.boran.com/security/it12-firewall.html and is highly recommended. A list of technical references on firewalls that goes beyond the scope of this book can be found at http://www.cert.org/ and is also highly recommended reading.

Most commercial concerns use pricey firewalls, such as Checkpoint, which has 40% of the market, and Cisco, which has 23% of the market. Others include IBM's Lotus Firewall for Windows NT, Network Associates Gauntlet, AltaVista's Firewall97, Raptor Eagle NT 4.0, Ukiah's NetRoard Firewall for NT, and numerous others.

As listed here, there are four basic kinds of firewalls, although most commercially available products are hybrids of these:

1. *Packet filtering.* This is the simplest and most common firewall. Packets are filtered based on user-provided criteria, such as where the packets are coming from or going to. As an example, packets that appear to be coming from known potential threats are prevented from passing through. Since the "from" portion (or any other portion, for that matter) of a packet header can readily be spoofed by a hacker, this is not a foolproof protection. No modification to a user's existing software is needed.

2. *Stateful inspection.* Stateful inspection corrects some of the most glaring weaknesses of packet filtering firewalls, by looking at sequences of packets and making decisions based on such sequences. As an example, if the packets do not arrive at the proper sequence, they can be blocked at the user's choice. This type of firewall, too, requires no change in the user's existing software. The popular Checkpoint firewall is of this type, with the addition of advanced features such as

network address translation (NAT), which shields one's protected network true addresses from an untrusted network. LanOptics' Guardian 2.2 also uses this approach.

3. *Application proxy.* This amounts to a go-between or "proxy" and checks all requests for everything that is trying to go through, compares it against its list of what is allowed and what is not, and acts accordingly. In other words, it operates at the "application layer" and as such, it requires the setting up of a separate such proxy for each application (such as FTP, and each custom application such as IP telephony—see Section 13.2.5—requires its own such proxy). Examples of such commercially available firewalls include AltaVista's Firewall 97, Raptor EagleNT 4.0, and Ukiah's NetRoad Firewall for NT.

   The advantage is that it provides the highest level of security among those firewalls listed above. The disadvantages are that some applications cannot work through a proxy and hence cannot work through this kind of firewall, and it can slow down the performance of a computing system.

4. *Circuit level gateway.* This is similar to the application proxy firewall. The firewall first authenticates the end points in an Internet TCP connectivity and then allows TCP and UDP data to go through between those two points. The best such firewalls use a standard developed by the Internet Engineering Task Force (IETF) called SOCKS (version 5 is the latest).

   The advantage is that it does not cause the slowdowns that the application proxy firewall does, because it does not function at the application layer. The disadvantages are that it requires one to modify either the application software being used or the so-called TCP/IP stacks (suitably modified stacks are available for most popular operating systems, such as Windows, MacOS, and Unix), and it involves a lot of work to configure a large network (such as a corporate network) to use this kind of firewall.

As with the testing of anything that is security related, one can never in clear conscience pronounce as "secure" that which is being protected. About all one can do is try to eliminate or reduce the known vulnerabilities. This applies to firewalls as well.

Firewalls are not a panacea. If one's computing system, for example, allows a "trusted person" to bypass a firewall in order to do system maintenance from afar, then the firewall cannot be blamed if that loophole is compromised. Firewalls cannot protect well against most viruses, because there are far too many ways whereby viruses can enter one's computer. Accordingly, one would be well advised to invest, at a minimal cost, in antivirus software. Also, a firewall that allows encrypted traffic to go through (e.g., encrypted e-mail, VPN; see Section 12.4) cannot possibly protect from the content of such encrypted traffic. Finally, a firewall offers no protection against an "insider threat."

12.16.1   Corporate Firewalls

Corporate firewalls are intended to protect entire internal networks, rather than individual computers and small home-office networks, and their prices reflect that.

The most notable ones as of the time of this writing include:

- **Checkpoint VPN-1 Appliance 330.** By Checkpoint Software Technologies (http://wwwcheckpoint.com/), its price is $4,000–$8,000, depending on the configuration. This is an Israeli-made firewall, reportedly codeveloped with Nokia, which is quite popular with the corporate world.

- **eSoft Interceptor.** By eSoft (http://www.esoft.com/); about $3,800. Includes a VPN server. It has minimal reporting and real-time monitoring capabilities.

- **Progressive Systems Phoenix Adaptive Firewall.** By Progressive Systems (http://www.progressive-systems.com/); about $3,000, plus $1,000 for an upgrade to include VPN and site-to-site capability. Lacks spam filtering.

- **Cisco Secure PIX Firewall 515-R-BUN.** By Cisco Systems (http://www.cisco.com/); about $5,200, including VPN with full-featured IPsec. It has excellent performance, but lacks a convenient graphical user interface and must be managed through a command-line mode.

- **WatchGuard LiveSecurity System 4.1.** By Watchguard Technologies (http://www.watchguard.com/); about $5,000. It has excellent performance and convenient management interface. It scored highest in an assessment in the June 27, 2000, issue of *PC Magazine.*

- **SonicWall Pro.** By Sonic Wall Inc. (http://www.sonicwall.com/); about $3,000. This is best for small offices. Lacks spam filtering.

It must be realized that any network firewall will slow down the throughput rate of a system to some extent, especially (and not surprisingly) during an attack on the firewall-protected network.

12.16.2   Personal Firewalls

High-end firewalls intended for corporate use are beyond the price range of most individuals. Firewalls whose price is within the plausible range for individual users include both hardware and software firewalls. The former are more expensive than the latter.

12.16.2.1   Personal Hardware Firewalls

A hardware firewall that is inexpensive and intended for users of high-speed Internet access (xDSL and cable modems) is made by D-Link (http://www.dlink.com/products/broadband/di701/) and sells for about $140. It sits in between one's computer and broadband modem using standard Ethernet connectors. Unlike software firewalls, which allow the protected computer to be visible to the Internet, the DI-701 acts as a go-between decoy. It can also allow up to 32 simultaneous computers to connect to the Internet through the same ISP account. It can be configured within a few minutes. It also uses Dynamic Host Configuration Protocol (DHCP) to provide dynamic allocation of IP addresses for up to 128 clients on one's network. It is basically what is known as a broadband gateway, and one can acquire such standard network products from numerous vendors, including http://www.sohoware.com/.

This particular product provides two levels of protection:

1. It masks any local user's IP address from the Internet (by assigning its own address through the DHCP); this makes it more difficult (though not impossible, since the DI-701's specs are public) for a run-of-the-mill hacker to target one's computer. No local computer is *directly* visible from the outside. As such, a port scanner will scan the DI-701's ports and not those of the protected computer.

2. It blocks and redirects certain ports, thereby limiting what outside users and hackers can access. A port that is open on one's computer will not be accessible from the Internet.

Its weakness is that it does not prevent anything from leaving one's computer, such as data that is surreptitiously sent out by any of the many adware programs (see Section 6.6.1). Because of this, it is best used in conjunction with a software firewall (see Section 12.16.2.2).

Caution: If one has a high-speed connection to the Internet (cable modem or DSL modem) *and* has to log in to the service provider (user name and password) just as if one dialed in with a regular modem, then the ISP is probably using PPPoE (Point-to-Point Protocol over Ethernet). PPPoE is not a "standard"; it prevents most hardware-based firewalls from functioning well; those that do, probably use PPPoE relay, which allows PPPoE packets to pass through with minimal checks; this compromises a firewall's security.

A more expensive alternative is WatchGuard from WatchGuard Technologies (http://www.watchguard.com/). The WatchGuard SOHO (Small Office, Home Office) protects one's networked computers and data from hackers with dynamic stateful packet filtering technology. It also provides network address translation (NAT), meaning that the IP addresses seen by the outside hacker are not the ones actually used in one's computer. VPN support is also available as an option.

The third hardware firewall—and the most expensive, approaching $800, versus $160 for the DI-701—that is available to individual users is WebRamp 700s by Ramp Networks (http://www.webramp.com/products/700s/). This allows multiple users to share a cable or xDSL modem, provides firewall protection against hackers, offers PPPoE support, and can be configured to block access to inappropriate Web sites; it offers an optional VPN IPsec upgrade for secure communication.

A simple but potentially effective augmentation to (or substitute for) any firewall is simply to disconnect one's computer from the Internet when not using it. This makes sense for xDSL and cable modem setups that default to being always connected. Simply removing the cable between these modems and the computer is not a viable solution because things don't usually work right after the cable is connected again until one reboots the computer. A product offered by www.firewallswitch.com for $50 is literally—as its name, Firewallswitch, suggests—a switch that disengages xDSL and cable modem lines when a connection is not needed. It is intended for xDSL and cable modems and not for dial-up modems.

12.16.2.2   Personal Software Firewalls

Personal software firewalls worthy of notice include the following:

- Signal9's **ConSeal.** Signal9 made two excellent firewall products: the ConSeal PC Firewall, which was sold through http://www.

consealfirewall.com/ as of the end of 2000, and which is available for Win9x, and NT; and the Personal Firewall, a product that was bought by McAfee, which sells it on a yearly subscription basis for about $40.

One should make sure to turn off the logging function, as it would be a goldmine for a forensics investigator. In addition, the Conseal Private Desktop has the annoying habit of making a log of every time it is turned on and off; this is a security hole and its makers should have known better.

As there is no way to get around it, one must manually wipe a file called *.log (where * is a month-and-year-dependent date) that resides in

C:\ProgramFiles\Signal9\Private Desktop

The ConSeal firewalls (http://www.consealfirewall.com/) do not work for Windows 2000.

- Symantec's **Norton Internet Security 2000** package (http://www.symantec.com/). This product bundles the firewall function with optional functions such as cookie blocking and parental Web control. Its high security option is quite effective; its parental Web control, like most all Web filters, is annoying and easily defeatable by any teenager who can route his or her Web browser through anonymizing proxies.

- NetworkIce's **BlackIce Defender** (http://www.networkice.com/). This is really not a "firewall" but a piece of intrusion-detection software. It is intended to bounce intruders off one's computer. It is prone to annoying false alarms when legitimate incoming traffic is mistaken as illegitimate. Worse yet, it keeps a record of all traffic downloads and a graphical line that shows the amount of traffic handled over the last 90 hours; this is a security weakness and its makers should have known better. It has very good documentation, though.

- Zone Labs' free **ZoneAlarm** (http://www.zonelabs.com/). In a nutshell, this product allows the user to specify which program(s) can access the Internet and locks all others out. Even though ZoneAlarm seems to be the most effective in preventing outbound unauthorized communication, it (like any other firewall), is not a guarantee of on-line security. ZoneAlarm is user-configurable in terms of what is allowed and what is not, as shown in Figure 12.1. The user can specify to always allow, always disallow, or to ask individual permission each time for any outgoing communication; this essentially negates many of the software programs that "call home."

Caution: After installing ZoneAlarm, uncheck the default "I want to check for updates automatically" in the Configure option, or risk keeping a port open that can be exploited remotely.

- **McAfee Personal Firewall** (http://www.mcafee.com/). This is what has become of the excellent personal firewall by Signal9. It continues to be a very good firewall but now requires a yearly fee.

- **WinPatrol.** Although not a firewall per se, Windows 98 users are highly encouraged to *also* consider using this small software application from http://www.winpatrol.com/. What WinPatrol does is alert the user anytime any new software starts running in one's computer without one's knowledge (such as adware), and asks the user to specifically permit or not permit this to happen. It also can readily display a list of all programs running in the background.

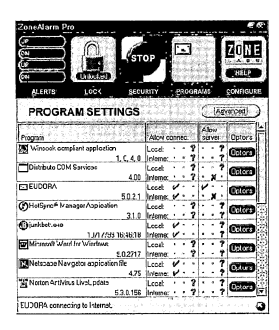

Figure 12.1   ZoneAlarm Pro allows detailed security customization. (Courtesy of Zone Labs.)

12.16.3 Windows 2000 Firewall

There has been some propaganda to the effect that Windows 2000 has, alleg-edly, a "built-in firewall" and, hence, that there is no need for anything else. This is not correct. Windows 2000 has IP filtering or IPsec that should not be used by most individuals. IP filtering merely blocks ports except for the ones that one specifies. If one wants to use IP filtering, all one has to do is to enable it and to fill in all the ports that one would be using, such as: 21 (for FTP), 25 (for SMTP outgoing e-mail), 80 (for Web browsing), 56&57 for DHCP, and so on. This is a far cry from the protection that one needs from a more comprehensive firewall.

12.17 Threats Posed by Ports

If a computer is a standalone entity that is not connected to any other com-puter through a network, such as the Internet, ports are not an issue and do not apply to it.

When a computer is connected to other computers through a network, however, some way must be agreed upon so that each will know how to con-tact each of the rest of them. This is analogous to a room full of people who want to communicate: Each has a different name. Similarly, for the tele-phone "network" to work, each telephone has to have a different number. In the case of the Internet, this unique "number" of each connected computer is its Internet Protocol Address, or "IP Address" in short, which is a string of 12 numbers separated in four groups of three numbers each.

Individual computers, unlike telephones, can do many different things, such as browsing the Web, sending/receiving e-mail, transferring files using the popular File Transfer Protocol (FTP), and so on. As such, each computer that deals with other computers has to have the equivalent of a "switchboard" function that will direct each incoming "telephone call" (data packet, in this case) to the correct "extension" inside the multi-function-capable computer. "Ports" are the computer equivalents of a telephone switchboard's inside extensions.

Since most computers that want to communicate with other computers have a set of standard functions (referred to as "services") that they all per-form (such as e-mail, FTP, and Web browsing), it makes sense that agree-ments have been made as to which port does what. This way, a remote computer that sends e-mail, for example, knows up-front not only to whom to send it (the IP address) but also to which "port" to send it.

There are three ranges of ports:

1. The well-known ones, in the range of 0 to 1023;
2. The registered ones, in the range of 1024 through 49151. These are ones that a number of "services" use, but they are also used for many other purposes.
3. The rest of them (used for private functions and also dynamically allocated by some software such as some VPNs) in the range of 49152 through 65535. No "service" is supposed to be assigned to any of these ports.

Complete lists of all the ports in the first two categories above can be readily downloaded from many Internet sites, such as http://isi.edu/in-notes/iana/assignments/port-numbers, and these lists run well over 100 single-space typewritten pages long. Similarly, http://advice.networkice .com/advice/Exploits/Ports has hyperlinks showing various ways in which ports have been exploited.

The commonly used "legitimate" ports are the following:

HTTP 80

HTTPS 443

SMTP 25

POP3 110

FTP 20-21

TELNET 23

REALAUDIO 1090

ICQ 4000

NEWS SERVERS 119

DNS 53

IRC 6667

VDOLIVE 7000

The following are open service ports for Windows NT, Terminal Server, and Exchange Server:

Functionality UDP TCP IP

Browsing 137, 138

DHCP Lease 67, 68

DHCP Manager 135

DNS Administration 139

DNS Resolution 53

Exchange Administrator 135

Exchange Client/Server Comm. 135

File Sharing 139

IMAP 143

LDAP 389

LDAP (SSL) 636

Logon Sequence 137, 138 139

MTA - X.400 over TCP/IP 102

NetLogon 138

NT Diagnostics 139

NT Directory Replication 138 139

NT Event Viewer 139

NT Performance Monitor 139

NT Registry Editor 139

NT Secure Channel 137, 138 139

NT Server Manager 139

NT Trusts 137, 138 139

NT User Manager 139

Pass Through Validation 137, 138 139

POP3 110

PPTP 1723 47

Printing 137, 138 139

RPC 135 135

SMTP 25

WINS Manager 135

WINS Registration 137

WINS Replication 42

But a port is an open gate to the outside world, and is therefore also exploitable as a pathway for a malicious outsider to penetrate one's computer.

It follows that any computer connected to the Internet (or any other network) should have all ports "closed" (meaning that the computer will ignore all attempts from either the outside or, as an option, even from mischievous software on the inside, to get data through those "ports") except for those that are absolutely required to do whatever function has to be performed; in fact, this is precisely what some firewalls do.

Ports 137, 138, and 139 are NetBIOS ports. Simply unbind NetBIOS from TCP/IP in your network settings. Not only do you not need them, but they are also a security concern. It may require a reboot to make the change effective.

Run

```
netstat-a
```

from command prompt and make sure that NetBIOS ports are now closed.

A complete port listing guide, as well as a lot of other useful information, is at http://members.cotse.com/helpdesk.

A "Trojan" is a program that pretends to be or do one thing, but in reality is damaging your data or sniffing your system for personal data. Back Orifice and (as of August 2000) Brown Orifice are probably the most notorious of such programs.

A list of the port numbers that are used mostly by Trojan and intrusion programs and should therefore be closely watched are provided in Appendix B (the list is courtesy of http://www.doshelp.com/trojanports.htm). A highly recommended detailed presentation of each individual main port's vulnerabilities and legitimate functions can be found at http://www.robertgraham.com/pubs/firewall-seen.html.

12.17.1 How to Use "Dangerous Port" Information

To detect if you are being probed or otherwise attacked through one of the ports, you need a firewall (see Section 12.16) that displays and/or logs all attempts to access any of the ports.

Caution: Just because a port shows some activity does not necessarily mean that you are being attacked.

Caution: Some of the latest attacks, notably involving adware (see Section 6.6.1), use legitimate ports (such as port 80 used by browsers to browse the Web) to get information out of your computer. Unless you have also installed a "sniffer" that actually allows you to look at all data going in and out of your computer *and* you are actually bothering to check all data leaving your computer at all times (which is highly unlikely because it is impractical), you will not detect such occurrences.

Caution: Be particularly careful about ports 137 to 139. If you are being scanned on these port there, chances are that someone is looking for your Microsoft Share Handles and shared folders and files.

12.18 Sniffers

A sniffer simply monitors and selectively records the data flow through a choke point. It can be used by a hacker to steal passwords, and it can also be used by an individual to detect if information is leaving his or her computer without permission (e.g., via adware/spyware and Trojans).

Most sniffers are primarily intended to debug (find flaws and correct them) network problems. They include:

RealSecure, for SunOS, Solaris, and Linux (http://www.iss.net/RealSecure);

Snoop, for Solaris;

Etherfind, for SunOS 4.1x.

For DOS-based systems, one can use:

Gobbler, for IBM DOS computers;

EthLoad v 1.04 for Ethernet monitoring (ftp://ftp.germany.eu.net:/pub/ networking/monitoring/ethload/ethld104.zip);

PacketView, by KLOS Technologies, Inc.;

Microsoft's **Net Monitor**;

Analyzer.exe, for Windows 95/98/NT/2000 (http://packetstorm.secu-rity.com/sniffers);

Anger.tar.gz, a challenge/response sniffer—see below—by L0phtCrack (http://packetstorm.security.com/sniffers);

Aps-0.14.tar.z, "COLD," coopersniff01.zip, dsniff, and a vast number of others, all available through http://packetstorm.security.com/sniffers.

It is not possible to detect the presence of a sniffer on one's network through software unless the sniffer is (unwisely) programmed to advertise its presence. The only real protection from a sniffer is to ensure that only encrypted data passes through the sniffer. If the concern is only about a sniffer detecting passwords being sent, this can be easily remedied (in conjunction with the server that one is logging to) by using an authentication system where a different password is needed every time. This can be done by using:

- "SecureID" tokens (a small device like a garage door opener, which generates a different set of numbers every few seconds that must be used as the password at any one time). The remote host has to have a duplicate of this device so that it can verify that the numbers entered as the password are the correct ones at any one time; such devices are usually used in conjunction with a PIN number so that if the device itself is stolen, the thief cannot gain access. One of many such vendors is Security Dynamics in Cambridge, Massachusetts.

- A software solution based on "challenge-response." The authorized user has a piece of software that accepts a random challenge (in the form of a few random symbols sent) by the server that one is trying to log in; this challenge is different every time; the software computes the response using a cryptographic algorithm and sends it to the server which has a duplicate of that software and verifies that the correct response was sent to the particular challenge. A typical implementation available worldwide is "S-Key" (ftp://ftp.nrl.navy .mil/ pub/security/nrl-opie/).

12.19   Software That Calls Home

Depending on their sophistication, detecting software that reports to its maker or a third party ranges from easy to very hard. Such software includes keystroke-loggers. As with any security issue, it is far easier to prevent the intrusion in the first place (through the "safe computing" practices detailed in Part II of this book) than to remove it after it has installed itself in one's inner sanctum.

Software programs such as REGRUN and WINPATROL can alert one to programs that started automatically at Windows startup without one's knowledge. One would be well advised to visit http://www.sysinternals.com/misc.htm#autoruns to obtain autoruns.exe, which searches system locations that can launch programs at startup. One should also visit http://grc.com/su-leaktest.htm to download a small benign test program that checks if one's computer does or does not disable most software programs that call home.

If one suspects that some software is connecting to some remote site through the Internet when one is on-line, one should go to the DOS prompt and type

```
netstat -a
```

This will show if there are any connections being made beyond what one expects. Interpreting the results takes some getting used to, especially if one is using proxies and firewalls that do address translation, so one should do this routinely to get used to the display when there are no surreptitious communications out of one's computer.

References

[1] Stevens, W., *TCP/IP Illustrated, Volume 1: The Protocols,* Reading, MA: Addison-Wesley, 1994; Stevens, W., and G. Wright, *TCP/IP Illustrated, Volume 2: The Implementation,* Reading, MA: Addison-Wesley, 1995; and Stevens, W. R., *TCP/IP Illustrated, Volume 3: TCP for Transactions, HTTP, NNTP, and the Unix Domain Protocols,* Reading, MA: Addison-Wesley, 1996, respectively.

[2] Comer, D. E., *Internetworking with TCP/IP, Volume I: Principles, Protocols, and Architecture,* Fourth Edition, Upper Saddle River, NJ: Prentice Hall, 2000; Comer, D. E., and D. L. Stevens, *Internetworking with TCP/IP, Volume II: Design, Implementation, and Intervals,* Upper Saddle River, NJ: Prentice Hall, 1998; and Comer, D. E., and D. L. Stevens, *Internetworking with TCP/IP, Volume III: Client-Server Programming and Applications-Windows Sockets Version,* Upper Saddle River, NJ: Prentice Hall, 1997, respectively.

[3] Burk, R., M. J. Bligh, and T. Lee, *TCP/IP Blueprints,* Indianapolis, IN: Sams Publishing, 1997.

[4] Postel, J., "User Datagram Protocol," STD 6, RFC 768, USC/Information Sciences Institute, August 1980. *See also* Postel, J., (ed.), "Transmission Control Protocol —DARPA Internet Program Protocol Specification," STD 7, RFC 793, USC/Information Sciences Institute, September 1981.

13

Encryption: The Empire Versus the Rebels

There are so few who can carry a letter of any substance without lightening the weight by perusal.

—Cicero to Atticus, 61 B.C.

13.1 Introduction

In the beginning, there was the mattress under which to hide things. And the safe, for those who could afford one. A decade or two ago, potent encryption, which had previously been available only to governments, militaries, and spies, became available to everyone.

There have always been legitimate reasons for confidentiality, beyond protecting the affairs of state, for example, to protect commercial trade secrets (such as those that have propelled the United States to technological excellence), medical records, and so on. The laws in practically all countries have even protected some material from the eyes of the state itself: Attorney-client privileged communication (but not confessions made to psychotherapists and the clergy) is such an example.

Until 10 to 20 years ago, the means available to nongovernmental individuals and groups for protecting secrets amounted to physical protection: placing things inside safes or in other hiding places. For most commercial and private needs, this used to be good enough, because what was being protected was a tangible physical object, such as a document or an occasional magnetic recording.

The transformation of society during the past decade to one that is entirely dependent on computers has resulted in the conversion of most of those sensitive physical objects into computerized data. In addition, the increasing acceptance of telecommuting has caused such sensitive information to be sent from one facility to another with increasing frequency. Finally, the sheer volume of sensitive corporate and personal information has increased vastly as a result of the use of e-mail, which is treated by most as a substitute for phone calls rather than as the permanent written record that it actually is.

It is self-evident that there is a legitimate need for technology to protect sensitive data in personal and office computers. Indeed there *is* a way to meet this need: potent encryption.

The problem is that, just like a kitchen knife, which can be used to slice bread or as a weapon, potent encryption can be used legitimately or illegitimately, to hide what courts and governments, rightly or wrongly, may want to see.

For example, an employee with access to highly sensitive corporate information would find it very easy to transfer that information to a floppy diskette, encrypt it, remove it, and pass it to a competitor; it would be very difficult for any evidence of this to be produced in a court of law. Conversely, a brutally totalitarian regime would very much like to be able to decrypt a file containing the names of the members of the underground opposition.

In the past, armed with a court warrant (or often without one, in some regimes), a state could easily force open a safe. Today, however, it is eminently possible for any individual anywhere in the world to use encryption, which is openly available worldwide, to encrypt text, voice, images, and anything that can be computerized, and to do so in a manner that cannot be broken by any physical force. (The term "unbreakable" is unfortunate; perishable information needs encryption to work only for the useful life of that information; on the other extreme, brute force cryptanalysis of openly available encryption has been shown to require computers to work for many times the expected life of the sun.) This amounts to an involuntary transfer of massive power from the state to the individual. Its social impact has not yet been fully felt.

Not surprisingly, every government in the world has been scrambling for ways to limit the spread of this new tool, citing assorted lofty principles. From a sovereign state's perspective, the existence of the Internet is bad enough in that it makes censorship extremely difficult; adding strong encryption to the brew makes the end result downright threatening to most governments.

Repressive regimes have realized the threat posed to their longevity by the use of strong encryption by dissident groups. Democratic regimes, too, have realized the potential threat to social order posed by the use of unbreakable encryption to facilitate out-and-out criminality, as well as to facilitate far lesser transgressions such as transmitting content deemed to be "inappropriate" by a state.

13.2 Availability and Use of Encryption

The sole purpose of encryption is to render a sensitive document ("plaintext") unreadable to all except those authorized to read it. This protection need not necessarily last forever; tactical information, whose usefulness to an adversary vanishes after some length of time, need not necessarily remain unreadable forever. This truism is often forgotten in debates about the relative strengths of various encryption algorithms and key lengths.

An attack on encrypted material is not limited to brute force attacks (i.e., exhaustive searches of all possible decryption keys). More often than not, it amounts to "cheating"; that is, an attack brought about through ways that the user never thought of. In other words, there is a lot more to protecting a sensitive plaintext than the encryption algorithm itself, as the following questions reveal:

- Has a copy of the plaintext been inadvertently left behind in one's computer?

- Has the decryption key been compromised?

- Is it possible that the encryption software being used has been compromised? If a password is used to enable the decryption key, is it easier to find that password than embarking on brute force cryptanalysis?

Unless each different file encrypted by a given sender (or sent to a given recipient by many senders) is encrypted in a different manner (using a different "key" and/or a different encryption method), the person attacking the encrypted file has an inherent advantage: If he or she can somehow read one such file from a given sender or to a given recipient, he or she can probably read many other encrypted files from the same sender or to the same recipient. This amplifies the infrastructure-related weaknesses of the encryption process (how people handle keys, procedures, and so forth).

Today, engineers who may be very competent in their respective fields but who have minimal experience in cryptography often implement encryption in software as an afterthought. What may seem to the author of an encryption algorithm as being an unbreakable scheme may well be (and has often turned out to be) an implementation that has serious exploitable weaknesses. Brute force cryptanalysis is only one of many possible attacks on an encryption system; other attack approaches include:

- *Exploiting the use of untested "proprietary" algorithms.* In general, only those encryption schemes that have successfully withstood the concerted analysis and assessment of experts over many years are to be used; the rest may seem secure until proven otherwise (or until they, too, have successfully withstood a similar scrutiny).

- *Exploiting weaknesses in the choice of the password itself.* If a password is used, it should be secure. A password should offer as much difficulty to a cryptanalyst as the encryption algorithm itself. Passwords should not be just a couple of dictionary words. A dictionary has less than 100,000 words in it. To get a password that is no more vulnerable to brute force dictionary attack than a 128-bit key, one would need about eight words randomly chosen from the dictionary.

- *Exploiting the hardware on which the encryption algorithm is used.* The hardware should itself be secure. In 1995, the "timing attack" became popular; in summary, it allowed someone with access to the hardware to make useful inferences from the precise time it took to encrypt a document using a particular class of algorithms. One can enlarge this class of attacks to include any externally observable hardware phenomenon, such as power consumption, unintentional RF radiation, and so on. This class also includes an assessment of what electronic paper trail is left behind if the hardware is caused to fail in the middle of an encryption or decryption.

- *Attacking the trust models.* Except in a small percentage of situations, the sender and intended recipient of encrypted messages never meet each other in person to exchange encryption keys; instead, they rely on third parties and processes that may well contain exploitable weaknesses.

- Exploiting the all too common human tendency to take shortcuts and to bypass security procedures in encoding and decoding sensitive documents.

In view of the above, the odds favor the person attacking an encrypted file, *unless* the person being attacked is very well informed in the ways of information security.

13.2.1 Old-Fashioned Encryption

Interestingly, provably unbreakable encryption was available long before computers entered the scene. A conceptually simple, yet potent, encryption scheme known as the "one-time pad" could be used by anyone willing to go through a manual process that, however, is quite onerous for long messages. Basically, one substitutes each symbol in a message to be encrypted (the plaintext) with another symbol, using a preagreed-upon conversion—that is known both to the sender and the intended recipient—which is never to be repeated (hence the name "one-time pad"). For example, both individuals can agree to substitute the first letter of the plaintext with the sequence number in the alphabet of the first letter of the first page of a certain edition of Mark Twain (e.g., "A" is 01; "B" is 02), the second letter of the plaintext with the sequence number in the alphabet of the second letter of the second page of the same book, and so on.

Amusingly, a one-time pad offers an interesting way of defeating a demand by authority to "decrypt that file": One can readily create and "reluctantly surrender" a fake one-time pad key which will convert that same encrypted document to something totally innocuous, like an excerpt from the Bible or the Bill of Rights.

The "solutions" to these problems have opened up a Pandora's box of new problems, new solutions, and a few hopes. Anyone today can obtain powerful encryption from the Internet or from software stores. It is of two fundamentally different kinds: symmetric and public key. Symmetric encryption refers to the fact that the same key is used to encrypt and to decrypt a message. The sender and the recipient must somehow find a secure way to share such a key. Public-key encryption refers to the fact that one key is used to encrypt a message, but a different key (which cannot be mathematically inferred from the first) is needed to decrypt that message.

Just like medicine, bad encryption looks like good encryption on the surface; one cannot tell the difference. "Proprietary," "secret," and "revolutionary" schemes that have not withstood the scrutiny of cryptana-lysts over time are to be avoided; the same goes for encryption with "recover-able keys" or that which is exportable. As already stated, since the recent liberalization of U.S. laws on the exportation of encryption, being exportable no longer implies weak encryption.

13.2.2 Conventional (Symmetric) Encryption

The Data Encryption Standard (DES) was developed in the 1970s and is still in extensive use worldwide, especially in the banking industry. It is a block cipher (64 bits/block) using 56-bit keys. By now, there is an extensive amount of open literature on DES cracking.

Double DES (encrypting the already DES-encrypted output, with a different key) does not add any measurable strength against brute force cryptanalysis to the end result; in fact, double encryption of most block codes is generally acknowledged to add little security. Triple DES, however, sub-stantively improves the resistance to cryptanalysis of the end result, making it a highly secure algorithm, albeit one that is slower than others. It is notewor-thy that most so-called triple DES implementations, however, use only two keys and not three: The first encryption uses key#1, the second uses key#2, and the third uses key#1 again. A true triple-key implementation is what should be used.

Other encryption algorithms from which a computer user is often asked to select include the following:

- IDEA (International Data Encryption Algorithm) uses a 128-bit key and was developed by ETH Zurich in Switzerland; its patent is held by Ascom-Tech, but noncommercial use is free. It is considered to be a good algorithm for all, except possibly the most well-funded, attacks. It is used, among others, in PGP and Speak Freely (voice encryption).

- BLOWFISH is a 64-bit block size block code having variable key lengths from 32 bits up to 448 bits. It was developed by Bruce Schneier in 1993 and it is also considered to be one of the best algo-rithms. Over 100 products use this algorithm already.

- TWOFISH is a more recent encryption algorithm which is reputed to be very strong, but which has not yet had the benefit of with-standing the concerted efforts and review of cryptanalysts.

- RC4 is a very fast algorithm of unknown security, which can accept keys of arbitrary length; key lengths shorter than about 40 bits result in encrypted output that is relatively easy to break.

Numerous other symmetric codes exist, many of which have historical value.

DES is headed for the dustbin. In October 2000, a new Data Encryption Standard was selected in the United States: Rijandel.

13.2.3 Public-Key Encryption

In conventional (symmetric) encryption, the same key is used to encode a message and to subsequently decode it. This has numerous practical disadvantages:

- Secure key distribution, as discussed earlier. The problem is compounded every time the keys are updated.
- Unless a voluminous one-time pad key is used, the repeated use of the same key for encrypting multiple different plaintext files favors the cryptanalyst.

An ingenious scheme that solves these problems (and introduces some new ones) was proposed in 1976 by Diffie and Hellman; it was reportedly devised earlier, in the early 1970s, in the United Kingdom, by James Ellis, Clifford Cocks, and Malcolm Williamson. It allows two entities, which never have the opportunity to exchange keys in some secure manner, to communicate with full encryption nonetheless.

In a typical implementation, assume that both Mr. A. and Mr. B have a copy of openly available software that implements public-key encryption. Initially, each directs their respective (identical or just compatible) copy of the software to "create key." What gets created (ideally using manual user input for true randomness) by each person is *a pair* of keys; it is significant that, in each pair, one key cannot be mathematically inferred from the other. The crucial concept is this: A file encrypted with one key of each pair can only be decrypted with the other key of that same pair. The implications of the last statement are far-reaching in that they allow:

- Encrypted file exchange between two entities without the need for any secure means to exchange keys;

- Sender authentication, also known as digital signature;

- Message integrity authentication.

This is shown in Figure 13.1.

Assume that Mr. A and Mr. B each elect to publicize any one of the keys of the pair generated by each, and appropriately name that publicized key as the "public key"; they each retain under tight control the other key in their respective pair and each calls that his "secret key." If Mr. A wants to encrypt a message that only Mr. B can read, Mr. A uses Mr. B's public key (which has been made available to anyone); that message can only be decoded by the other key in the pair, namely, Mr. B's secret key. The converse process (encrypted message by Mr. B to Mr. A) is clear. What has been achieved is that Mr. A and Mr. B can now exchange encrypted files without the need for any secure means to exchange keys.

Sender authentication (digital signature) is just as easy: Mr. A sends any message he wishes to the world after encrypting it with his secret key. The world uses Mr. A's public key to decrypt that message, thereby validating that it could only have come from Mr. A.

Message authentication (validation that the message received is indeed an unaltered copy of the message sent) is also easy: The sender (Mr. A, for example) performs a digital summary ("digest") referred to as a cryptographic "hash function" on his outgoing plaintext message (an elaborate version of a checksum) before encrypting it; this cryptographic hash function, such as the very popular MD5 (which was developed by RSA and extracts a digital digest from a file of arbitrary length into a 128-bit value) and SHA (which hashes a file into a 160-bit value and was published by the U.S. government), compresses the bits of the plaintext message into a fixed-size digest or hash value of 128 or more bits. The hash function is such that it is extremely difficult to alter the plaintext message without altering the hash value. The sender then:

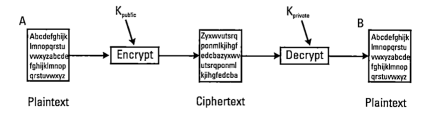

Figure 13.1 Public-key encryption.

- Encrypts the plaintext with the intended recipient's public key;

- Encrypts the above hash value with his own secret key;

- Sends both to the intended recipient.

The intended recipient:

- Decodes the received plaintext using his own public key;

- Decodes the received checksum digest by using the sender's public key, thereby confirming sender authenticity;

- Compares the received checksum with one that he performs locally on the just-decrypted plaintext, thereby confirming message integrity.

This is depicted in Figure 13.2.

Public-key encryption has been a part of any Web browser for the last few years, for automatically providing end-to-end encryption between an Internet user and select Web sites (e.g., when sending credit card information to an on-line vendor for a purchase through a Web browser, or when sending e-mail using the standard S/MIME protocol and a "security certificate" that one can obtain from on-line commercial vendors or that can be created locally by some software).

Public-key encryption is not without shortcomings. It is orders of magnitude more computationally intensive (read: slower) than conventional symmetric encryption. As a result, practically all implementations use the following "trick," which involves using both conventional symmetric encryption and public-key encryption for the same message:

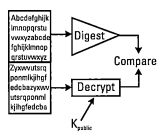

Figure 13.2 Message integrity authentication.

1. Encode the outgoing plaintext with strong conventional symmetric encryption, such as using IDEA, BLOWFISH, or Triple DES, and using a locally generated symmetric encryption key.

2. Encode only that locally generated symmetric encryption key with public-key encryption.

3. Send both of the above to the intended recipient. In addition, perform the ancillary functions just described for permitting message authentication and sender authentication.

The obvious question that comes up then is, "If the symmetric encryption algorithm used is such-and-so and its key length is x bits, what is a good public-key encryption algorithm and how many bits should its key have so that both are of equal strength?" A good 128-bit block code like IDEA is roughly comparable in resistance to brute force cryptanalysis to a 2,304-bit public-key encryption algorithm like RSA.

Another shortcoming of public-key encryption is that it is subject to the same logical conundrum as any encryption when the two parties to the communication have not had a secure channel to allow each to confirm the identity of the other. If Mr. B receives a public key (or a conventional symmetric key) ostensibly coming from Mr. A, Mr. B has no way to affirm that this key does not, in fact, belong to a third party (Mr. C, the so-called "man in the middle"). There is no "technical fix" to this logical conundrum: Mr. A and Mr. B must find some *independent* way of verifying that the keys indeed belong to each other as claimed.

One of the most commonly used public-key algorithms is RSA (Rivest-Shamir-Adelman, initially published in 1978). Its security is based on the difficulty of factoring large prime integers. At present, a key length of at least 1,024 bits is generally considered secure enough. However, RSA has been claimed to be somewhat vulnerable to chosen plaintext attacks (namely, when known plaintexts and the corresponding RSA-encrypted ciphertexts are available to a cryptanalyst) and to timing attacks.

Another public-key algorithm, used mostly for key exchange, is Diffie-Hellman. Its security is based on the difficulty of the discrete logarithm problem, which is considered to be equivalent to the difficulty of prime number factoring. It is generally considered secure if sufficiently long keys and proper generators are used. It, too, is vulnerable to a new timing attack.

The most popular implementation of public-key encryption is PGP (Pretty Good Privacy). See Section 14.3 for details on installing and using PGP securely. Philip Zimmerman created PGP as a sociopolitical statement that potent encryption should be widely available. It has now become a mainstream product of a reputable corporation, although freeware versions continue to be available from the Internet throughout the world.

Like all implementations of public-key encryption, PGP uses strong conventional symmetric encryption (typically 128-bit IDEA) to encode the plaintext with a session-specific key, and then uses public-key encryption to encode that key. This means that any two encryptions of the same plaintext to the same recipient will be different.

Even though it was stated above that a 128-bit IDEA encryption is comparable to a 2,304-bit public-key encryption, one should use a public key that is longer than this 2,034 value; this is so because, in PGP, breaking the symmetric encryption key (e.g., IDEA) compromises a single message; whereas breaking the public-key encryption compromises all messages to a given recipient.

Over the years, there have been numerous versions of PGP. Not all versions are compatible with the others. Early versions of PGP were made for DOS, whereas late versions are for 32-bit operating systems. PGP has been ported to numerous non-Windows operating systems as well, such as Apple OS and Unix.

13.2.4 Elliptic Curve Encryption

The architecture of typical microprocessors is not efficient for software implementations of encryption. While this is not a problem for personal computers, it is a problem for new classes of handheld devices needing encryption, such as the wireless version of 3Com's Palm Pilot. A new class of encryption algorithms, known as elliptic curve encryption, appears to provide encryption strength equal to that of the earlier-mentioned ones but using a smaller key and an arithmetic which is easier on microprocessors than either symmetric or public-key encryption, and also requiring far less memory. Being a new type of encryption, its security must withstand the concerted scrutiny of experts before it is accepted.

13.2.5 Voice Encryption On-Line

Until only a few years ago, the Internet was viewed as a means of exchanging text messages and files. Today it is also handling a vast amount of voice and even slow-scan-video traffic.

Telephony over the Internet started as a fringe underground technical application. Today it is a legitimate mainstream industry; even well-established telephone companies have begun to use it and to offer it to their non-Internet customers. Communications between Internet users are free. Communications to or from non-Internet-connected parties are billed at rates lower than those of the conventional telephone companies.

In countries where the telephone service has been a government-protected monopoly, this was viewed as a revenue threat. Attempts to eliminate it have been unsuccessful. Section 16.1 deals with Internet telephony at length.

In addition, conventional broadcasting of audio (speech and/or music) has also taken off, totally undermining the control that governments used to have over licensing radio broadcasting within their respective territories; in fact, Internet "radio" has a worldwide reach, unlike local conventional RF broadcasts, and can be done with no budget. This has caused understandable consternation on the part of repressive regimes, which were used to being able to control the news media.

Merging powerful encryption with digitized telephony over the Internet was an inevitable simple step. Indeed, anyone today can use fully encrypted voice communications with any other user connected to the Internet. Perhaps the most advanced, yet totally free, software is Speak Freely, available worldwide (http://www.speakfreely.org/). Its latest version allows users to select IDEA and/or DES and/or BLOWFISH encryption. Unlike some mainstream nonencrypted voice-over-the-Internet software, such as the technically impressive Internet Phone by Vocaltec Communications Ltd, which routes the data through its own servers, thereby opening a possible security weakness, Speak Freely and some other software, such as PGPfone, allow Internet users to communicate directly and with strong encryption as a built-in option.

13.3   The Empire Strikes Back: Attacks Against Encryption

Practically every organization needs discipline to function, be it the military, the Church, a government, or a commercial organization; this, in turn, implies a "stovepipe" organizational structure to ensure command and control. The Internet undermines this time-honored structure by allowing low-level subordinates to bypass the entire chain of command to communicate with any level of management. As if that were not threatening enough to traditional organizations, such communication can be encrypted.

The forcefulness of most governments' opposition to the use of encryption by individuals, however, suggests a more fundamental reason why governments have been so opposed to it: the loss of the ability of a state to exercise censorship. Even the most enlightened and democratic regimes have topics that are patently disallowed. Even the most staunch opponents of censorship have no problem supporting censorship of what they consider "obviously offensive," even if it is victimless; depending on the country, such topics could be related to religion, to criticism of the head of state, to sexuality, and so on; ultimately, censored topics follow from religious or political taboos. Encryption by individuals makes censorship unenforceable, and this loss of control is unacceptable to most sovereign states, sort of like having two rude guests at your dinner table who whisper secrets into each other's ears.

Given the dual use of both the Internet and of encryption for legitimate goals, for goals to which individual governments take offense, and also for out-and-out criminality, most governments engage in a triple-pronged counteroffensive to limit the use of encryption: on the technical, legal, and social fronts.

13.3.1   On the Legal Front

On the legal side, there have been enactments of a flurry of new laws intended to criminalize numerous acts related to strong encryption.

The interested reader can find a country-by-country summary of laws on encryption at http://www.epic.org/reports/crypto2000. As previously stated, the United Kingdom has enacted legislation, known as the RIP, which permits the police to compel a person to decrypt an encrypted file or face a two-year jail term; worse yet, its Clause 13 requires the recipient of such a demand to "keep secret the giving of the notice, its contents and the things done in pursuance of it" under penalty of a five-year jail term. This law's definition of encryption is extremely broad and includes what some consider to be a mere "data protocol." Along similar lines, the Clinton administration drafted the Cyberspace Electronic Security Act (CESA), which would have given officials the ability to use search warrants or court orders to access encryption keys.

This class of approach, which sounds simple on the surface, has two fatal flaws:

1. If the very commonly used public-key encryption has been used to encrypt a file to an intended recipient, the sender is physically unable to decrypt that file; only the intended recipient can; that is in the nature of public-key encryption.

2. If a commonly occurring crash of one's hard disk containing a conventional symmetric key has occurred, one is again physically unable to decrypt a file.

On August 20, 1999, the *Washington Post* reported that the U.S. Justice Department had prepared a request to Congress to enact laws to authorize federal investigators to secretly enter private residences and offices in order to covertly override encryption programs on personal computers. This could turn into "Spy vs. Spy," according to the director of George Washington University's (Washington, D.C.) Cyberspace Policy Institute; knowledgeable computer users could take countermeasures.

The October 1999 version of the U.S. bill CESA allowed police to present a text in court and claim that it is the decrypted version of an encrypted file, but does not require the police to show how it was decrypted. As cryptography expert Bruce Schneier, of Counterpane Internet Security Inc., points out in his October 1999 *Cryptogram*, a free monthly electronic newsletter sent gratis by this company to anyone who requests it: "This means that the police could present decrypted plaintext in open court, but refuse to reveal to the defendant how that plaintext was obtained. This, of course, means that the defendant can have a hard time defending himself, and makes it a lot easier for the police to fabricate evidence. The ability to receive a fair trial could be at stake."

In Australia, according to Attorney General Daryl Williams' spokeswoman Catherine Fitzpatrick, a bill passed in December 1999, and waiting for the largely ceremonial approval of Australia's governor general before it becomes law, allows the attorney general to authorize legal hacking into private computer systems, as well as copying data and even altering data to conceal surveillance, as long as the attorney general has reasonable cause to believe that it is relevant to a "security matter." It also authorizes "reasonably incidental" activities. Greg Taylor, vice chairman of Electronic Frontiers Australia, views this bill as "getting around the problems that strong cryptography presents law enforcement," in that "now they can attack the problem at the source before the data even gets encrypted." Also, according to Taylor, such a law "opens to question all computer evidence if there has been the potential for legalized tampering of it."

Unlike most any other human institution, the Internet is inherently transnational in nature. While any nation could elect not to allow the Internet within its borders, a simple assessment of the economic benefits that it brings has caused practically every nation on earth, including the most repressive ones, to connect to the Internet. Besides, "keeping the Internet out" is no more feasible than wishing the wind away; any country's citizens can access the Internet through foreign Internet service providers by merely dialing them up; this applies to a considerable degree to the situation when individual countries have elected to filter out select Internet material.

13.3.1.1 Crypto Law Survey

Some countries control cryptography's export; others control its import; still others control its use; some control a combination of the above.

The *importation* of cryptography is controlled to varying degrees by Vietnam, France, most of the former Soviet states, and a handful of other governments. The *exportation* of at least some kinds of cryptography is controlled to varying degrees by the United States, Canada, Australia and New Zealand, France, the former Soviet states, and a few others. The *use* of cryptography is controlled to varying degrees by the former Soviet states, and to a lesser degree by France, Italy, South Africa, and a few others. In the United States at the present time, the use of cryptography of any strength is legal but its export is controlled by:

- *The Arms Export Control Act (22 USC Sec. 2778).* While cryptography is not mentioned, the law empowers the president to designate any items to be included as "defense articles" or "defense services."

- *The International Traffic in Arms Regulations (ITAR).* These regulations explicitly mention cryptography as being heavily controlled.

- *Munitions Control Newsletter #80* (a 1980 newsletter elaborating on the application of cryptography export regulations to scientific and technical speech vis-à-vis the First Amendment).

- *Numerous Commerce Department export guideline documents.* While these documents do not mention cryptography per se, they apply whenever the State Department passes jurisdiction of some specific cryptography export matter to the Commerce Department.

The Coordinating Committee for Multilateral Export Controls (COCOM) was an organization of 17 member states (Australia, Belgium, Canada, Denmark, France, Germany, Greece, Italy, Japan, Luxembourg, The Netherlands, Norway, Portugal, Spain, Turkey, the United Kingdom, and the United States; additionally, Austria, Finland, Hungary, Ireland, New Zealand, Poland, Singapore, Slovakia, South Korea, Sweden, Switzerland, and Taiwan were "cooperating members"), whose purpose was to control the export of items and data which were viewed as "dangerous" to particular countries. In 1991, COCOM, with the notable exception of the United States, allowed the export of mass-market and public domain cryptography. In March 1994, COCOM was dissolved, and in 1995, it was replaced by the Wassenaar Agreement between (as of last count) 32 countries (Argentina, Australia, Austria, Belgium, Bulgaria, Canada, Czech Republic, Denmark, Finland, France, Germany, Greece, Hungary, Ireland, Italy, Japan, Luxembourg, The Netherlands, New Zealand, Norway, Poland, Portugal, Republic of Korea, Russian Federation, Slovak Republic, Spain, Sweden, Switzerland, Turkey, United Kingdom, Ukraine, and the United States).

It is significant that the Wassenaar Agreement is not a treaty and it therefore cuts out review by any country's legislature.

The laws pertaining to encryption in various countries are quite convoluted in that they are full of exceptions and qualifications (e.g., based on the number of bits, on whether or not it is "for personal use," and so on), which are periodically revisited and changed. In Sweden, for example, encryption importation and use is free and so is its export to all but a few countries; the authorities may search one's premises for the decryption key but may not compel one to assist in one's own investigation by providing that key to the authorities.

13.3.1.2   Can Encryption Bans Work?

Can encryption bans be effective in their intended purpose? No, for the following simple reasons:

1. The penalty for using encryption (if caught) is likely to be far lower than the penalty for openly disclosing what was deemed sensitive enough to have warranted encrypting it. This is similar to the situation where, even though "lying under oath" in any court is a "crime" (if one is caught), people still routinely lie under oath simply because the penalty for admitting to a more serious crime by not lying is often much higher.

2. There is a class of openly available techniques, known collectively as steganography, that allows anyone to hide data "in plain view," whether encrypted or not. Such techniques often make the issue of banning or not banning encryption irrelevant.

3. Detection of the existence of sophisticated encryption can be impossible. Who can prove that the innocuous sentence "The temperature in the garage was 75°" means "Meet me behind Joe's

garage on July 5"? Who can detect new advanced custom-designed steganography schemes?

4. The existence of the Internet makes it easy for encryption technology to circumvent bans on its proliferation. Indeed, former U.S. Attorney General Janet Reno is alleged to have stated so in writing in a May 1999 letter (openly available on the Internet) to the German Federal Secretary of Justice, Herta Doubler-Gremlin, in which she allegedly stated that "The use of the Internet to distribute encryption products will render Wassenaar's controls immaterial."

5. Banning software encryption is unenforceable against savvy users. In most (though not all) countries, one can bring encryption software in a diskette to any one of many publicly available computers connected to the Internet, such as public libraries or Internet cafés, and transmit the encrypted files quite anonymously to a recipient who can retrieve them in a similar manner just as anonymously. Obtaining encryption software in the first place can easily be done in the same manner, anonymously, through thousands of Internet servers that openly provide a large collection of such software.

6. Potent encryption is available indigenously in dozens of countries; as such, controls on exporting it from select countries are pointless.

In fact, the big to-do about attempts to ban encryption may be having an effect that is opposite to what was intended. This is so because individuals who may not have otherwise been sensitized to the vulnerability of their plaintext material are now aware enough and may be encrypting what they otherwise would not have.

The bans on the exportation of encryption are even less effective in their stated goals, even though the stated goal of making encryption unavailable to terrorists is laudable. It makes good sense for a country to ban the exportation of something that it alone possesses or it alone can create which could be used against it; it makes no sense for any one country to ban the export of what other nations produce locally, too. Potent encryption is available indigenously in many countries, notably including the United States, Israel, Russia, France, India, Ireland, Australia, and some 30 others as well.

A recent survey conducted by George Washington University's Cyberspace Policy Institute identified 805 products (hardware and software) that use encryption, developed in 35 different countries. That same study states that "on average, the quality of foreign and U.S. products is comparable" and that "in the face of continuing U.S. export controls on encryption products,

technology and services, some American companies have financed the creation and growth of foreign cryptographic firms.... With the expertise off-
shore, the relatively stringent U.S. export controls for cryptographic products
can be avoided since products can be shipped from countries with less strin-
gent controls."

The technicalities of U.S. law pertaining to the exportation of encryption, while understandable in a legal and historical context, make the ban on
the exportation of encryption even more porous. While it is illegal in the
United States to export potent encryption in software form without the
appropriate license, constitutionally guaranteed rights make it perfectly legal
to export the source code of that same encryption if it is printed on paper.
The printed source code is then optically scanned across the ocean using
standard optical character recognition (OCR) technology, and it is then
compiled into the same executable code that was illegal to export directly.
This has, in fact, been done legally on a number of well-documented
occasions.

The concept of "escrowed encryption," namely, where a third party
accessible by the state would be able to decrypt material belonging to a user,
seemed reasonable from the perspective of a government that presumes itself
to be trusted, but unreasonable from any user's perspective. The arguments
against it are basically the following:

- A citizen often does not trust the government.
- Even if a credible case can be made for the government to obtain the
  decryption key to read a particular document, it is difficult to see
  how that key, once obtained through escrow, cannot be copied and
  used by the government to look at other documents by the same
  user in the future, for which a credible case for viewing them could
  not be made, or conceivably to impersonate the user.

The counterargument by some government representatives to the effect
that "escrowed keys should be a welcome service to a user in case he loses his
own decryption keys" has been invariably met with polite bemusement.

Today, even governments are backing away from the concept of
escrowed encryption, for the following reasons:

- Those who matter most to law enforcement (narcotraffickers, terrorists, and so forth) are most unlikely to oblige law enforcement

officials by using encryption that is openly advertised to be readable by the government.

- The transnational nature of the Internet requires a global key-escrow system; this is not palatable to sovereign states, which have their own equities to protect.

- Steganography and related data-hiding techniques that can conceal the mere existence of files, whether encrypted or not, make the debate almost irrelevant.

- The logistics of who keeps the escrowed key for what keys, who has authority to demand the release of such escrowed keys to whom and under which conditions, and so on, become unmanageable for vast numbers of encryption keys.

As a result, escrowed encryption is basically dead both in the United States and in practically all other countries. As of May 1999, for example, the U.K. prime minister's office has abandoned a similar proposal; a report by the House of Commons Trade and Industry Select Committee into the Electronic Commerce Bill, concluded that "U.K. electronic commerce policy was for so long entrapped in the blind alley of key escrow that fears have been expressed that the UK's reputation...for electronic commerce is now severely damaged."

Worse yet, the notion of escrowed encryption seems to have backfired in two ways:

1. Individuals who would not have otherwise encrypted their data due to their former lack of awareness of the threats have now been sensitized to it by the extensive press coverage of escrowed encryption and now routinely encrypt their data.

2. Entire nations have realized that escrowed encryption where the keys are kept by another nation is an obvious threat. In early 1999, in a reversal of its position on encryption, the German government started actually *encouraging* its citizens and businesses to use strong unescrowed encryption. "Germany considers the application of secure encryption to be a crucial requirement for citizens' privacy, for the development of economic commerce and for the protection of business secrets. The Federal Government will therefore actively support the distribution of secure encryption. This includes in particular increasing the security consciousness of

citizens, business, and administration," according to a report
released in early 1999 by the German Federal Ministry of Economic Affairs and Technology. In a departure from the U.S. position, this report stated that it understands that encryption can be
used to criminal ends but that it felt that the need to protect the
economic concerns of that nation takes precedence.

The reader may misconstrue the above verbiage as being slanted in
favor of libertarian privacy and at the expense of the legitimate concerns of
law enforcement. Quite the contrary is true. The point being made is that
some legitimate concerns of law enforcement can only be met through provably effective means and not through simplistic and ineffective cosmetic measures such as provably ineffective attempts to ban encryption.

It is, perhaps, in realization of all of the foregoing that, in September
1999, the U.S. government came up with a new policy that removes many of
the bureaucratic burdens to companies wanting to export encryption; a
"one-time review" of each encryption product is still required, though,
before it can be exported; this has caused the cynics to suspect that only
products with an identifiable weakness may receive the requisite export
license. Furthermore, this new policy will have little practical impact because
the most contentious encryption, namely, freeware encryption, is *not* affected
by it. This policy is hotly debated because, among other reasons, it does not
define key terms in its provisions, such as what a "low-end user" is or what a
"government-affiliated" buyer is (Is Fiat, the well-known private automaker,
which has a substantial investment from the Italian government, a
"government-affiliated entity"?); it interprets "retail" as excluding sales over
the Internet, and so on.

At the same time, that new policy criminalizes the refusal of any individual to surrender a decryption key in response to a court order; yet, providing
the authorities with such a key is inherently impossible for public-key-
encrypted files sent to anybody else since only the intended recipient (and
never the sender) can decrypt such files. Furthermore, the new policy exempts
law enforcement from having to disclose how a decrypted version of a document was obtained; this has obvious legal implications when, for example, the
defense questions the authenticity of such documents.

13.3.2   On the Social Front

On the social side, there have been numerous strong campaigns by various
law enforcement organizations to demonize the Internet, anonymity, and

encryption. Some regimes have branded the Internet "an American imperialist tool," allegedly out to corrupt the moral fiber of society. Others have taken offense to the fact that most Internet activities are in English; some have even criminalized the operation of Web sites on their soil if such sites are solely in English. Still others have been outraged by the availability of this or that on the Internet, be it nudity, religious commentaries considered blasphemous, political discourse viewed as threatening or critical of a regime, and so on. Nearly all regimes, including democratic ones, have taken offense to the free flow of encrypted data which could contain any one or more of the above, or which could be facilitating terrorism or other generally agreed criminality.

Encryption has been equally demonized with simplistic arguments of the type, "If you have nothing to hide, then you do not need encryption"; ergo, if you do use encryption, you are up to no good. This argument ignores the legitimate national and societal needs for protecting trade secrets, privileged attorney-client information, patient medical record privacy, and so on, in the face of a huge number of documented attacks on such computerized data.

13.3.3 On the Technical Front

On the technical front, there have been public reports even in responsible journals, such as *Business Week,* of extensive government ongoing activity in intercepting digital communications. Given the minimal, if any, likelihood of any effectiveness in banning encryption, governments appear to have concluded that a much more effective tool would be to capitalize on the fact that most traffic is in fact not encrypted, and to try to derive information from massively expanded monitoring of the unencrypted traffic. Even in the case of encrypted traffic, a lot of information can be derived from what is almost always unencrypted: Who is communicating with whom and when. The only exception to this is if traffic uses concatenated anonymizing remailers.

In 1998, according to A. Oram in his August 1998 article, "Little-Known International Agreement May Determine Internet Privacy" (http://www.oreilly.com/people/staff/andyo/ar/cypto_wassenaar.html), the International Police (Interpol) decided to implement a system known as ENFOPOL, intended to have access to any and all kinds of electronic transmissions, specifically including the recently launched (and more recently bankrupt) Iridium global satellite phone system.

On October 16, 1999, however, it was reported that ENFOPOL was being scrapped by the member states. Even so, according to a November 8,

1999, *Telepolis* (Germany) report by C. Haddouti, ENFOPOL plans remain integrated into Article 11b of the European Legal Aid agreement. That article stipulates "remote access" of national monitoring measures "regarding telecommunications connections on a state's own territory under engagement of national service tenderers by means of remote control in another member state which has the appropriate ground station." It also stipulates that all telecommunications member service offerers make "possible the execution of national monitoring arrangements." Article 12 of the same legal aid convention stipulates that another member state can be obligated to make a technical monitoring of telecommunications traffic "in real time" or deliver monitoring recordings already existing.

Independently, for the last few years, a number of Internet Usenet forums (the bulletin-board-like "newsgroups" on the Internet) and even reputable media organizations such as ABC News, have been alleging the existence of a multinational surveillance network named Echelon. In June 1999, Duncan Campbell, a British investigative journalist, submitted a report (*Interception Capabilities 2000*) to the European Parliament's Science and Technology Options Assessment (STOA) panel assessing that panel's concern about such a network. Following that report, the Australian government confirmed its participation in it in related interviews.

According to Campbell's report, a law-enforcement-oriented organization, the International Law Enforcement Telecommunications Seminar, is involved in coordinating and sponsoring related activities. A different report, *An Appraisal of Technologies of Political Control*, dated January 6, 1998, authored by Steve Wright of the Omega Foundation, a British human rights organization in Manchester, England, and written for a research unit of the European Parliament department for the STOA, asserts that "Echelon ... [is] a global surveillance system that stretches around the world." Public inquiries about it have been made by numerous politicians on both sides of the Atlantic, such as Representative Bob Barr (R-Georgia, and a former federal prosecutor) and Glyn Ford, a British Labor party member of Parliament. According to the United States–based Federation of American Scientists Internet Web site, Echelon "searches through millions of interceptions for pre-programmed keywords on fax, telex and e-mail messages."

In his book *Secret Power*, Nicky Hager asserts that this system facilitates the "monitoring of most of the world's telephone, e-mail, fax and telex communications" and that "it is designed primarily for non-military targets," thereby "potentially affecting every person communicating between (and sometimes within) countries." He asserts that "every word of every message intercepted gets automatically searched—whether or not a specific telephone number or e-mail address is on the list."

Independently, according to a spokesman for the U.S. National Security Council (NSC), a 140-page draft plan by the NSC calls for setting up a Federal Intrusion Detection Network ("FIDNet") that would monitor traffic on both government and some commercial networks, as a means of safeguarding the United States' critical information infrastructure. According to a counsel for the Washington-based Center for Democracy and Technology, this network would also monitor citizens who visit federal Web sites, and might involve tracking e-mail, use of certain computer programs, and remote access to government as well as commercial networks; the same counsel has stated that the chances that FIDNet will be established are good.

On a much smaller scale, of course, it is certainly well within any one country's power to use its own laws (or influence) to require select Internet service providers (ISPs) to track and report on the activities of specific clients of theirs, and/or to use criteria to identify users meeting particular on-line profiles.

If large interception systems do, in fact, exist, then one can understand why encryption, which negates them, is disliked so intensely by governments involved in such systems.

13.4   Countermeasures: The Rebels Regroup

The right and, indeed, the obligation of any responsible government to protect its citizens from terrorism and from out-and-out criminality are unquestionable. The only issue is how to do this effectively without trashing the very institutions in which a democratic government takes justifiable pride.

Political correctness makes discussion of countermeasures to surveillance inappropriate in polite company. The philosophical positions between those who advocate state interception of personal data and those who oppose it have had the rigidity of religious debates that ultimately appeal to nebulous higher principles for their justification. In practical terms, the law enforcement side has the benefit of the power of the various laws. The privacy-protection side has the benefit of technology, which evolves and allows numerous creative ways of negating interception, let alone decryption.

What is contested is not merely whether or not two individuals should have the ability to communicate information that the state cannot decipher, but whether individuals and organizations should have the ability in the first place to encrypt and store encrypted information that the state cannot decipher.

The two main classes of techniques that have evolved to defeat attempts by nations to either ban encryption or to force the disclosure of decryption keys are: (1) steganography, which hides the mere existence of a hidden file (see Section 14.5), and (2) anonymity, which hides the author or originator of a file (see Chapters 8 through 12).

13.5   The Plot Thickens: State Support for Encryption

In March 1999, the French government, which had been strongly against the use of potent encryption by the public in the past, issued a decree specifically encouraging its use by French citizens. In May 1999, Germany surprisingly announced that it would actually promote the use of potent encryption throughout Germany, even though this would hamper eavesdropping by law enforcement. Since the Wassenaar Agreement is not binding on its member states, the Federal Minister of Economic Affairs and Technology recently released a report stating that "[Germany] considers the application of secure encryption to be a crucial requirement for citizens' privacy, for the development of electronic commerce, and for the protection of business secrets." In fact, this document also states that "[f]or reasons of national security, and the security of business and society, the federal government considers the ability of German manufacturers to develop and manufacture secure and efficient encryption products indispensable."

In other words, Germany now considers the use of strong encryption by its citizens as something that furthers, rather than hinders, the interests of its national security. Indeed, the German Ministry of Economics and Technology, to its credit, is now actively sponsoring and funding the development of encryption software known as GnuPG, whose "innards" (source code) will be openly available for inspection to anyone who wishes to satisfy himself or herself that there are no hidden features, and will be knowingly unbreakable by that government (or anyone else, for that matter).

The motivation for both of these fundamental policy changes seems to have been the realization by individual countries that the protection of their respective data from each other outweighs the law enforcement concerns.

Independently, Canada's Minister of Industry, John Manley, announced last on October 1, 1999, that the Canadian government would not seek to regulate the domestic use of encryption and would restrict exports only as far as Canada's Wassenaar obligations require. The Irish government has announced the same policy.

To their credit, Hong Kong police were reportedly handing out the pro-encryption sticker shown in Figure 13.3 during the 1999 Internet Convention.

The significance of these transcends the boundaries of any one nation: The global interconnectivity of the Internet makes it extremely easy for encryption software to travel between countries despite controls. If one or more major countries elect not to enforce encryption controls, then the effectiveness of attempts to control encryption software by any country becomes highly questionable.

13.6   The Future of Encryption

No matter what wondrous encryption schemes come along in the future, one should never lose sight of the fact that the specific process of encrypting information is only a small part of what needs to be done to protect that information from the eyes of someone having no authorized access to it.

Figure 13.3   Hong Kong police support for encryption.

The availability of computers to implement the encryption arithmetic has actually made the overall problem of protecting something through encryption *more* difficult and not less. This is so because the complexity of the operating systems of contemporary computers has created a plethora of exploitable security weaknesses once a sensitive plaintext can be accessed by a computer.

Many openly available modern (and certainly future) cryptographic algorithms are adequately strong in and of themselves. Instead, the real weaknesses are in:

- The handling, processing, and removal of the unencrypted plaintext in the computer;

- The propensity of modern user-friendly operating systems to do things without one's knowledge, such as creating housekeeping files, swapping information between memory and hard disk, and so on;

- The human tendency to cut corners, such as enabling "fast key generation" in public-key encryption systems based on factoring large prime numbers, in favor of precomputed prime numbers, or using easy-to-remember weak passwords;

- The vulnerabilities created by connecting a computer to a network;

- The vulnerabilities created by running untrusted software in the computer, such as some software downloaded from the Internet and bootlegged software from friends, which could quietly steal passwords and keys;

- The vulnerability introduced by doctored encryption software;

- The serious vulnerability of ensuring that a key (whether the public key in public-key encryption or the key in conventional symmetric encryption) indeed belongs to the person one thinks it does;

- The serious vulnerability of securely distributing a conventional symmetric encryption key.

13.6.1   Quantum Cryptography

The basic precepts of quantum cryptography were discovered in the early 1970s. In the 1980s, Charles Bennett of IBM and Gilles Brassard of the University of Montreal published a number of papers on the subject; they gave a demonstration of it in 1989.

Quantum cryptography is not an encryption algorithm. Instead, it is a means for the secure distribution of a key using single photo transmission, and for the creation of such a random key. The basic idea, according to its proponents, is that, according to the Heisenberg uncertainty principle, the communicating photons cannot be diverted from the intended recipient to the interceptor without disturbing the communications system to the point of creating an irreversible change in the quantum states of the system.

Since the secret key cannot be intercepted without evading detection (because the interception of the photons will raise the error rate of the key above an alarm threshold), it can be viewed as a secure means of encrypted communications over open channels. As such, the fundamental security of quantum key distribution (QKD) is based on the fundamental principles of quantum physics. The optical distribution path can be free space or optical fiber.

Numerous teams have been working on quantum cryptography for the last decade, including teams at various universities such as Johns Hopkins in the United States and the University of Geneva; at U.S. national laboratories such as Los Alamos; and in the corporate sector, such as British Telecom.

Curiously, the lack of any overwhelming interest in the deployment of the technology has not helped expedite the progress. This underscores a significant point: Encryption strength today is where it is because there is no need for it to be any stronger. Unless some cryptanalytic breakthroughs occur which challenge the fundamental mathematical assumptions behind modern encryption, such as the difficulty of factoring large prime integers, it is quite easy to increase encryption strength by merely adding bits to the encryption key; this would increase the brute force cryptanalytic effort nearly exponentially.

13.6.2 Quantum Computing

According to the late Nobel Laureate Richard Feynman and others, binary numbers can be represented by orthogonal quantum states of two-level quantum systems; a single bit of information in this form was then called a "qubit." Having more than one qubit, one can then think of quantum logical gate operations as building blocks for a quantum computer. The advantage over conventional computer architectures is that the quantum gate operations can be performed simultaneously rather than serially. Cryptanalysts' interest was piqued in 1994 when it was shown that this "quantum parallelism," if implemented in a practical "machine," could factor the products of large prime integers, which are the basis of many (but not all) cryptographic algorithms today.

Despite extensive work in academia and the national labs, quantum computing is nowhere close to resulting into a practical reality. This is so because:

- It is difficult to engineer the quantum states needed.

- Even if created, those quantum states lose their coherence properties (which are necessary for quantum computing) when interacting with the environment.

- It is difficult to engineer the means to read out the end quantum states that contain the result of a computation.

Elaborate "workarounds" to the problems above are continuing to evolve. Realistically, a practically useful device for factoring large prime numbers cannot be expected for at least a decade or more.

Even if prime number factoring becomes a reality, however, there are numerous other encryption algorithms that do not depend on prime number factoring for their strength, such as one-time pads or quantum cryptography, to cite a couple. As such, quantum computing will not spell an end to encryption, as has been claimed by its proponents on occasion in the literature.

13.6.3   DNA-Based Encryption

The first step in this technique is to convert each letter of the alphabet into a different combination of the four bases that make up the DNA. This is followed by synthetically creating a piece of DNA spelling out the message to be encrypted in addition to short marker sequences at both ends of the DNA chain. Finally, this can be slipped into a normal fragment of a human DNA of similar length. The end result can be dried out on paper and cut into small dots; only one DNA strand in about 30 billion will contain the message, thereby making the detection of even the existence of the encrypted message most unlikely; for this reason, DNA-based encryption is basically a data-hiding technique that is the modern equivalent of the microdot of World War II fame.

13.7 Comments

Governments have been trusted with the obligation to protect their citizens from terrorism and from out-and-out criminality, but not to use that power to squelch dissent by labeling it as criminality. Controlling encryption is not an effective means of meeting this obligation and may actually hurt vital economic national interests, as some Western governments have recently realized, and are now actually encouraging their citizens to use strong encryption.

The transformation of modern society into one that is increasingly and vitally dependent upon computers makes it a matter of national economic survival for corporate and personal sensitive information to be protected through potent encryption. Furthermore, there is an increasing legitimate need to continue protecting the confidentiality of such personal information as attorney-client privileged information, medical privacy, and the like through strong encryption.

While cryptography, like anything else, can be used for illegitimate purposes (e.g., to hinder valid investigations by the police), the fact that it is also used to prevent crimes and make society safer is often overlooked by law enforcement officials interested merely in getting evidence to result in a conviction at all costs.

To be sure, there *are* situations where there is a legitimate need for specific third parties to have a way to read an encrypted file (whether through escrowed keys, backup keys, or other means): These include work-related employee documents in an organization, as well as some personal records (e.g., life insurance information) in case one dies and a spouse needs to access that information. In the case of data encrypted for transmittal to an intended individual recipient, it is hard to conceive of any justification for a third party to have any right to see that data; this is merely an extension of one person's right to whisper a secret in someone else's ear; the distance between the first person's mouth and the second person's ear should have no bearing on the right to privacy of what is being transmitted.

The indigenous availability of potent encryption in most of the world's nations and the global interconnectivity provided by the Internet makes the control of software encryption an unattainable goal. Independently, the development of data-hiding techniques, motivated by the commercial applications of digital watermarking, will continue. Effective data-hiding techniques will make the debate about encryption irrelevant.

While encryption, just like other technologies such as commercial telecommunications, automobiles, and assorted devices, can be used for terrorism and criminality, outright banning of any of these technologies is ineffective and has a major negative economic impact on any nation. The alarmist prose used by today's law enforcement to solicit support for banning encryption is rather unconvincing; if one were to change only a few words, that same prose could have been used in the 1930s to claim a need to ban horseless carriages and the telegraph ("criminals escape using horseless carriages..."; "criminals conspire and communicate at the speed of light using the telegraph...").

The solution may be in criminalizing the use of encryption in the commission of generally recognized serious criminal acts only, and in actually encouraging its use in all other activities.

Selected Bibliography

The rate at which most aspects of encryption and the Internet advance is such that books on the topic become obsolete almost as soon as they are published. The Internet offers the most current information on the subject. While these Web sites referenced were in existence at the time of this writing, it is inevitable that they, too, will change with time; the reader's best option is to access Internet search engines, such as http://www.google.com/, http://www.excite.com/, and http://www.hotbot.com/, and perform keyword searches on the topics of interest (e.g., anonymous remailers and steganography).

Selected Bibliography on General Encryption

Curtin, M., "Snake Oil Warning Signs," Ohio State University, cmcurtin@interhack.net.

Kosiur, D., "Keep Your Data Secure from Prying Eyes: An Encryption Primer," http://www.sunworld.com/swol-03-1997/swol-03-encrypt.html.

"The Passphrase FAQ," http://stack.nl/~galactus/remailers/passphrase-faq.html.

Schneier, B., *Applied Cryptography*, Second Edition, New York: Wiley, 1996.

————. "Security Pitfalls in Cryptography," Counterpane Systems, http://www.counterpane.com/pitfalls.html.

On DES cracking: http://www.replay.com/mirror/cracking_des/chap-1.html and http://cryptome.org/.

On other encryption cracking: http://www.stack.nl/~galactus/remailers/index-crack.html.

Selected Bibliography on Encryption Software and Algorithms

On blowfish algorithm: ftp://ftp.psy.uq.oz.au, ftp://ftp.ox.ac.uk.

On elliptic curve encryption: Smart, N., et al., *Elliptic Curves in Cryptography,* London Mathematical Society Lecture Notes, Cambridge, England: Cambridge University Press, 1999.

On hashing algorithms: ftp.funet.fi:/pub/crypt/hash.mds/md5, ftp.funet/fi:/pub/crypt/hash/sha, and http://www.esat.kuleuven.ac.be/~bosselae/ripemd160.html.

On PGP: http://www.pgp.com and http://www.pgpi.com/ for the United States and international versions, respectively.

On PGP versions: http://www.stat.uga.edu/~rmarquet/pgp/ and http://www.paranoia.com/~vax/pgp_versions.gif.

On public-key encryption: http://www.cesg.gov.uk/about/nsecret/possnse.htm.

On voice encryption: http://www.speakfreely.org/.

Selected Bibliography on Legal Controls on Encryption

ftp://ftp.cygnus.com/pub/export/export.html.

http://cwis.kub.nl/~frw/people/koops/cls-sum.htm.

http://cwis.kub.nl/~frw/people/koops/lawsurvy.htm.

http://www.dfat.gov.au/isecurity/pd/pd_4_96/pd10.html.

On applicable U.S. laws: ftp://ftp.cygnus.com/pub/export/aeca.in.full and ftp://ftp.cygnus.com/pub/export/itar.in.full.

On cryptography in Europe: http://www.modeemi.fi/~avs/eu-crypto.html.

Selected Bibliography on Technical Countermeasures by Governments

Markoff, J., "U.S. Drafting Plan for Computer Monitoring System," *New York Times,* July 28, 1999, http://www.nytimes.com/learning/general/featured_articles/990729thursday.html.

"They're Listening to Your Calls," *Business Week,* May 31, 1999, pp. 110–111. See also http://cryptome.org/.

Selected Bibliography on Data Hiding and Steganography

http://ise.gmu.edu/~njohnson/Steganography

http://www.jjtc.com/Steganography/

http://www.psionic.com/papers/covert/covert.tcp.txt

http://ww2.umdnj.edu/~shindler/telemedicine.html

Selected Bibliography on Future Trends in Cryptography

Bancroft, C., C. T. Clelland, and V. Risca, "Genomic Steganography: Amplifiable Microdots," *Fifth International Meeting on DNA-Based Computers,* Massachusetts Institute of Technology, Cambridge, MA, June 14–15, 1999.

On quantum cryptography: http://p23.lanl.gov/Quantum/images/qcrypt.gif.

14

Practical Encryption: Protecting Proprietary and Confidential Information Against Hostile Penetration

14.1 Introduction

By now, it must be quite clear from the vast number of ways that sensitive information can be left behind on one's hard disk that the odds are stacked in favor of the computer forensics expert. This is as it should be for civilized societies that must defend against out-and-out criminality, the evidence of which may be hidden in computer files.

However, there are perfectly acceptable situations, like those listed as follows, in which honorable individuals may want to maintain the privacy of their files and protect themselves against malicious computer forensics.

- An individual in a patently repressive, totalitarian regime, or a regime known for its intolerance to religious or other individual preferences, who feels the need to keep overzealous investigators from either inserting incriminating evidence in his or her computer or otherwise manipulating stored data;
- An individual who connects his or her computer to the Internet or to any other network and who is therefore vulnerable to having his or her confidential files stolen, vandalized, or otherwise accessed without authorization, by any savvy hostile remote site;

- A businessperson who travels with a laptop that contains proprietary corporate information of interest to an unscrupulous competitor;

- A professional who stores information entrusted to him or her by his or her clients, such as a physician, a mental health practitioner, or a lawyer;

- An individual who stores legitimate personal information in his or her computer, such as tax returns and personal correspondence;

- An individual entrepreneur who uses his or her computer to store confidential lists of clients, creative new designs, ideas for which patent protection has not yet been applied, copyrighted material that could be stolen, and so on;

- An individual who uses his or her computer to store intellectual property, such as scientific publications, laboratory test results, and artistic creations.

Since the odds are stacked in favor of the computer forensics examiner, a user who falls within the above categories may elect to take the safe yet easy way out by having his or her entire hard disk encrypted. This will do away with most of the subtleties and threats detailed in this book, including:

- The proclivities of Windows to create temporary files all over one's hard disk;

- The difficulties of keeping track of entries made by Windows 95/98/NT in the registry and the difficulty of cleaning the registry (see Chapters 4 and 9);

- The swap (paging) file;

- The data stored by assorted applications software in nondescript files on one's hard disk (e.g., Network Navigator/Communicator's netscape.hst file, and others discussed in this book);

- The data left behind in cluster tips, or slack; see Section 4.2.1.

And so on, and so on.

14.2 Entire-Disk Encryption

Encrypting the entire disk is quite different from creating an encrypted file or encrypted disk partition, such as can be done with PGP-disk, ScramDisk, E4M, and others discussed in this chapter; these schemes do not solve any of the problems listed in Section 14.1, although they do provide a "hiding place" for some files.

Encrypting an entire disk is not a panacea, however. One is still vulnerable to all of the following threats, which carry through from the normal Windows-user list of threats:

- Commercial keyboard-capturing software (see Sections 6.4 and 6.6);

- Commercial keystroke-capturing hardware (see Section 6.3);

- Commercial hardware for intercepting Van Eck radiation (see Section 6.7);

- All on-line threats while one is connected to a network such as the Internet, because the encrypted hard disk is just as accessible to the remote malicious hacker while one is on-line as it is to the legitimate user sitting in front of the keyboard;

- Adware/spyware that "calls home" via the Internet after it has been installed (see Section 6.6.1).

Even so, this is a far smaller and more manageable list of vulnerabilities than if it were to include computer forensics after physical possession of one's hard disk by an adversary.

There are two promising commercial solutions to the problem of encrypting an entire hard disk:

- **SafeBoot**, from Fischer International Systems Corporation in the United Kingdom; this software has been acquired by Control Break Europe Computer Security Consultants, http://www.control-break.co.uk. It is compatible with Win3.1x, 95/98, and NT. As an option, it can work with a smart card through one's PCMCIA port or a smart card reader that works through one's floppy disk drive using that company's SmartySmart card reader/writer.

- **PCGuardian** (http://www.pcguardian.com/support/faq_hd.html). This author has not had success in getting this product to work on a Windows 98 laptop, and the manufacturer's technical support was unable to remedy the problem. As with any software, it may well be that there was some incompatibility that has yet to be resolved and that the software may work with others' computers.

14.3   Encrypting for E-Mail: PGP

PGP[1] is an encryption program that is available over the Internet, worldwide, at no cost. A commercial version is also available for purchase. A detailed list of frequently asked questions (FAQs) about PGP can be found at: http://www. cryptography.org/getpgp.htm and http://www.pgp.net/pgpnet/pgp-faq/.
Additional information about it can be found at:

- http://www.cryptorights.org/pgp-help-team/hello.html;
- http://www.mit.edu:8001/people/warlord/pgp-faq.html;
- http://www.freedomfighter.net/crypto/pgp-history.html.

Official PGP documentation in several languages can be found at:

- http://www.pgpi.com/;
- http://www.geocities.com/Athens/1802/ (German);
- http://www.geocities.com/SiliconValley/Bay/9648 (French).

PGP started as a political statement by its creator, Phil Zimmerman, to make encryption available to everyone. Unlike the version available for purchase, whose source code (the human-readable sequence of steps that it does) is not made available, all of the many free versions have made the source code available to anyone for analysis and scrutiny. It is considered an extremely good piece of encryption software, and all known attempts to "break" (cryptanalyze) PGP-encrypted cipher have been withstood.
At the same time, no encryption software can protect a user from sloppy usage. Specifically:

---

1. The best authority on PGP is Tom McCune. He has an extensive on-line set of tutorials on PGP, along with current information and relevant links. See http://www.mccune.cc/ PGPpage2.htm#Why.

1. PGP, like any encryption software, encrypts and decrypts. It is not a "security suite" (except for the new NAI versions 7.x, which are *not* recommended, for reasons stated in detail in Section 14.3.10) that is intended to take care of the inherent security flaws of Windows or DOS. Similarly, it does not protect a user from himself or herself, such as if the user forgets to wipe the unencrypted plaintext version of a message that was (foolishly) stored on hard disk.

2. PGP, like most any encryption software program, does not counsel the user not to use easily guessable pass-phrases such as one's name or birthday.

3. PGP, like most any encryption software program, presumes that the user is versed in the many security precautions discussed in this book (e.g., commercial software or hardware that can capture a pass phrase entered on a keyboard). The reader is referred to the condensed list below for such "Gotchas!"

A false sense of security is far worse than no security at all, because a false sense of security motivates one to entrust a computer with information, while a person who believes that there is no security would act accordingly. Because of this, the reader is strongly cautioned to understand the ancillary "ifs, buts, and howevers" outlined below *before* assuming that encryption will meet his or her needs.

As with all software that has evolved over more than a decade, PGP has gone through numerous versions, not all of which are compatible with the others. The interested reader is referred to http://www.paranoia.com/~vax/pgp_versions.gif for a list of such compatibilities; knowledge of such is really not necessary, however, as shown next.

- *Caution:* PGP, like many encryption products, makes it very clear in its encrypted outputs that PGP was used. This may be highly undesirable if one is in a situation where the mere use of PGP is incriminating. For those cases, one can use STEALTH V1.1 by Henry Hastur (http://www.unicom.com/pgp/s-readme.html), which removes the telltale headers from a PGP-encrypted message (and allows the intended recipient to add them back before decrypting a message). This is not foolproof, however, as PGP-encrypted messages have a structure that, to the trained eye, immediately reveals that PGP was used. A user would be well advised to use steganography as the outer "envelope" of an encrypted message in such cases.

- *Caution:* (Repeated from Section 11.3 due to its importance.) Users of PGP encryption should not use the PGP plug-ins for either Eudora or Outlook/Outlook Express (in fact, Outlook/Outlook Express should not be used at all, with or without PGP, due to a long history of security flaws announced by Microsoft in its many security warnings); instead, encrypt the clipboard and cut and paste the ciphertext into the e-mail software program's window.[2] The danger is that the "out" mailbox saves on the hard disk—under some conditions—both the plaintext and the ciphertext; this is about the worst scenario from a security perspective.

- *Caution:* Avoid using encryption plug-ins for e-mail software, be it a Web browser or anything else. While no evidence of an actual exploitation exists, it is quite possible for a smart-enough plug-in to compromise the security of the encryption in any one of numerous ways.

14.3.1 How PGP Works

PGP uses a combination of conventional (symmetric) and public-key encryptions (see Chapter 13); this is standard for most programs using public-key encryption. Specifically:

- Upon initial installation (and at any time thereafter), PGP creates a public and private key pair. You provide (by whatever appropriate means) to the intended recipient the public key part, and store the private key securely. See Figure 14.1.

- To encrypt a file, you need the intended recipient's PGP public key, which he or she must first have provided to you by some appropriate means. The software will ask you "to whom shall this unencrypted file be encrypted?" and you provide that information.

- Since public-key encryption/decryption is much slower than conventional key encryption, PGP dreams up a conventional encryption "session key," which it uses to encrypt the file in question; it then encrypts that session key using public-key encryption with the public key of the intended recipient, and sends out both the

---

2. Easier yet, use the Current Window feature of Windows; see Tom McCune's excellent tutorial at http://www.mccune.cc/PGPpage2.htm#usecurrent, where a shortcut is shown for this cut-and-paste ritual.

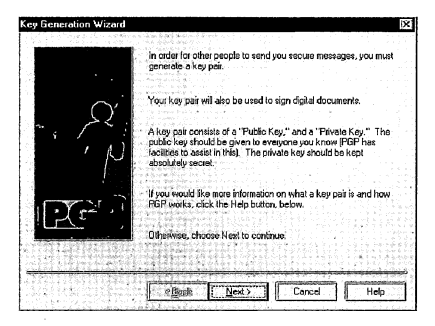

Figure 14.1 PGP key generation.

conventionally encrypted file and the public-key-encrypted key of that conventional key encryption. The session key then evaporates into thin air. Since the session key is unique to each encryption and is random, you can encrypt the exact same file to the exact same recipient and you will end up with two totally different-looking end results, both of which will be perfectly valid.

• As an option, you can digitally authenticate your message so that the recipient knows that it really came from you. The way this is done is this: Your copy of PGP will first form a brief digital summary of your message, and will encrypt it with your private key; this becomes part of the overall encrypted file to be sent. On the receiving end, if the recipient who has your public key can decrypt this digital sum-mary, it means that it could only have been encrypted by you with your private key (or else it wouldn't be decryptable with your public key). As a side benefit, the intended recipient's PGP compares the digital summary you sent him or her with the one he or she gener-ates locally on your decrypted file, and if the two are identical it means that the message was not doctored by anyone along the way.

- Given that one way for someone trying to break encryption is to try many possible "keys" until he or she hits upon the correct one, and that the easiest way to tell is if readable text comes out, PGP in essence prerandomizes what is to be encrypted in a manner that is transparent to both the sender and the recipient.

Once installed, PGP usage is easy and intuitive; all one has to do is to click on the PGP icon on the lower right corner of the screen, at which time a self-explanatory list of options appears. See Figure 14.2.

14.3.2   Do's and Don'ts of PGP Installation and Use

14.3.2.1   Windows Version

Here is a list of do's and don'ts of PGP installation and use for Windows.

- *Do not* accept the default "faster key generation" option; uncheck it. See Figure 14.3.
- Set the "temporary" disk to be a RAM disk (see Chapter 9) so that no interim steps get written onto the hard disk.
- It is recommended that the public keys and especially your own secret keys not be stored in the computer, as per Figure 14.4, but on a floppy disk that is carried separately if needed and is stored in a physically secure and especially nonobvious location when not needed.
- *Do not* use plug-ins for assorted e-mail programs. Instead, to encrypt, write the plaintext in RAM disk using a simple text editor

Figure 14.2   PGP primary menu.

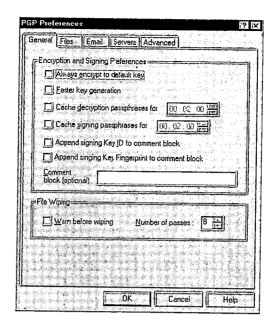

Figure 14.3 PGP preference setting.

such as the one that Windows provides to create a new text file, as shown in Figure 14.5. Edit/Cut, and then use PGP's "Encrypt Clipboard" option, as in Figure 14.6. Edit/Paste into the text window of your favorite e-mail program. To decrypt, Edit/Cut from your e-mail program's inbox; then select "Decrypt & Verify Clipboard," as per Figure 14.6. Then make sure that you key the "Empty Clipboard" option as shown in Figure 14.7, to minimize the likelihood of plaintext spillage into the swap file.

- *Do not* use the latest (as of September 2000) versions 7.x, for the following reasons:
    - They are much slower than earlier versions.
    - Their source code is far too long to be subjected to scrutiny.
    - Their source code has not been released by its manufacturer, NAI Inc.
    - Phil Zimmerman, who pioneered PGP, had left NAI in February 2001. While he asserted up until the time of his departure that versions 7.x are safe, one cannot assume he would give this assurance now.

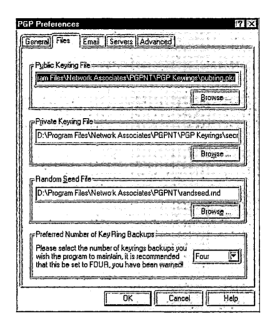

Figure 14.4 Secure off-site storing of PGP keys can be specified.

Figure 14.5 Creating a new text file in RAM disk.

- The PGP folder is now in "My Documents."
- One is not able to open and close PGPtray.
- Key rings are now locked and not copy-able.
- They are memory-hogging.

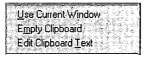

Figure 14.6 Encryption/decryption options.

Figure 14.7 Cleaning the clipboard from plaintext.

- They create error messages on boot if one hides the key rings.
- Direct CD is incompatible with PGPdisk.
- Reported vulnerability to ADKs continues because its commercial maker wants the same software code for the industry version—which wants ADKs.
- They have numerous reported incompatibilities.

Caution: The DOS versions of PGP are the most secure. The Windows versions should only be used as the outside envelope—if at all. This is not a reflection on PGP but a reflection on Windows.

- When using PGP from within Windows, don't bother with the plug-ins for a handful of popular software programs, such as Eudora or Outlook Express, and do not use them. Instead, simply use the little icon on the lower right corner of the screen and:
  - In the case of encryption, copy plaintext file to clipboard, then opt for "encrypt clipboard," and then Edit/Paste the (encrypted) clipboard contents onto the message window of whichever e-mail program you are using.
  - In the case of decryption, Edit/Copy encrypted file from the e-mail into the clipboard, opt for "decrypt and verify," read it, and

do not save it. Then make sure you overwrite the e-mail that brought this message.

- Abide by the recommendations provided in Chapter 9 about setting up Windows securely. In particular:

  - Have enough physical RAM memory so as to set the virtual memory to zero. This prevents any sensitive data, such as passwords, from ending up on disk.

  - Ensure that your computer has no software or hardware enabled that can capture keyboard strokes (see Chapter 6).

14.3.2.2 DOS Version

The DOS version is preferable from a security perspective because it is not vulnerable to the many security problems of the Windows environment; however, like all DOS programs, it requires the use of unintuitive commands.

- Create a RAM disk (see Chapter 9).

- Print out and read the lengthy document that comes with the software; it is highly informative, though a bit verbose. Do not be intimidated by its length or apparent complexity; once you become accustomed to using PGP, you will find that it takes only a few seconds to encrypt or decrypt a file.

- After installing PGP, go to the folder where it resides, find config.txt, open it with a text editor, and set the temporary directory to point to that RAM disk letter. This will prevent writing sensitive information on hard disk, and will also speed up the program's execution.

- PGP uses several special files for its purposes, such as pubring.pgp and secring.pgp, the random number seed file randseed.bin, the PGP configuration file config.txt, and the foreign-language-string translation file language.txt. These special files can be kept in any directory, by setting the environmental variable PGPPATH to the desired pathname. If using MSDOS, the following command must be inserted in the standard AUTOEXEC.BAT file using any text editor, assuming that these files are in C:\PGP\:

    SET PGPPATH=C:\PGP

14.3.2.3 Both DOS and Windows Versions

Here is a list of do's and don'ts of PGP installation and use for both DOS and Windows.

- Get your PGP copy from a trusted source, such as http://www.pgpi .com/ or (for the long keys) http://www.ipgpp.com/. Just because the version you got from an unknown source appears to work fine and be compatible with PGP messages going in and out, it does not mean that it has not been compromised; it is quite possible, for example, for a version to select the encryption keys from a list of, say, 100 keys only, as opposed to a repertoire of a quadrillion choices or more; the end result would still be compatible with every PGP message going in or out, and it would also be trivial for an interceptor to break merely by trying 100 keys.

- Follow the simple instructions about validating the integrity of the file you just downloaded (usually this amounts to checking a CRC or hash value, which in PGP parlance is the "digital signature").

- Make sure that whatever you compose to be encrypted is composed on RAM disk and not on magnetic disk; if it is sensitive enough to warrant encryption, it has no business being on a magnetic disk and risking being found there.

- Select a key length of no less than 1,024 bits. If compatibility with unknown other users of PGP is not an issue (and it shouldn't be, because you don't know "unknown" people and hence you cannot trust that they are who they say they are, as per discussion of the "man in the middle problem" below), opt for a key length of 2,048, 4,096, 8,192, or even 16,394 bits. The Windows versions from CKT (http://www.ipgpp.com/) support very long keys. Expect the time it takes to generate those keys to be quite long if you have a slow computer (it can even take half a day or more—depending on the key length desired—with slower computers), but key generation is only done once and has nothing much to do with how long it will take to encrypt or decrypt files later on.

- Select a pass phrase that is truly not guessable, nor amenable to a brute force dictionary search attack done by numerous commercially and freely available software on the Internet, such as those listed in Section 14.6.

- *Do not* store the PGP files on the hard disk, and certainly not the "key ring" files that contain your secret key. Instead, store them on a floppy disk (with a backup on another floppy disk), which should be kept separately in a physically secure place. Make sure that you specify in your setup where PGP is to look for those files.

- *Do not* "publish" your public PGP key anywhere; doing so is pointless and dangerous. A recently discovered bug in PGP allows one to doctor up your PGP public key so that any messages encrypted with it can be decrypted by ADKs. Since you don't want to be dealing with total strangers, anyway, due to the man in the middle problem, there is really no reason to publish your PGP key. Simply give it to the select few that you want to communicate with using PGP.

- *Do not* accept someone's PGP public key from the Internet unless you have some *independent* way of verifying that it truly belongs to whomever it is alleged to belong and has not been altered. This, too, is to prevent the man in the middle problem.

- *Do* have at least two PGP key pairs, one for "low trust" communications and one for "high trust" ones. For highest sensitivity communications, create a key pair immediately, use it, and destroy it securely shortly thereafter.

- Delete (read: wipe) PGP key pairs on a regular basis (such as at least monthly, preferably more often) so that you could not possibly be compelled to decrypt this or that file by anyone after a few days (or minutes if you are a member of the opposition in a repressive regime).

- Depending on the level of threat under which you think you may be, you may also want to consider periodically verifying that your copy of the PGP software and public and private keys have not been altered. You can do this by running CRC or some other hashing program on your files (see Section 14.7 on how to do this); make sure that you keep those CRC or hash values in some secure place.

- *Do not* opt for encrypting an outgoing message to yourself as well as to the intended recipient. (This may be phrased as a "save outgoing files" option, which is not desirable at all because it makes you able to comply with a demand to decrypt a file sent.) In other words, uncheck the option of "always encrypting to default key" as shown in Figure 14.8.

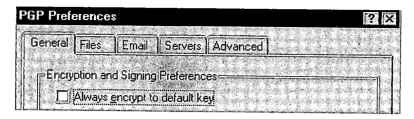

Figure 14.8 Defeating forced decryption of outgoing PGP messages.

- You *can* encrypt an already-PGP-encrypted file for additional security, but this is really pointless if you have abided by the recommendations of this section; if you have not abided by them (e.g., not
  protected against keystroke-capturing software), then you can
  encrypt a file a hundred times over and this will not make it any
  more secure.

- Keep in mind that a PGP-encrypted file does not hide the fact that it
  is a PGP-encrypted file, as shown in the partial message reproduced
  in Figure 14.9. Because of this, it may attract unwanted attention on
  its way to the recipient. To get around this, consider steganography
  (see Section 14.5).

- Also keep in mind that neither a PGP-encrypted e-mail nor any
  other encrypted e-mail hides the "from whom" and "to whom"
  information. If this is an issue, consider the information on anonymity in Chapters 8 through 12.

- If you have an attachment to a PGP-encrypted e-mail using your
  favorite e-mail software, the attachment will not be encrypted by
  default; you have to encrypt it separately prior to attaching it, as
  follows:

  From Windows Explorer (or any other way) select the file you
  want to encrypt; it could be an executable file or any other type.
  Edit/Copy.

  From the little PGP lock icon in the tray on the lower left, select
  "encrypt" (or "encrypt and sign," if you wish to sign it too).

  Select and drag the intended recipient's name to the lower window
  of PGP. Click OK.

```
-----BEGIN PGP MESSAGE-----
Version: 6.0.2CKT b-6

qANQR1DBw04DQ2KWr5oNP8EQD/4gFs+jLMFB204gSg5uDbrsAKzdBZPY9nqfzFIT
cF63/rK3KgMJcYpZcnTe+LuRiFyD4WB6N/CpEVapyFTFx0AdKVb2g5YXm9ZVxzMd
cRKnRFqG2p8Mqs3KNmtSOWSoP77Cg7R78vKL44z/mviSxmhXiBKgwwFbfcVFEqB2
P1OFfYm5z1isNstu+XtgzlfRb7wllcqb91fCRdnGVX40a+ApD/LhMLtxksR8QEJM
```

Figure 14.9   PGP-encrypted messages stand out.

The PGP encrypted file will be saved as a new file in the same folder that the unencrypted one was, as shown in Figure 14.10. Use the "attach file" option of your favorite e-mail program. *Do not* Edit/Paste.

- Keep in mind that no encryption software protects from someone who can make inferences based on the mere fact that encrypted messages are being sent (or received), when some other publicly observable event, such as activity by freedom fighters in a repressive regime, occurs.

- Never keep both an encrypted and a decrypted version of the same file.

14.3.3   The Need for Long Keys

It has been estimated in papers available on the Internet (see http://www.interhack.net/people/cmcurtin/snake-oil-faq.html) that a 128-bit symmetric key is about as resistant to brute force cryptanalysis as a 2,304-bit RSA public key; the corresponding equivalences for various key lengths are reported in Table 14.1.

Some (amazingly, even the often revered originator of PGP) have inferred incorrectly from this that the public-key length need not be longer

video.exe   video.exe.pgp

Figure 14.10   PGP encrypting any file, including executables.

Table 14.1
Bit Equivalences

Symmetric Key Size (bits)	Public Key Size (bits)
56 bit	384 bits
64 bit	512 bits
80 bits	768 bits
112 bits	1,792 bits
128 bits	2,304 bits

than 2,304 bits. This is incorrect for the following reason: If someone were to break the symmetric session key of PGP (see Section 14.3.1), then only that one encrypted file would be compromised. However, if one were to break the public key of PGP, then *all* encrypted files to that recipient would be compromised. Because of this, the public key length should be much stronger than the symmetric key; that is, much longer than 2,300 bits. It is for this reason that this book recommends PGP key lengths of 4,096 or longer, and this is possible with the PGP versions from Cyber Knights Templar.

At the same time, users should realize that if they want to be compatible with the majority of other PGP users, the use of ultralong keys will have to be reserved for those who have PGP versions that can handle long keys.

14.3.4 The Man in the Middle Problem

The man in the middle problem has nothing to do with PGP per se; it is a logical security problem inherent in all public-key encryption schemes. If you received an e-mail (or floppy disk or other document) with a public key that claims that it belongs to Mr. XYZ, this act in and of itself does not prove that it belongs to Mr. XYZ, even if you can exchange messages with Mr. XYZ using it. The key could very well belong to Mrs. ABC, who receives your message to Mr. XYZ, decrypts it, and reads it (because what you think is Mr. XYZ's public key belongs, in fact, to Mrs. ABC), and then she, in turn, encrypts it with Mr. XYZ's public key and sends it on its way without Mr. XYZ being any the wiser. The reverse path works just as well.

You need to have some independent way of verifying that a key that is claimed to belong to XYZ does in fact belong to XYZ and not to some go-between, or man in the middle. Such an independent way depends on the specifics of the situation.

If you know XYZ personally, you could talk with him on the phone, and he could confirm that "the key that goes like this [and here he could read the public key aloud to you, which is OK because it is "public"] is mine."

If you don't know XYZ personally, you can use someone you trust to vouch for the fact that this is the case. This, in fact, is the basis of authenticating a public key among people who do not know each other: a "web of trust," where each person in the web trusts another person, who trusts another, and so on, that the key belongs to XYZ. This is formalized in PGP by having each person in the web of trust "sign" (digitally) a key for the person that they can vouch for.

In practice, nobody pays too much attention to this web of trust, and the only way for you to know for a fact that a key belongs to XYZ is for you to find some independent way of satisfying yourself that the key in fact belongs to XYZ.

14.3.5 DH or RSA?

Many versions of PGP allow the user to select between Diffie Hellman (DH) and RSA encryption [1]. (Actually, PGP uses a variant of DH known as El Gamal.)

DH's security is based on the difficulty of factoring and computing discrete logarithms [2] (the "Discrete Logarithm Problem"), whereas RSA is based on the difficulty of factoring large numbers into the prime number components (the "Prime Integer Factorization Problem" [3]). Both were covered by patents that have expired (DH's patent expired on September 6, 1997, and the RSA patent expired on September 20, 2000); because of this, both algorithms are now in the public domain; this is significant because the main reason why there have been so many versions of PGP has to do with the fact that the RSA patent was in force in some countries but not in others.

The benefits of DH over RSA are as follows:

1. A longer RSA key (in terms of the number of bits) is required to result in the same security as a given-length DH key [4].

2. DH has the benefit of a more solid mathematical foundation; this is not to say that RSA keys are weak, however.

3. If someone were to forcibly obtain your DH-using PGP key, he or she would be able to read your e-mail but he or she would not be

able to impersonate you by digitally signing outgoing e-mail, because a different algorithm (DSS) is used for that; RSA keys, by comparison, do both functions.

The disadvantage of DH in PGP implementations is that it is more amenable to the recently discovered weakness whereby an ADK can be inserted by a third party (see Section 14.3.8).

14.3.6 What About DSS?

Digital Signature Standard (DSS) is an algorithm for generating a fixed-size (1,024 bits) digital summary of a message of arbitrary length, to allow detection of any alteration of the message. It is considered "safe" for another couple of decades. Even though a 1,024-bit key may appear to be weaker than, say, an 8,000+-bit DH key, PGP does not use DSS for encryption only for message authentication.

Of more concern should be the fact that, according to the open literature (e.g., http://www.scramdisk.clara.net/pgpfaq.html), DSS keys suffer from a weakness known as "subliminal channels" [5]; this is a term used to denote the existance of unintended pathways that can leak information that can be advantageous to an adversary.

14.3.7 Selecting IDEA, CAST-128, 3DES, or Another Encryption Algorithm

IDEA, CAST-128, and 3DES are very secure algorithms and are well implemented in PGP. The choice comes down to compatibility with the version of PGP that one's correspondent is using. While CAST-128 is about twice as fast as IDEA, which, in turn, is about three times as fast as 3DES, it really does not matter in typical usage of an average-length message every few days.

Both CAST-128 and IDEA are 128-bit algorithms, and they are about equally secure; IDEA has been around for longer and there is more "comfort factor" associated with its use, but there are some minor patent issues that make it free only for noncommercial use.

3DES is often implemented with only two, rather than three, different 56-bit keys (encrypt with key#1, decrypt with key#2—which causes further encryption since it is the wrong key—and reencrypt the result with key#1 again); this is a sloppy and totally unnecessary shortcut, which does not save any computation time. In the case of PGP, 3DES is implemented with the full three different keys. There is debate as to whether its effective equivalent key strength is 168 bits or 112 bits; the latter is associated with the assumption that a "meet in the middle" cryptanalytic attack is possible; this is a specific attack documented in the open literature that exploits the specific construction of 3DES.

14.3.8   The Flaw in PGP

In August 2000 there was a big to-do [6] about a "discovery" of what has really been common knowledge among software encryption professionals: that if a hostile entity gets hold of one's public key, that public key can be downright changed (the man in the middle problem, explained earlier), or (and this was not as well known) altered so that messages encrypted with it can be decrypted by others in addition to the intended recipient.

This is nothing new. The trouble started when a major company that started making PGP for profit had the most unfortunate idea of increasing PGP's appeal to the corporate marketplace by providing for an additional decryption key (ADK) so that an employee's supervisor could also decrypt the employee's incoming PGP-encrypted messages. In fact, some versions of this PGP for corporate customers were openly advertised as having this feature, which appealed to law enforcement as well.

The problem is that, unless the PGP user is savvy about the technical details of PGP at a fairly esoteric level, he or she is most unlikely to spot the existence of such ADKs in his or her public key.

Worse yet, and this is where PGP can be rightfully blamed, there were ways in most versions between 5.5 and 6.5.3 whereby such ADKs could be added by third parties onto one's public key at a later time (e.g., when one's public key is stored in a "public key directory" server), thereby enabling such third parties to read messages encrypted to that unsuspecting user's public key.[3]

For this to happen, the following conditions have to be met:

---

3. Adding an ADK can, reportedly, be done from the command line by adding the following line in the PGP.CFGpgp.cfg file:
    ADKKEY=0X28A635C6 [put the ADK here]
    ENFORCEADK=ON
   Now create a new key in the usual manner (i.e., with the command)
    pgp—kg
   Add the ADK to this new key with the command
    pgp—kg+ADDKEY=0x28a653c6+ENFORCEADK=ON
   The author has not verified this process.

1. The attacker has to gain access to the victim's public PGP key. (This can be done if that key is deposited in a public key directory server, something that this book already advised against, or even if that public key was merely stored in one's computer that is connected on-line to the Internet or is physically accessible by others—in both cases all the files in the computer are vulnerable, specifically including encryption keys.)

2. The attacker has the know-how to add the ADK and repost or replace the doctored public key where the undoctored one was before.

3. The attacker can either access incoming e-mail sent to the victim (physically, by a tap, or any other way described in Chapter 6), or has modified the e-mail software to send e-mail to the attacker as well.

New versions of PGP (such as PGP 6.5.8) are advertised as having "fixed" this bug. This may lull one into a false sense of security, because the logical conundrum of any encryption key has not been and cannot be fixed: One has to have some independent means of verifying that an encryption key does indeed belong to the person it is supposed to belong to and has not been modified.

Some have stated that PGP's hubris in having claimed for so long that it is unbreakable has been punished and that PGP has irrevocably lost the confidence of users. Perhaps the opposite is true: Users and would-be users have had a crash course on the logical and procedural weaknesses of any encryption; as a result of that forced-upon new awareness, any encrypted communications will now be that much more secure.

Users of PGP 6.x for Windows and MacOS can easily test for the presence of ADKs in a certificate by right-clicking on the certificate and selecting "Key Properties." If the ADK tab is present, the key has one or more ADKs and might be a malicious certificate. There is no easy way of finding ADKs in the Unix command line version of PGP 5.x or 6.x.

To negate the ADK threat:

1. Never post a PGP public key anywhere. First of all, do a quick CRC or hash check on it (see Section 14.7), or simply digitally sign that public key. Then hand-carry it to the intended other user with whom one needs to exchange secure e-mail, or send it by secure

e-mail; in the latter case, the recipient should do a quick CRC (or hash or PGP-digital-signature) check of the received public key and compare the result with you through some independent means whereby you and he or she can ensure that you are talking with the right "other person."

2. Never store a PGP public key (let alone the PGP private key) on a computer that either goes on-line or can be accessed by others. Store it in a floppy disk in a secure place.

3. For particularly sensitive communications, create a PGP key pair for that occasion only. Destroy it afterward.

4. If at all possible, do not use any of the Windows-based PGP versions. Instead, use the DOS versions (2.3a up through 2.6.x) available from the Internet worldwide. If you really want to use the Windows-based versions, consider applying a "repair" tool from http://www.pgp.com/other/advisories/adk.asp.[4]

14.3.9 PGP Weaknesses

Other PGP weaknesses refer to the fact that it does not protect one from making unsound decisions, for example:

- A user can select an easily guessable password.

- A user can leave copies of unencrypted text in the hard disk.

- A user may not elect to independently verify that the public key he or she is using does, indeed, belong to the person to whom it purports to belong.

- A user may elect to use a very short-length public key.

- Pass phrase entry is susceptible to keystroke capture (see Sections 6.3–6.7).

- A user may forget to encrypt, and end up saving or sending unencrypted text.

---

4. The technical subtlety that the PGPrepair1.0 fixes is this: ADKs added to PGP keys in some versions can escape detection because they are appended after one "digitally signs" his or her public key, thereby eluding detection because the digital signature still validates the public key despite its having been doctored. An ADK should never sit outside the hashed part of the self-signature of the sender.

- PGP does not ensure that all cache is encrypted; the user must do that.
- PGP does not ensure wiping of buffers; the user must do that.

14.3.10 Beware of PGP Version 7

There have been unconfirmed allegations that PGP version 7 communicates with outside Internet addresses. This can be blocked with one's firewall.
PGP version 7 is not recommended for other reasons as well, namely:

- It is a security "suite" and not merely an encryption program. As such, its source code is huge and highly unlikely to be subjected to the intense scrutiny to which earlier versions (such as 2.3–2.6.3) have been subjected.
- It is a commercial product by a commercial vendor. It is quite possible that, in the interest of having a single core code serve corporate customers, too, that the ADK feature may still be there.
- It is much slower than all earlier versions.
- The source code has not been released by NAI. Because of this, it cannot be independently verified that it has no security flaws. Avoid *any* encryption software that does not release the source code as well.
- The PGP folder now is in "My Documents."
- One is not able to open and close PGPtray.
- The key ring files are locked, and one is not able to copy them.
- It uses way too much memory.
- It generates error messages on boot if one hides the key rings.
- Direct CD is incompatible with PGPdisk *if* one writes to the CD.
- Even though it is supposed to be a security product, it has the temerity to "call home" unannounced on a regular basis.
- If a user elects (as one should) to keep the key ring files on a floppy disk, PGP7 copies them over to the hard disk; this is unacceptable.
- Its "personal firewall" option is too rigid to be useful. Typically, if one opts for a nondefault filter-set, the rule details cannot be examined nor can new rules be added or deleted. Also, when an attack does occur, one cannot see the details of just exactly what data was received and on what port.

On the positive side, PGP 7.x versions have the desirable option of autosecure-wiping upon deletion.

At the expense of being repetitious, it is emphasized yet once more that the mere use of encryption software programs without an understanding of the multitude of ways that a third party can work around them gives a novice a false sense of security that is worse than not using any encryption at all.

14.3.11   Easy-to-Use E-Mail Encryption

It is a self-evident truism in any form of security, whether computer-related or not, that convenience and security pull in two opposite directions.

In the case of encryption software, if one does not want to be bothered with knowing a thing or two about what the threats are and how they are addressed (or not addressed) by a particular piece of software, one has to place one's entire faith on the maker of the software. Unlike freeware, with respect to which one can inspect the source code (or at least have the assurance of knowing that it has been inspected by competent and unbiased professionals), commercial software is usually "proprietary," which means that there is no independent review possible and one has to depend on the manufacturer to ensure that all possible "Gotchas" have been resolved.

It is in the above spirit that the following e-mail encryption software programs are discussed.

14.3.11.1   ZixMail

With ZixMail (http://www.zixmail.com/), both communicating parties have to have the software (which is freely obtainable) installed; encrypted e-mail to someone without ZixMail is also accommodated, but the recipient must access the ZixMail server, which, of course, will display it unencrypted.

A concern with ZixMail is that every time one encrypts something to a ZixMail recipient, the software calls home (to ZixMail) to get the recipient's public key. This makes it very vulnerable to man in the middle attacks; if ZixMail wanted to, and this is not to insinuate that it does, it could read everything one encrypts to a ZixMail recipient. This cannot be "fixed," because a fix would remove ZixMail's ability to control things.

ZixMail's source code is not open for independent review. In other words, you have to take the vendor's word for everything, and it is against the law to even try to find out if it really works. If you are new to the crypto subject, be sure to see http://www.interhack.net/people/cmcurtin/snake-oil-faq.html.

ZixMail's notion of sending "secure" mail to a person who does not have the ZixMail software is to post it as a password-protected Web page; the intended recipient can then retrieve it through an SSL-encrypted connection to the ZixMail Web site. Of course, ZixMail can also read that e-mail if it so elects.

While this author has no factual information about the specifics of any of these commercial proprietary systems, the fact that they are proprietary and not open to peer review raises the legitimate concern that they just might have "escrow keys" and "backdoors" associated with them, not to mention the possibility of security flaws in the implementation of the encryption. It is emphasized that these are mere concerns and not factual findings; these programs, and ones like them, may well be excellent; however, the fact that they cannot be subjected to peer-review scrutiny makes them inadvisable for any serious security considerations.

In summary, if one wants to use ZixMail, 1on1mail, or most any of the other similar programs that attempt to make encryption and security "easy," one would be well advised to preencrypt what is to be sent using one's own encryption software, and use these programs' encryption as the outer envelope only.

14.3.11.2   Zero Knowledge

One of the most promising commercial entities for enhancing privacy is Zero Knowledge Systems (http://www.freedom.net/). It is no better—and probably more insecure—than using mixmaster concatenated remailers in conjunction with Private Idaho, for example, but is considerably easier to set up for the average user.

There is lingering suspicion that, being a commercial entity and a reputable one at that, it would be vulnerable to a legal subpoena by a local court. That company's counterargument is that it cannot comply with any such court order because its setup is such that the company itself has no way of knowing who sends what to whom. To this effect, it has reportedly posted the source code of its software; this is no guarantee, however, as one has no way of knowing if the source code posted is all that is being used.

There is also some concern that it may be vulnerable to traffic analysis of its small number of servers. This concern has increased since May 2001, when Zero Knowledge reduced from three to two the number of remailers through which an e-mail can sequentially pass.

Caution: To preserve anonymity, Zero Knowledge software should not be traceable to the eventual user, meaning that it should not be purchased from its manufacturer by the intended buyer with a credit card, nor sent to the intended user's address.

14.4   Encrypting One's Own Files: ScramDisk

Any businessperson or responsible individual who wants to protect the privacy of digitized files from unscrupulous competitors, from overzealous prosecutors in totalitarian regimes, and from thieves of intellectual property, must contend with two classes of threats:

1. Theft of data while in transit (e-mail);
2. Theft of data while in storage in one's computer.

PGP, discussed in Section 14.3, being public-key-encryption–based, is primarily intended for e-mailing encrypted messages or attached files to another party. Of course, one can always encrypt to one's own public key and save the encrypted output locally; by so doing, however, one surrenders one major benefit of public-key encryption (when properly set up), which is that the sender is mathematically unable to decrypt a file that he or she has encrypted to an intended recipient's public key and, hence, cannot be forced to do so.

A number of encryption products are available, the intended purpose of which is to encrypt files for one's own use. The most common are:

- BestCrypt;
- E4M ("encryption for the masses");
- FlyCrypt;
- F-Secure FileCrypto (part of the F-Secure Workstation Suite);
- Invincible Disk with Data Lock;
- PGPDisk (the only part of PGP that is not recommended, due to "bugs"); while versions of PGP since 6.02 have ostensibly corrected the problem, this author has had continuing difficulties with PGPDisk in later versions as well);
- SAFE Folder;
- SafeHouse;
- S to Infinity;
- McAfee PC Crypto;

- ScramDisk.

BestCrypt seems to work well with Windows 95/98, NT, and 2000. Its configuration panel, shown in Figure 14.11, is quite intuitive and straightforward, and it has received good reviews from the "typically picky" users that post on the various Usenet forums related to computer security and privacy.

The best of these encryption products, which also happen to be free, is ScramDisk, assessed at length here. The interested reader is encouraged to see a comparison of most of these products in the article, "On-the-Fly Encryption: A Comparison," by S. Dean, at http://www.fortunecity.com/skyscraper/true/882/Comparison_OTFCrypto.htm.

ScramDisk is available worldwide (including from http://www. scramdisk.clara.net/) and is intended primarily for encrypting files for one's own use. As with most PGP versions, its source code has been made available for review and scrutiny. As of October 2000, it was available only for Windows 95/98 and not for NT or Windows 2000. It can use any one of a large number of established reputable encryption algorithms, and it is considered an excellent software product. Figure 14.12 depicts the ScramDisk user interface.

ScramDisk for Windows 2000 and Windows NT is available from its creator, Shaun Hollingworth, on a purchase-basis only, for $20. Interested parties can contact: FAO Paul Kirk, Krisalis, 47 Moorgate Street, Rotherham, s6o 2hD, United Kingdom.

Caution: To preserve anonymity, payment should be made by bank check (not personal check), postal money order, or cash. Obtaining the software anonymously can be done by using a throwaway free e-mail address obtained pseudonymously for just this occasion from a public PC, such as a

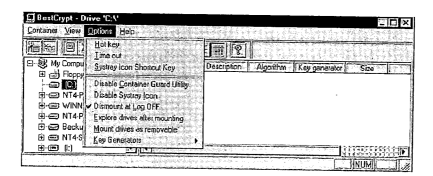

Figure 14.11   BestCrypt configuration panel. (Courtesy of Jetico, Inc.)

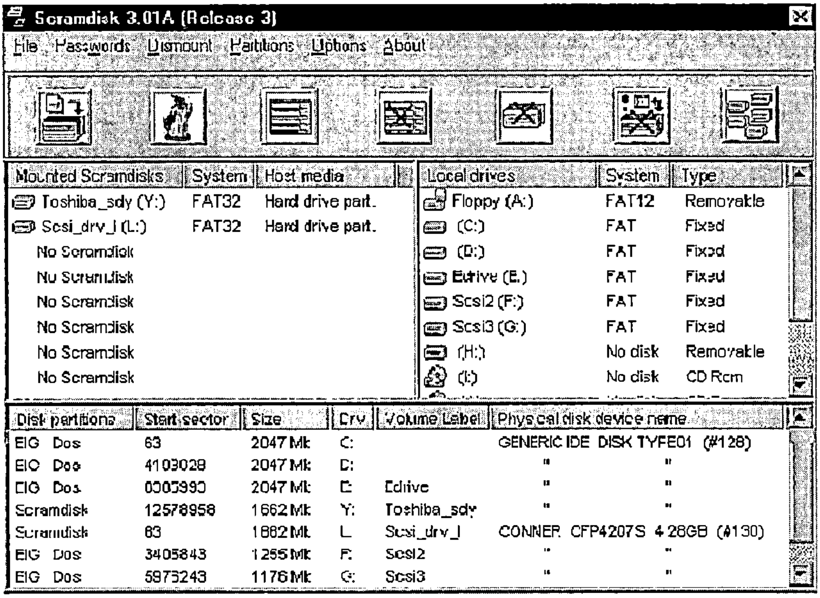

Figure 14.12 ScramDisk user interface for encrypted disk partitions. (Courtesy of Shaun Hollingworth.)

library or Internet café, and having the software sent to a friend's address (e-mail or physical), or asking the vendor to post it encrypted on a news server with a preagreed encryption key; in this case, the recipient should download a number of posted messages and not only the one of interest.

Caution: As with any encryption software, one should be very concerned that a "keystroke logger" can capture the pass phrase or encryption keys used, thereby rendering all such encryption useless in its intended purpose. One such program, KeyKey (see Chapter 6), was able to capture ScramDisk (version 2.02h) passwords entered even in the protected "red screen mode," presumably by operating at a sufficiently low level through the use of "vxd."

As its own Web site succinctly states,

Scramdisk is a program that allows the creation and use of virtual encrypted drives. Basically, you create a container file on an existing hard drive which is created with a specific password. This container can then be mounted by the Scramdisk software which creates a new drive letter to represent the drive. The virtual drive can then only be accessed with the correct passphrase. Without the correct passphrase the files on the virtual drive are totally inaccessible.

Once the passphrase has been entered correctly and the drive is mounted the new virtual drive can then be used as a normal drive, files can be saved and retrieved to the drive and you can even install applications onto the encrypted drive.

ScramDisk goes considerably beyond the conceptually simple task of encrypting one's files, by including the following functionalities intended to conceal the fact that it is being used.

1. It is computationally infeasible to prove that a large file held on a drive is a ScramDisk virtual disk container without knowing the pass phrase. The ScramDisk container files do not have to have a standard file extension and contain no file headers that indicate the file is anything but random data. *Caution:* While this is true, the registry of a computer on which ScramDisk has been installed has unmistakable evidence to that effect.

2. Unlike the Windows versions of PGP, some of which are about 8-MB long, the ScramDisk executable program is very small and can be carried on a three-and-a-half-inch floppy disk.

The following key points are of direct interest to any potential user of ScramDisk:

- Passwords are protected from ending up on the swap file.
- ScramDisk files cannot be identified as such. They look like random data. A user should have a plausible story as to what that random data is. One could, for example, create a digitized long file of, say, an old 33-rpm audio disk,[5] and seamlessly append the ScramDisk file to it. Regardless, one must have a believable reason as to why there is a large file of random data in one's hard disk.
- ScramDisk partitions are readily identifiable for what they are. Don't use them.
- To obscure the telltale evidence of ScramDisk, one should rename the device driver (SD.VXD) to something plausible, such as DRV45GX.DLL. Do likewise for the executable portion of

5. Not from a CD because of the identifiable high quality of the CD recordings.

ScramDisk. Also, make sure that there is no scramdisk.ini anywhere; this is created only if one alters the standard configuration of Scram-Disk, in which case that file, too, should be suitably renamed.

- ScramDisk volumes have the .SVL filename extension, but one can name them anything at all.

- Since ScramDisk counts the number of times that a volume has been mounted along with the time and date that this occurred (albeit in encrypted form), the user may well wish to prevent this by making the volume file a read-only file.

- Do not use the "fast shutdown" option in Windows 98 Second Edition. Disable this option if using Windows 98 Special Edition.

- Use the "red screen" option for password entry. It defeats some (but not all) keyboard sniffers openly available. This works only for the standard QWERTY keyboards and not others (such as Dvorka, French, German, or other).

- Use the latest version of ScramDisk. Older versions have a security weakness that allows one to reset the passwords of an encrypted volume to the original ones when the volume was created.

- *Do not* leave the computer on unattended after dismounting a ScramDisk volume.

- Consider availing yourself of the security benefits of a (free) companion utility called SecureTrayUtil from http://www.fortune-city.com/skyscraper/true/882/SecureTrayUtil.htm.

- If you use ScramDisk's steganography option, select the 4/16 bits option and not the 8/16 bits option.

14.5 Steganography

In our youth, most of us delighted by writing secret messages on a piece of paper with lemon juice as ink, then using our parents' iron for the really useful purpose of making the lemon ink become visible. What made it more fun was if the paper we used had a perfectly innocuous letter written on it to disguise the existence of the secret message.

For applications other than entertainment, the microdots of World War II fame are well known. In earlier years, leaders often wrote secret messages to distant recipients on a messenger's shaved head and then waited for that messenger's hair to grow before sending him on his way. Some popular printed images that, if stared at long enough from the right distance, suddenly reveal a previously invisible three-dimensional image, are yet another example of techniques for hiding information in plain view.

These techniques are collectively referred to as steganography, which is a means of hiding data.

Unlike encryption, which hides the content of a message and often does it in an alerting manner unless additional steps are taken, steganography hides the mere existence of something hidden. Computers are clearly well suited for implementing a broad collection of techniques having the same end purpose: to hide information in plain view. The type of techniques that can be used is limited only by one's imagination.

There is nothing inherently disreputable or subversive about steganography. It is just one example of a class of information technology techniques known as "data hiding," and there is even a very proper annual international professional conference on the subject. Also, it is the technical basis for digital watermarks, namely, hiding a digital watermark on a copyrighted image or in a sound file, and in a way that would not "wash out" if such files were tinkered with.

Openly available software programs, available worldwide, for implementing steganography tend to take advantage of three classes of techniques:

1. If one were to change the least significant bit of most digitized samples of a sound file, the ear certainly would not notice. One can therefore hide one bit of sensitive information for every digitized sample of sound. The resulting file would still sound the same and would be no bigger and no smaller than the file with which one started.

2. If one were to change the least significant bit of a digitized value that represents the brightness of a picture element ("pixel"), the eye would most likely not notice the change in brightness by 1 out of a typical 256 levels, let alone if it is by one of over 32,000 levels. Typical images use 256 levels of brightness and hence 8 bits/pixel for black and white or, in the case of color images, 8 bits for each of the three primary colors (red, green, and blue) for each pixel. It is simple arithmetic to show that one can hide a lot of data in a typical image of 1,024 by 768 pixels. The image in Figure 14.13 depicts the concept.

3. One can also hide data in normally nonaccessed portions of a computer disk (floppy or hard disk). Such portions include the

Figure 14.13 One steganography concept: data hidden in an overt image.

free space (which usually includes so-called deleted files), the slack (the space between the end of a file and the end of a cluster), and normally unused tracks on a disk. This point is worth explaining: A computer disk is divided into clusters, which are like bins where information is placed. Their size depends on the operating system and on the disk file system used and ranges typically from 512 bytes (a collection of 8 bits of data) to over 32,000 bytes. When a file is saved onto a disk and it uses a portion of such a cluster (possibly in addition to an integral number of other clusters), the remaining space between the "end of file" and "end of cluster" is commonly referred to as slack; it is not normally accessed by the computer because DOS and Windows operating systems do not save more than a single file (or portion thereof) per cluster. Even though it is not normally accessed, that space is nonetheless readily accessible with special software; as such, it is comparable to placing the key to the front door under the doormat.

While the concept of steganography sounds very appealing on the surface, it is not the panacea it may appear to be. This is so for two basic reasons:

1. Having on one's computer—or, worse yet, sending via the Internet—many innocuous images or sound files can be quite alerting unless one's normal daily activities are such that warrant this content and conduct (e.g., being a musician or a painter or a professional photographer). If such files are coupled with the existence of steganography-related software in one's computer, then the files are alerting despite one's conduct.

2. While images and sound files used to hide steganographically hidden files may look natural to the eye and sound natural to the ear, they are not necessarily undetectable by special mathematical implementations of techniques devised to home in on the weaknesses of most. This is discussed in more detail below.

The most commonly used steganography software tools, which are available worldwide, are:

-   **Hide and Seek** by Colin Maroney;
-   **Steganos** (shareware) by DEMCOM (initially authored by Fabian Hansmann), the interface for which is depicted below;
-   **StegoDos** by an anonymous author;
-   **White Noise Storm** by Ray Arachelian;
-   **S-Tools for Windows** by Andy Brown;
-   **Jpeg-Jsteg**;
-   **Stealth** by Henry Hastur;
-   **SFS (Steganographic File System)** for Unix computers, by R. Aderson et al.

The encryption software ScramDisk (see Section 14.4) also includes the option of hiding a file with steganography.

Each of these software packages has its own strengths and weaknesses; it is not the purpose of this book to do a comparative evaluation. For such an assessment, the reader is referred to numerous publications on this topic by Neil F. Johnson of the Center for Secure Information Systems at George Mason University.

Numerous commercial steganography packages, such as Invisible Systems Pro by East Technologies (http://www.east-tec.com/ispro/index.html), are now entering the marketplace. *Caution:* Practically all of the commercially and openly available steganography tools are not safe against steganalysis (the science of determining if an innocent-looking file contains steganographically hidden information). See Section 14.5.2.

14.5.1   Practical Considerations

The extent of the detectability of a file that contains steganographically hidden information is, amusingly, somewhat proportional to the popularity of the software package. The more extensive its usage, the more resources are devoted into detecting its footprint. Steganography is treated by law enforcement like a virus: Once it hits the market in a significant manner, tools are developed to detect it.

Conversely, if a new method were to be devised privately and used sparingly, chances are that its existence would never become alerting enough to be subjected to scrutiny which could lead to techniques for its detection. As an example, a recent telemedicine-related article discusses hiding a sensitive file in the images of echocardiograms. With a little imagination, one can conceive of steganographic techniques having nothing to do with either image or sound files. As another example, the reader is referred to an interesting paper, "Covert Channels in the TCP/IP Protocol Suite" (http://www.watermarkingworld .org/WMMLArchive/0011/msg00015.html) by Craig H. Rowland of Psionic Company, which discusses hiding information in TCP/IP packet headers.

From the perspective of the traveling businessperson who would rather not alert a prospective data thief to the existence of valuable information in his or her computer, the steganographic strength of the software being used is far less important than maintaining a low profile and not attracting attention to oneself. This applies even more if one uses steganography in e-mail from countries with knowingly repressive regimes. While it would be plausible for one to explain sending "a couple of digitized photos of the local scenery" to the family at home, sending the exact same photograph every day at 7 P.M. would raise suspicions even in the mind of the least unimaginative interceptor.

14.5.2   Detecting Steganography: Steganalysis

Users of some amateurish steganography software, satisfied by their own inability to detect the existence of hidden information, assume that nobody else can do so either. The result of this dangerous self-deception is that law enforcement can reap the benefits of information that would never have been entrusted to a particular steganography software program if its users knew just how alerting it was.

Whether the existence of a steganographically hidden file is visible to the eye or perceptible by the ear should never be the criterion of steganographic strength. Instead, the sole criterion should be whether or not mathematical tools can be deployed on a file to determine if it includes steganographically hidden data.

Steganalysis is a potent tool for law enforcement that is only now beginning to find its way, slowly, into the toolbox of computer forensics experts. Interestingly, the identical same tools can be used to identify the existence of perfectly legitimate "digital watermarks" that are placed on copyrighted material by their owners to identify illegally proliferating copies. This is rapidly becoming "big business" in music, photography, and literary prose as more and more of such copyrighted content is traded openly over the Internet.[6]

Since there is no single steganography scheme, there is no single steganalysis scheme. Some steganographic schemes can be readily detected, while others cannot. Due to the nature of steganography, this will be remain the state of affairs: New steganographic software programs will continue to be developed, and as soon as they become popular enough to pique the interest of law enforcement, steganalysis software will follow, and the cycle will be repeated.

Steganography is viewed as a serious threat by some governments, as evidenced by the fact that one sees on the Internet mention that even the U.S. Air Force's Research Laboratory has subcontracted with Binghamton University's Center for Intelligent Systems and WetStone Technologies, Inc. to "develop algorithms techniques for detecting steganography in computers and electronic transmissions, as in digital imagery files, audio files, and text messages." According to the Air Force Research Lab site, "The goal is to develop a set of statistical tests capable of detecting secret messages in computer files and electronic transmissions, as well as attempting to identify the underlying steganographic method. An important part of the research is the development of blind steganography detection methods for algorithms."

---

6. The reader is reminded of the ongoing legal and ethical battles involving Napster, Gnutella, and the publication of the De-CSS algorithm [i.e., the algorithm for decrypting the Content Scrambling System used by the major studios in digital video disks (DVDs)].

14.5.3   How Steganography Can Be Detectable

Clearly, if the original unmodified file (image or sound) used as a "cover" by the steganography software is available to an investigator, then all one has to do is a bit-by-bit comparison with the suspect version in order for the existence of steganography to become apparent. It is for this reason that one should never use commonly available digital files (such as sound files from CDs, or classical images from the Internet), because the difference would stand out right away.

Independently from the above, most of the steganography software available on the Internet modifies the least significant bit of a color image, often an 8-bit color image. To understand the problems caused by this simplistic scheme, one must first understand the notion of "palettes"—the list of allowable colors; changing the least significant bit in 8-bit images often results in a color that is not in the original palette. Using 24-bit images allows one to get around this problem somewhat, but at the cost of dealing with an image that takes much more space on the disk and hence much more time to send.

Numerous least significant bit–based steganography tools have been shown to be detectable in an excellent paper by Neil F. Johnson, "Steganalysis of Images Created Using Current Steganography Software," available at http://debut.cis.nctu.edu.tw/~yklee/Research/Steganography/Sushil_Jajodia/IHW98.html.

Shortly after the United Kingdom passed the RIP law, which empowers authorities to demand that one surrender the decryption key to a file, numerous countermeasures appeared on assorted Usenet forums about ways to defeat the spirit of that law. One such message, for example, urged readers to fill their hard disks with digital noise so as to inundate the British authorities with "suspicious" files that, in fact, contained nothing at all.

Another message proposed the scheme whereby one would have two one-time pad keys for the same encrypted message: One key (which would be surrendered to the authorities upon demand) would decrypt the suspect file into something totally benign, such as a passage from the Bible; the other key (the existence of which would never be disclosed) would decrypt the exact same suspect file into the true hidden content. Since a one-time pad is really a simple one-to-one transformation, then

$$\text{Ciphertext} = \text{One-Time Pad Key1} + \text{True Sensitive Message} \qquad (14.1)$$

$$\text{Ciphertext} = \text{One-Time Pad Key2} + \text{Passage from the Bible} \qquad (14.2)$$

Hence:

$$\text{One-Time Pad Key2} = \text{Ciphertext} - \text{Passage from the Bible} \qquad (14.3)$$

As soon as one creates the ciphertext from (14.1), one uses (14.3) to create the bogus one-time pad to be surrendered upon demand while keeping silent about the existence of Key1.

14.5.4   Recommendations for Maintaining Privacy Through Steganography

Here are a few recommendations on how to maintain privacy through steganography:

1. *Do not* use the software commonly available over the Internet.

2. Read the paper on steganalysis by Neil Johnson mentioned in Section 14.5.3, which details the weaknesses of specific popular steganography software.

3. Realizing that some regimes take extreme exception to anyone hiding things from the eyes of the state, ensure that you have a very good explanation for the presence and/or transmittal of whichever files you use to hide others through steganography.

4. Have a good explanation with respect to why your hard disk contains steganography software. Remember that even if you "remove" such programs (with the Software Add/Remove feature of Windows), they usually leave traces behind in the registry; it goes without saying that the removed files must be wiped, as per Chapter 9).

14.6   Password Cracking

Passwords are used to "protect":

1. Documents created with popular commercial software (e.g., Microsoft Word and WordPerfect).

2. Public encryption keys (such as in PGP). Since the keys in public-key encryption are much longer than in conventional encryption (see Chapter 13) and one cannot remember the long public key, which is a very long sequence of random symbols, such "keys" are "activated by" entering a smaller password. Clearly it is far easier for one to try to crack a shorter sequence of symbols (the password) than the much longer sequence (the key).

3. The document itself, encrypted with conventional encryption. Conventional encryption, such as IDEA, typically uses 128 bits (128:8 = 16 alphanumeric symbols); one can try to remember it if it is a sequence that can be remembered. A 128-bit password, if (and only if) it is a truly random sequence of 128 bits (ones and zeroes), cannot be found through exhaustive search; the number of possibilities is simply too many ($2^{128} = 3.4 \times 10^{38}$; i.e., 34 followed by 37 zeros); even if a computer tries a billion different keys every second, it will take 1.08×10^{28} years to go through all the keys; by comparison, the life left in the Sun is a mere 10^9 years.

However, if one unwisely selects those 128 bits to be a word like "I hate passwords" (which is about 128 bits long), then an adversary would not find it too difficult to break it using openly available "dictionary search" software and a cheap personal computer. In password selection, as with anything else, technical knowledge is no substitute for common sense.

14.6.1 For the Law Enforcement Professional

Numerous password-cracking software programs that basically do exhaustive searches of dictionary words are available through the Internet. Additionally, companies such as Access Data Corporation in Utah (http://www.access-data.com/) sell software that break the password protection of such popular software as PKZip, WinZip, Word, Excel, WordPerfect, Lotus1-2-3, Paradox, Q&A, Quattro-Pro, Ami Pro, Approach, QuickBooks, Act!, Pro Write, Access, Word Pro, DataPerfect, dBase, Symphony, Outlook, Express, MSMoney, Quicken, Scheduler+, Ascend, Netware, and Windows NT server/ workstation.

Most people tend to use passwords that they can easily remember, such as permutations of family member names, birth dates, and so on, often abbreviated or spelled backward.

The following password-cracking software tools are openly available on the Internet:

wordcrk.zip (attacks passwords of Microsoft Word documents);

c2myazz.zip (spoofs Windows NT passwords);

pwdump.zip (dumps the hash function values from NT .sam files);

Pwdump.zip (obtains password information from the .sam file);

Samdump.zip (same);

Pwlcrack.zip (obtains password information from memory);

Pwltool.zip (attacks .pwl files);

95sscrk.zip (attacks WindowsNT passwords);

Winpass (breaks windows screensaver passwords);

Wfwcd (attacks passwords used in Microsoft Word);

Wpcracka (same, for WordPerfect files);

sharepw.c (attacks Windows 95 share passwords);

sharepwbin.c and **.exe** (attacks Windows 95 share passwords);

Glide (decrypts .pwl files);

Crackerjack (cracks Unix passwords in PCs).

At the time of this writing, all of the above were downloadable from http://www.cotse.com/winnt.htm.

Openly available on the Internet is the following list of backdoor CMOS BIOS passwords:

AWARD BIOS

Award

AWARD_SW

SW_AWARD

AWARD?SW

LKWPETER

lkwpeter

j262

j256

AMI BIOS

AM

AMI

A.M.I.

AMI_SW

AMI?SW

OTHER BIOS

Syxz

oder

Wodj

bios

cmos

alfaromeo

14.6.2   Recommendations for the Security-Conscious Professional

It follows from the foregoing that one should choose a password that is both easy to remember and long enough to be at least as hard to break through known means as a 128-bit truly random sequence of bits. If one goes through a little arithmetic, this amounts to 107 truly random alphabetical letters, if no distinction is made between upper and lower case. That is not easy to remember either. And this is precisely why passwords that can be remembered are breakable and encryption keys (if truly random) are not.

Clearly, the more random the password, the better. But the more random the password, the harder it is to remember.

Do not:

- Use phrases from poems or stories;
- Depend on the password protection of commercial software such as MS Word, WordPerfect, and so on—use full-blown encryption instead;
- Use phrases from common foreign languages;
- Use words, names, or dates that are related to your family and that others could figure out with minimal effort;
- Use the same password for more than one piece of software;
- Use the same password for a long period of time (beware of key-stroke capture, as per Sections 6.3–6.7);
- Write the password or pass phrase on anything.

Do:

- Select a pass phrase that includes upper- and lower-case letters in unexpected places, and punctuation marks, and numbers.
- Select a pass phrase that cannot be remembered, yet which you can reconstruct. For example, the tenth word of the eleventh page of the first 22 books on your bookshelf, in the precise order that the books

are arranged. If an assertive intruder ransacks the books, the password is gone forever—(or you can claim that it is).

- Abide by the security precautions listed in Chapters 9 through 12 to preclude the possibility that your prized pass phrase may have been captured on your hard disk (swap or slack or keystroke-capturing software).

The interested reader is referred to an excellent paper on the subject, "The Passphrase FAQ," at http://www.stack.nl/~galactus/remailers/passphrase-faq.html.

14.7 Ensuring the Authenticity of Digital Files: CRC and Hash Functions

Given the ease with which it is possible to alter any digital document, there is an obvious need for ways to detect such alterations in such situations as:

1. *E-mail text.* There is all the difference in the world between a message to one's stockbroker that directs him or her to "Buy 10 shares of stock" and one that says "Buy 10,000 shares of stock."

2. *Encryption software.* One would clearly like to know if the encryption software that is being trusted with sensitive information has been "doctored" since the time when it was known to be "good."

Simply running a "checksum" that detects whether the number of "ones" is even or odd is not good enough.

A mathematically more elaborate version of a checksum is cyclic redundancy check (CRC). A mathematical operation is performed on the entire digital file of interest and a digital summary is generated in the form of a sequence of a few numbers. An additional advantage of CRC over a checksum is that it is "order sensitive," meaning that the strings "ABCD" and "DBCA" will produce totally different digital summaries. The odds that two different digital files can be created that will have the same CRC digital signature are about 1 in 4 billion.

Indeed, CRC is exactly the technique used by most hard disk drives to check on the integrity of every sector (a sector has 512 bytes). The CRC value is computed (and stored along with the data) when the data is stored in that sector, and it is recomputed again when the data is read from that sector; if the two CRC values differ, it means that there has been a disk read/write error.

One can readily obtain CRC.COM through a vast number of servers from the Internet. It is in the public domain and free.

Caution: Early versions of CRC had flaws.

Given the odds that CRC can be spoofed (1 in 4 billion is not all that small a probability when it comes to security), an even more robust mathematical algorithm has been replacing it: the MD5 hash; "hashing" refers to the process of obtaining a digital digest or summary from a digital file. MD5 is an upgrade from MD4, which has been reported in the open literature to be broken [7].

The MD5 hash has 16 symbols (bytes) and is therefore $16 \times 8 = 128$ bits. It was originally developed by RSA and it is in the public domain now. The odds that two files can be concocted that have the same MD5 hash digital signature are about one in 10^{38} (i.e., one in 10 followed by 37 zeros).

Software programs for computing the MD5 hash of a file are also available from multiple sources on the Internet by doing a keyword search for MD5. The reader is strongly encouraged to download and use such software to verify the integrity of key files (such as encryption-related ones). It is a simple process and it is well worth the minimal effort to do it. The savvy user should first determine the MD5 (or CRC) value of each and every sensitive file of interest, label and store those digital digests in some safe place other than the computer in which the files themselves reside, and periodically recheck by recomputing the MD5 or CRC values of the same sensitive files and comparing.

A better algorithm, yet for digital message digests, is SHA-1. Its output is 160 bits, and has withstood the scrutiny of competent specialists. It is offered in both PGP and S/MIME (see Sections 14.3 and 12.7.1, respectively), but it is roughly twice as slow as MD5 to compute, all else being equal.

14.8   Emergencies

14.8.1   Protecting Sensitive Data from a Repressive Regime

Obviously, in an emergency, there is seldom time to wipe magnetic data from disks and tapes; the only viable safe practice is not to write sensitive data on magnetic media in the first place. There are two alternatives, which are not mutually exclusive:

1. All keyboard input should go to RAM and not to magnetic media. This means:

a. Have enough physical RAM in the computer so that the swap file (virtual memory) can be disabled altogether, as per Chapter 4.

b. Direct all temporary files to be in a RAM disk (Chapter 9). If using software that sets its own location for temporary files, consider using some other software. For example, instead of using Microsoft Word, use Secure Office, discussed earlier in this book. Ideally, do not use Windows at all; use MS DOS instead and a RAM disk.

c. Since file names often get stored in locations other than—and in addition to—those associated with the files themselves, do not use file names that are descriptive of the content.

2. If sensitive data must be stored in magnetic media, it must be encrypted automatically "on the fly" and not as a separate step that one would have to do manually. This means:

a. Using full-disk encryption software (see Section 14.2). This way, anything written to disk is encrypted, specifically including the swap file, the registry, and the slack (see Chapter 4).

b. As an alternative, using MS DOS and a simple test editor with no "smarts" (i.e., no temporary files and no activities running without a user's knowledge), rather than any version of Windows, working with a RAM disk on the sensitive files, and encrypting all things that are to be saved. In the worst case, you can turn the computer off and anything not encrypted will disappear.

14.8.2 A Word of Caution

The following point has already been made and cannot be overemphasized. Resources in even the most repressive regime are limited; everyone cannot be physically surveilled all the time.[7] It follows that one should not attract attention to oneself by engaging in such readily observable alerting activities as routine use of encrypted e-mail, exchanging inflammatory e-mail with others on topics that the local regime considers threatening, posting of inappropriate messages in Usenet forums, frequenting Web sites and forums that a local regime finds offensive, and the like.

---

7. However, technology today makes it eminently possible for some regimes to surveil the Internet and other telecommunications activities of everyone all the time (through automated procedures that scan for preprogrammed "suspect activities" or words).

If you travel to repressive regimes, avoid bringing your own computer for use with respect to anything that could land you in a local jail. For your communications needs, consider patronizing other's computers, such as public libraries or Internet cafés (to see if one is available in your area, check http://www.cyber-café.com/icafesearch.asp), and carry your encryption software in an encrypted floppy disk.

14.8.3   Getting "Discovered" as a Desirable Persona

Realistically, no one personifies pure virtue. Because of this, it behooves one to have some carefully crafted "secret" that can be reluctantly surrendered to overzealous computer forensics investigators so that they do not go away empty handed, and mostly so that they can feel satisfied that they have done their job and not pursue a forensics investigation further. Such a surrenderable secret must be one that is believable and mildly embarrassing, but not one of the kind that would land one in jail. There is an even greater importance to having such a sacrificial lamb: It helps explain the reason for having encryption software in the first place.

And what if you live in a totalitarian regime and find strong evidence that your computer has been compromised? Obviously, there can be no "one-size-fits-all" advice, since the prudent course of action would depend entirely on the specific circumstances. You would be well advised, however, to view this as the opportunity that it is, and not as a cause for alarm. It is an opportunity because you have been provided with a direct pipeline to the regime, and you can use this pipeline to ensure that the image you present to the regime—or whoever is monitoring you on its behalf—is precisely the one that *you* want to present, and not the one that the totalitarian regime might suspect; not too many "suspects" have this opportunity!

So, do *not* disable whatever mechanism you have discovered that is monitoring your computer habits. Leave it alone, and let it monitor and inform on that side of your life that you want to advertise. Clean all of your magnetic media of anything remotely incriminating. This may also be a good time to plan a politically correct and graceful exit to another country.

14.9   Computer Biometrics: A False Sense of Security

One already can buy small fingerprint-readers that connect to a computer's serial, parallel, PCMCIA, or USB ports; some are already integrated into laptops, mouse devices, and keyboards. An example of such a device, this one by Ethentica Inc. (http://www.ethentica.com), is depicted in Figure 14.14.

Some competing products use voice recognition, and some upscale ones intended for commercial and government applications use iris recognition, palm-print recognition, or face recognition. The short answer is that, if used to replace passwords for access to one's computer, these techniques, known as biometrics, provide absolutely no security protection from hostile computer forensics. This is so because computer forensics analysis never bothers with log-in to one's computer or disk in the first place; instead, it makes a magnetic copy of the magnetic media being investigated, and then analyzes the data on a track-by-track and sector-by-sector basis.

Biometrics used as a substitute for (or augmentation of) conventional manually typed password entry into a standalone computer is only an issue of convenience for the user and not security. About the only security enhancement afforded would be from keyboard-capturing software or hardware (see Sections 6.3 and 6.4), which would have captured a manually entered password, but such tools are almost never used in computer forensics.

14.9.1   State-of-the-Art Identification

14.9.1.1   Fingerprint-Based Systems

Fingerprint-based systems for computers are already available for around $100 or $200. They are quite dependable. They do not look for the loops

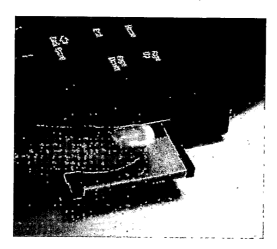

Figure 14.14   Semi-integrated fingerprint reading by Ethentica Inc. (Courtesy of Ethentica Inc.)

and twirls of fingerprints that were used in years past as the basis for finger-print classification; instead, they look for the "minutiae," which are the *relative locations* of two things only: bifurcations (where one ridge becomes two in a Y fashion) and ridge endings. These relative locations of the 10–50 such minutiae can be abstracted into a very short file of 100–800 bytes (i.e., equivalent alphabetical symbols, which correspond to eight times that much in bits); these abstracted bytes are, typically, stored in an encrypted manner in the computer, and are checked against a fingerprint whenever that finger-print is presented for access. A typical implementation, by Anadac Corporation (http://www.anadac.com/), is intended for high-volume usage.

14.9.1.2 Iris-Based Systems

The science behind iris recognition is that the pattern of a human iris (the circular area between the center black opening of the eye and the white of the eye) is different for every human being, and does not change from the time one is about a year old. This technology requires a simple passive imaging of the eye and is entirely different from the technology that shines a light into the eyeball and looks for the pattern of cells and veins inside the eye. Two examples, marketed by IriScan Inc. (http://www.iriscan.com/), are shown in Figures 14.15 and 14.16.

Commercial products for this technology are bulkier and more expensive, and are therefore mostly intended to control access to buildings and rooms rather than to computers.

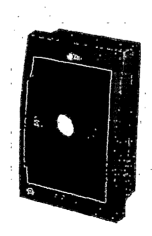

Figure 14.15 Iris-matching biometric system by IriScan Inc. (Courtesy of Iridian Technologies Inc.)

Figure 14.16 Table-mounted iris-matching system by IriScan Inc. (Courtesy of Iridian Technologies Inc.)

14.9.1.3 Face-Recognition Systems

These systems abstract key measurements of one's face (e.g., precise distance between pupils and length and relative position of nose and mouth). For authentication purposes with willing participants, they are useful in the mode of supplementing other authentication means, such as personal identification numbers or passwords; the technology is not mature enough whereby face-recognition systems can be depended on as the sole means of authentication.

With unwilling participants, face-recognition schemes can be easily defeated with face-distorting grimaces, extensive makeup, dark glasses, adding or removing mustaches, and so on.

14.9.1.4 Voice-Recognition Systems

Voice-recognition schemes suffer from the obvious shortcomings of:

- Voice changes (intentional, or unintentional due to laryngitis or head colds);
- Distortion introduced by different channels (e.g., the difficulty of comparing direct voice with that heard through a telephone);
- Individual enunciation of words.

The degree of effectiveness of voice-recognition systems depends entirely on the degree of sophistication of the algorithms (the "mathematical recipe") used in making a determination as to whether two voice samples came from the same person or not.

14.9.1.5 DNA

The ultimate biometric is, of course, DNA. The process required to analyze it, however, is very equipment-intensive and requires machinery, expertise, and time that make it impractical for any short-term authentication application.

Individuals "shed" DNA cells all the time while going about normal life. Because of this, collection is quite simple in principle; in practice, of course, one has to make sure that the right person's DNA is being collected; hence the use of tightly controlled collection processes.

References

[1]   See the excellent write-up by S. Simpson, "PGP DH vs. RSA FAQ" at http://www.scramdisk.clara.net/pgpfaq.html.

[2]   Tsiounis, Y., and M. Yung, "On the Security of El Gamal-Based Encryption," *PKC '98*, LNCS. Springer-Verlag, 1998, http://citeseer.nj.nec.com/tsiounis98security.html.

[3]   Menezes, A. J., P. C. van Oorschot, and S. A. Vanstone, *Handbook of Applied Cryptography,* Boca Raton, FL: CRC Press, 1997.

[4]   Schlafly, R., "Re: El Gamal vs. RSA," sci.crypt USENET posting, March 11, 1999.

[5]   Young, A., and M. Yung, "The Dark Side of 'Black-Box' Cryptography or Should We Trust Capstone?" *Crypto '96*, 1996.

[6]   Senderek, R., "Key Experiments: How PGP Deals with Manipulated Keys, An Experimental Approach," August 2000, http://senderek.de/security/key-experiments.html.

[7]   RSA FAQ v4, 1998. Available at http://www.rsa.com/.

Selected Bibliography on Steganography

Anderson, R., (ed.), "Information Hiding: First International Workshop," Cambridge, U.K., *Lecture Notes in Computer Science,* Vol. 1174, New York: Springer-Verlag, 1996.

Anderson, R., and F. Petitcolas, "On the Limits of Steganography," *IEEE Journal on Selected Areas in Communications,* Vol. 16, No. 4, May 1998, pp. 474–481.

Aura, T., *Invisible Communication,* EET 1995, Technical Report, Helsinki University of Technology, Finland, November 1995, http://deadlock.hut.fi/ste/ste_html.html.

Bender, W., et al., "Techniques for Data Hiding," *IBM Systems Journal,* Vol. 35, Nos. 3 and 4, MIT Media Lab, 1996, pp. 313–336.

Johnson, N. F., and S. Jajodia, "Exploring Steganography: Seeing the Unseen," *IEEE Computer,* Vol. 3, February 1998, pp. 26–34.

Petitcolas, F., R. Anderson, and M. Kuhn, "Attacks on Copyright Marking Systems," *Second Workshop on Information Hiding,* Portland, OR, April 1998.

Selected Bibliography on Steganalysis

Kuhn, M., "Watermark and Steganography Analysis Tools," 1997, http://www.cl.cam.ac.uk/~fapp2/watermarking/image_watermarking/stirmark.

Sanders, D., "Stegodetect," steganography detection software tool, 1997.

"unZign," watermarking testing tool. (See http://altern.org/watermark/.) Information available through unzign@hotmail.com, 1997.

Selected Bibliography on Steganography Software

Arachelian, R., White Noise Storm&trade (WNS), shareware, 1994, ftp://ftp.csua.berkeley.edu/pub/cypherpunks/steganography/wns210.zip.

"Black Wolf": StegoDos, Black Wolf's Picture Encoder v0.90B, in the public domain; ftp://ftp.csua.berkeley.edu/pub/cypherpunks/steganography/stegodos.zip.

Brown, A., S-Tools for Windows, shareware, 1994, ftp://idea.sec.dsi.unimi.it/pub/security/crypt/code/s-tools4.zip.

Digimarc Corporation, PictureMarc&trade, MarcSpider&trade, http://www.digimarc.com/.

Hansmann, F., Steganos, Deus Ex Machina Communications, http://www.steganography.com/.

Hastur, H., Mandelsteg, ftp://idea.sec.dsi.unimi.it/pub/security/crypt/code/.

Kutter, M., and F. Jordan, JK-PGS (Pretty Good Signature), Signal Processing Laboratory at Swiss Federal Institute of Technology (EPFL), http://ltswww.epfl.ch/~kutter/watermarking/JK_PGS.html.

Machado, R., EzStego, Stego Online, Stego, http://www.stego.com/.

Maroney, C., Hide and Seek, shareware, ftp://ftp.csua.berkeley.edu/pub/cypherpunks/steganography/hdsk41b.zip (version 4.1), http://www.rugeley.demon.co.uk/security/hdsk50.zip (version 5.0), http://www.cypher.net/products/ (version 1.0 for Windows 95).

MediaSec Technologies LLC, SysCop&trade, http://www.mediasec.com/.

Repp, H., Hide4PGP, http://www.rugeley.demon.co.uk/security/hide4pgp.zip.

Signum Technologies, SureSign, http://www.signumtech.com/.

Upham, D., Jpeg-Jsteg, ftp://ftp.funet.fi/pub/crypt/steganography.

Selected Bibliography on Passwords

Reinhold, A., "Diceware: (A Passphrase Generation System)," http://world.std.com/~reinhold/diceware.html.

RFC1750 Randomness Recommendations for Security, http://www.clark.net/pub/cme/html/ranno.html.

Schneier, B., *Applied Cryptography,* New York: Wiley, 1994.

Ward, G., "Creating Passphrases from Shocking Nonsense," www.cert.lu/cert-web/security/bibliography.html.

Williams, R. T., "A Simple Random Noise Source," July 1, 1995, posted to sci.crypt and alt.security.pgp at http://www.finerty.net/pjf/crypto/passphrase.txt.

Part III
Legal and Other Issues

15

Legal Issues

Disclaimer: Laws obviously vary widely from one country to another, and even within one country from one day to another. Nothing in this section should be construed as legal advice. The reader needing legal advice should consult a local attorney who is specifically knowledgeable about the legal issues surrounding electronic evidence.

15.1 Why Electronic Evidence Is Better Than Paper Evidence

Electronic evidence is superior to paper evidence for the following reasons:

- It is far easier to search and catalog. For example, one can use software such as MIMEsweeeper by Content Technologies, Inc. (http://www.mimesweeper.com/) to scan all corporate e-mail for evidence. Once the desired data has been collected, it is much less labor-intensive to prepare it for presentation in a court than is paper evidence.

- Documents are individually stamped with the date and time of creation or last modification. In some cases one can even see the entire sequence of modifications.

- It may well be that there is no paper evidence for the particular instance requiring verification. Many "documents" exist only in electronic form today.

- E-mail tends to be casual and includes gossip, conspiracies, and so on. It is also permanent.

- Whereas it is often hard to identify the author of a typed paper document, it is almost always possible to identify the author of a document entered on a computer.

- Some information that exists in the electronic version of a document may not show up on the printed version. Examples include author's name, date it was last updated, the actual formulas used in the computation of entries in a spreadsheet, and annotations (which can take the form of Post-It notes on paper documents, which are easily removed or lost).

It follows that even a staunch traditionalist lawyer would be well advised to opt for an electronic record rather than a printout of what is ostensibly that same record.

At the same time, both prosecutors and defense attorneys and especially judges must realize that electronic records can easily be altered; if the person doing the altering is an expert, such alteration will never be discovered; if it is done by an amateur, it will add to his or her woes.

Electronic evidence does not reside only in personal computers. It also resides in personal electronic organizers such as the increasingly popular Palm line of devices, Internet service providers' records and archives, corporate and other organizational databases, and, in those cases when organizations have elected to outsource their data storage, with third parties.

Additionally, given the increasing popularity of IP telephony (i.e., telephone conversations handled through one's computer), and of digital telephone-answering machines (implemented as part of one's PC, or more often as a standalone device) and of digital fax-storage-and-forward machines, the evidence may also include records of telephone conversations and of complete faxes.

In view of the above, let alone of the rest of the material in this book, today's lawyer absolutely has to be (or become) fully versed in these technologies, or he or she will be doing a disservice to the client. Such education cannot be perfunctory; it must be in depth, precisely because cases are won or lost on technical details that answer the following types of questions: "Could the electronic date of this document have been altered?" "Exactly how was the chain of custody of the confiscated hard disk handled?" "Who else might have kept an electronic copy of a document that the opposition claims to be unable to locate?" and so on. Without a thorough schooling in such matters, a lawyer will have no idea what to ask for, what is inconsistent, how to make sure that the electronic evidence being sought is not purged—thereby depriving the lawyer's client of possibly the only proof—what is false and why, and so on. A law school that graduates lawyers who are not savvy about such matters is graduating unqualified lawyers.

Since practically everything is committed to computer memory today, there is hardly anything that cannot benefit from computer forensic evidence. Classic examples include but are not limited to:

- *Product liability cases.* Subpoenaed electronic records can show if the manufacturer was aware of any flaws in the product and failed to correct them, if there was any conspiracy to defraud or misrepresent, and so on.

- *Discrimination cases.* Internal corporate computer records can show if there was awareness that decisions about an employee were made that were influenced by that employee's "religion, race, creed, color, sexual orientation, or ancestry" (in the case of the United States) or whatever other criteria exist in other countries.

- *Sexual harassment cases.* Computer forensics can show if an employee sent inappropriate or suggestive e-mails to others, if he or she patronized adult Web sites at work, and so on.

- *Divorce cases.* Although the laws depend highly on where one lives, one recalls the case where allegations of a spouse's infidelity were supported by the subpoenaed records that showed that she was having a "cyber-affair" with someone else.

- *Criminal cases.* There have been cases when an individual's guilt or innocence was proved with the help of detailed forensic examination of computer hard disks (e.g., a claimed "suicide note" whose electronic date was after the victim died).

But even the most qualified attorney in the world cannot be expected to know the particular setup that the opposition has in terms of procedures, hardware, software, policies, administration, and so on. The first step would be to "discover" those, by taking a deposition from the system administrator ("sysadmin") or whoever functions in that mode.

Perhaps even more difficult than collecting and presenting the electronic evidence is the task of convincing a nontechnical jury or judge of the validity of the evidence. It is understandable why such juries and judges hate listening to highly technical conflicting testimony about the validity of electronic evidence in a case: They simply cannot form an opinion because they don't have the background to do so. It is the lawyer's job to present such testimony and evidence in plain language that anyone can understand; to do so requires a thorough skill in these technologies, as anyone who has tried to explain complex scientific or technical concepts to nonspecialist audiences will attest.

Judges asked to approve subpoenas for producing electronic records have to be themselves convinced that what is sought is truly relevant and needed, and that it is not "unduly burdensome"; the Advisory Committee Note to the Amendment to Federal Rule 34 states succinctly that courts should ensure that discoveries are not abusive.

In the United States, the trend for courts has been increasingly in favor of interpreting the term "document" (even "written document") to include computer files.[1] This is so even though the discovery rules have minimal explicit reference to computer files. The Federal Rule of Civil Procedures and the Superior Court Civil Rule 34 merely state that "Documents ... [include] other data compilations from which information can be obtained, translated, if necessary, by the respondent through detection devices into reasonably usable form." In other words, a defendant providing a plaintiff with undecipherable machine language code in response to a request for production is not in compliance, and courts have so decreed.

In Canada, a recent review by the Canadian Department of Justice found that roughly half of the most relevant 600 federal statutes seemed to apply to paper as the means for exchanging information; proposed legislation would update those statutes to include electronic means of information exchange. Even so, in at least one case [1] in 1988, an Ontario high court found that a computer disk fell within the definition of a "document."

15.2   Civil Legal Discovery Issues

Knowing what to look for and where is not a simple matter in computer evidence. While paper medical documents can be reasonably expected to be in

---

1. Even as early as 1973, in *Union Electric Company v. Mansion House Center N. Redevelopment Co.,* 494 S.W. 2d 309, 315 (MO), the court stated that "computerized record keeping is rapidly becoming a normal procedure in the business world." Also, in *Crown Life Insurance Company v. Kerry Craig,* U.S. Court of Appeals, Seventh Circuit 92-3180, the court rejected the assertion that "written documents" excluded magnetic media.

the folder marked "medical" in one's home file cabinet, computer evidence about an alleged crime by an organization can be spread over numerous physical locations, not to mention numerous magnetic storage devices within any one location.

There is an entire professional field within information technology (complete with its own journals, professional societies, and so on) known as knowledge management (KM). This is an acknowledgement of the fact that information about any one issue is spread all over, and it takes computer-assisted help to pull this information together from disparate places. Today's standard Web searches by an individual wanting to learn about, say, lymphoma are scattered throughout the world; one uses a good search engine (such as http://www.google.com/ or http://www.metacrawler.com/) to do the search and provide the locations of what is sought (which usually number in the thousands or more). Most large organizations have an analogous situation within them for handling their own records. But that is not enough; what an attorney wants during the discovery process is often stored in unadvertised locations, such as in individual users' hard disks and in intentionally mislabeled electronic folders.

The attorney who is conducting the discovery must know (or learn) the opposition's hardware and software well enough so that the correct electronic media can be subpoenaed; hardly any reasonable judge will bless a request to subpoena all of an organization's computer software and hardware in a "fishing expedition."[2] Some software programs store data in readily readable form (known as ASCII text); others store it in a form that is not readable without the proper software—and the lawyer must know what that software is; others store it in password-protected form, and the lawyer must know how to read *that* (see Chapters 4, 6, and 7 and Section 14.6).

As an example, Netscape used to have an electronic forum where Netscape employees vented personal feelings, presumably without repercussions. Yet it was precisely this forum's records that Microsoft subpoenaed to show that many Netscape employees privately felt that Microsoft had a better Web browser. This underscores the importance of a lawyer knowing what to look for and where.

Subpoenaing electronic documents is an art form based on solid science of which the lawyer must have a good command. If one attempts to

---

2. CIBA-Geigy requested the court to restrict the plaintiff's request for electronic documents, as it was "overly broad." Case 94-C-987, M.D.L. 997 (N.D. Ill 1995). Also: Appellate Court decision in *Strausser v. Yalamachi*, 669 So. 2d 1142, 1144–45 (Florida Appellate Court, 1988).

subpoena entire databases (because one lacks a knowledge of which portions of a database are most relevant), chances are that the subpoena will be denied or fought as either too onerous and disruptive or as a request for material that is irrelevant to the case pending. Conversely, if one's subpoena is too specific, chances are that it will miss a lot of relevant electronic evidence; for example, a request for an electronic document may not result in getting the electronic attachment that was appended to that document or the e-mail that precipitated it.

Electronic discovery of "groupware" (software that is intended to help numerous individuals in a group organize and coordinate their activities), such as Meeting Maker and Lotus Notes, with about 40 million installations worldwide, poses yet a different problem because the data sought is spread over many sites and different databases and magnetic media; since, by its nature, it contains information about many individuals' activities, subpoenas can be legitimately objected to on the basis of covering data about matters that have nothing to do with the case at hand.

A goldmine of data usually exists in organizations' backup archives, which all organizations—and individuals—must keep to protect themselves and be able to recover from a catastrophic "crash" of the computing system caused by any one of a multitude of reasons. Most backups do not go back all that far. Individuals typically keep only one or at most two sets of backups. Organizations may keep from 5 to 10 of them. All recycle them, meaning that the oldest one is used as the new medium for the next backup. Typically, backups go "back" only about a month. It follows that, from any savvy lawyer's perspective, time is of the essence; at a minimum, a lawyer must take steps to inform the opposition that no record should henceforth be purged until a formal subpoena is issued.

Even in the worst case, however, there may still be hope. As any individual computer user who has to go through the drudgery of backup-making will attest, backups on tape take many hours to complete; because of this, most individuals (and many organizations) back up only the changes since the previous backup; as such, records that are very old may well still exist for the benefit of forensics evidence. (Hint to the individual or organization: To avoid this, use full backups every time, preceded by a full wiping of the previous backup.) The reader is referred to Chapter 4, which details where data can be stored in one's computer.

Finally, the so-called anonymous free e-mail offered by assorted commercial organizations is emphatically not anonymous. It is not free, either: One pays by providing these companies with a pair of eyeballs that will read assorted advertisements that will pop up on the screen every time it is accessed. Unless a user of such services has taken knowledge-based extensive steps to shield himself or herself from disclosing his or her identity, most of those organizations have a fairly precise idea who the "anonymous" user is and provide it in response to a subpoena; if they don't know who a given anonymous user is, they can find out in response to a court order by any combination of the following techniques:

- Retrieving through the user's Web browser the true e-mail address of the user (e.g., in the configuration of the Netscape setup or of the corresponding setup for Microsoft Explorer);
- Readily observing the user's ISP at each connection, and asking that ISP (with the force of a legal subpoena) to show who was accessing the free e-mail server at a particular instant in recent time;
- Caller-ID information, if a direct call.

A savvy attorney can subpoena any such commercial organization's records, and many have been doing so in rapidly increasing numbers. (AOL, even though it is not free, has had its share of individuals logging in with fake or stolen credit cards, and has been served with—and had to comply with—numerous subpoenas; it can be safely assumed that other ISPs are being faced with subpoenas as well.)

Many individuals disclose a lot of information about themselves and their personal preferences on-line, such as in chat rooms (digital one-on-one communications through the Internet, which are also archived and monitored)[3] and in "profiles" they complete about themselves. Such information can be of use to the attorney in the discovery phase.

Other sources of digital information in civil discovery are openly available to the well-informed attorney and require no subpoena whatever. There are, for example, some 40,000 or more digital bulletin boards, known as Usenet forums, on an equal number of different topics, and anyone can post his or her opinion on them. They range from the very useful (e.g., suicide prevention, cancer information, and so on) to the absurd.

Individuals post their opinions under a true or an assumed name (which can be discovered most of the time through computer forensics of the individual's hard disk). Luckily for the investigator, there are numerous

---

3. In *U.S. v. Charbonneau*, No. CR-2-97-83, 1997 WL 627044, S.D. Ohio, September 30, 1997, the Court stated that there is no Fourteenth Amendment protection of privacy in AOL "chat rooms."

organizations that tend to store all such postings (a vast amount), and anyone can access such organizations to find, for example, everything that a given "username" (true or assumed) has posted over the years. One such organization is http://www.deja.com/ (formerly dejanews.com).

Most proxy servers (see Section 12.5) are not as tight-lipped about their clientele as their users assume. Unless the person using them is knowledgeable enough to have taken all the necessary steps to launder his or her identity before it reaches the proxy server, and to prevent the proxy server from finding it while that user is connected, proxy servers collect and store the information of who connected through them and to what eventual Web site. Subpoenas served upon them can produce these records, but only if the attorney involved moves fast enough.

At a minimum, a savvy plaintiff's attorney should send the opposition a written demand not to delete or otherwise tamper with evidence that is likely to be subpoenaed, or better yet (in the United States), serve a detailed and specific "Request for Production of Documents and Things" (which must spell out what information is to be found where, including archiving media and backups); this should be augmented with a formal request to abstain from any routine procedures (such as routine deletions and defragmenting of hard disks) that could affect the data sought, followed by a Rule 30(b)(6) deposition of whoever knows most about the computers of the party being sued.

In the extreme, a plaintiff's lawyer can go as far as obtaining and serving upon the defendant a restraining order to prevent the destruction of any data of interest as well as by a hearing to get an even more formal injunction by the court.

15.3   E-Mail

E-mail is used by practically 100% of U.S. businesses and 90% of Australian businesses [2]. Even though e-mail does not represent the official position of an organization, it can be every bit as damaging; witness the unofficial Microsoft e-mail that allegedly stated something to the effect that the company would cut the air supply of (rival) Netscape, the trials and tribulations of Ollie North during the Iran-Contra hearings as a result of e-mail, and numerous other situations.[4] Contrary to popular belief, employee e-mail

---

4. *Bourke v. Nissan Motor Corporation,* No. B068705 (California Court of Appeals, July 26, 1993). The court asserted that there is no inherent right to privacy for e-mail.

enjoys zero privacy.[5] An employer has every right (in the United States, anyway) to read employee e-mail, and many do.

Unlike an official organizational document that can have numerous ghost authors and editors before it is finalized, e-mail has an identifiable single author who, more often than not, mistakenly believes that it is "private" (it most emphatically is not), and may use language that betrays biases and other illegalities that can be used against its author.

Until recently, organizations tended to proudly preserve such electronic "skeletons in the closet" for many years through the routine process of making archival backups of the entire organization's databases. As some organizations' legal liabilities that were proved with the help of such archived e-mail became known, many reputable organizations sought a way to clean up those closets for good measure. To minimize the plausibility of an accusation that this is done for illegal purposes, it was usually declared that storage costs for obsolete e-mail were high (which is quite amusing in these days of rock-bottom prices of archival magnetic storage) and that, therefore, e-mail would be purged from organizations' records after rather short lengths of time (often as little as one month). This can "work" only for as long as the organization that does it cannot be held liable for purging records that are subject to subpoena (e.g., during the discovery phase of a lawsuit already filed or as part of an ongoing investigation of which the organization has been made aware). If e-mail is sent out of an organization, the problem is compounded because the organization loses all control of such e-mail and has no way of making it disappear.

It is not at all clear if the attorney-client privilege that protects the confidentiality of verbal communication between an attorney and his or her client extends to e-mail. A third party that obtains a copy of such communication (e.g., an ISP that routinely keeps backups of all e-mails going through its circuits) may well have to turn over such ostensibly "privileged" communication if subpoenaed or be found in contempt of court. Laws are not clear on this, nor have they been tested enough.

Also legally unclear is the status of e-mail sent or received by officials in their *personal* (rather than office-provided) computers that pertains to their official duties as government employees or even corporate employees (e.g., employees working from home or otherwise telecommuting): Can they remove such "official" e-mail from their personal computers or is that e-mail

---

5. For example, in *Smyth v. Pillsbury Company*, 1996 WL 32892 (E.D. Pennsylvania, 1996), when the court stated clearly that employer reading of employee e-mail does not constitute an invasion of privacy.

an "official record" whose preservation is covered by applicable laws? And what if the personal computer in which these "official" e-mail records were legitimately kept, crashes or is sold or is disposed of?

It is quite evident that laws have not kept up with the rapidly advancing popularization of the Internet and even of internal organizational networks. Perhaps an organization would be well advised to protect itself by creating and enforcing clear-cut policies in regard to the use of computers and especially e-mail,. and in particular e-mail that may leave the organization's perimeter (either electronically or physically), just as there have always been established procedures before an official letter on the organization's letterhead could be sent out.

Such policies should clearly state:

- What is not allowed in the organization's e-mail (e.g., illegal acts such as harassment or discriminatory or defamatory prose);

- Procedures for originating and handling what would be proprietary or otherwise confidential e-mail content;

- Time after which all e-mail that has not been specifically marked for retention will be purged, and the procedure and approvals needed for marking some e-mail for retention; ·

- Procedures for allowing e-mail to be released outside an organization, and means for detecting and handling transgressions.

15.4   The Digital Millennium Copyright Act of 1998

In the United States, the Digital Millennium Copyright Act of 1998 makes it illegal to try to circumvent "technical self-help protection measures." This act, along with UCITA (the act passed by the legislatures of the U.S. states of Virginia and Maryland and might be adopted by others as well), is a giant step in precisely the wrong direction for the following simple reason: These laws make it illegal for legitimate users of software to identify and publicize security flaws of such software for the purpose of having such flaws corrected. Given the sickening litany of security-related "bug fixes" in practically all software of any consequence today (e.g., Microsoft operating systems and Microsoft Office), these laws increase the vulnerability of every nation to cybercrime.

The Digital Millennium Copyright Act also has had two unintended amusing effects:

1. Some U.S. pro-encryption individuals precede their encrypted files with a legal warning that quotes this 1998 act and reminds anyone inclined to break the encryption that doing so would be a "federal offense"; a typical such message reads as follows:

   > LEGAL WARNING NOTICE: The encrypted file below contains copyrighted material. In accordance with the Copyright Act, 17 USC 108(a)(3), as amended by the Digital Millennium Copyright Act (P.L 105-304) and the Copyright Term Extension Act (P.L. 105-278), any attempt by anyone other than the intended recipient to circumvent the encryption protection on this copyrighted material is a crime that is punishable severely by law. END OF WARNING NOTICE.

   It is unknown what the legal implications of this would be in the United States on, say, local law enforcement trying to circumvent someone's encryption under some conditions.

2. One can conceive of situations in which a company lightly encrypted information that it wanted to protect, so as to be able to claim a violation of this federal law if a whistle-blower disclosed that information to the public.

15.4.1 UCITA

The Uniform Computer Information Transactions Act (UCITA) is a draft law (already adopted in the states of Maryland and Virginia[6]—enacted by the latter on July 1, 2001) sent in July 2000 to all U.S. states and territories for "consideration." It is plagued by controversy, for good reason.

This act benefits a single sector of society, software makers, and would be more aptly named the Software Industry Protection Act. For example:

1. UCITA allows software companies to avoid liability for damage caused by defective software, even if the problems were not disclosed to the customer at the time of purchase.

2. In its original draft—from which UCITA has since backed off as a result of massive opposition—UCITA allowed the manufacturer of software to remotely shut down a buyer's software if the buyer was

---

6. This is done for purely selfish economic reasons, namely, to entice software makers to move to Maryland and Virginia so that these states can reap the obvious tax benefits.

deemed by the manufacturer not to have upheld the software licensing agreements.

3. UCITA prohibits the transfer of software between companies, even in mergers and acquisitions.

4. UCITA obligates buyers to abide by terms that were not disclosed prior to the purchase of the software. This is what is colloquially known in the United States as "buying a pig in a poke."

5. The notion that UCITA is intended to create uniform rules across all states (to favor software makers) has already been killed by the fact that the legislatures of two states, Hawaii and Illinois, have considered UCITA and have decided not to move ahead with it.

6. UCITA obligates a buyer of software not to use reverse engineering on the purchased software in an attempt to identify and correct security-related or other software flaws. The software buyer is therefore prevented from having any control over what software is running in his or her computer.

7. UCITA prohibits a software user who discovers flaws in a purchased software program from disclosing them. This flies in the face of the United States' (and every other nation's) need to enhance information security and protect its critical information infrastructure. One is therefore witnessing the spectacle whereby software manufacturers, through UCITA, are actually undermining the U.S. Presidential Directive 63 about the protection of the U.S. critical infrastructure. Besides, this, as well as all other UCITA provisions, is a toothless monster in that any U.S. company can send overseas software that it has purchased in the United States for reverse engineering there. For example, under the European Union fair-use laws, software can be reverse engineered in Europe.

15.5 International Policy on Computer-Related Crime

The fact is that the Internet is an inherently transnational communications network. One can as easily cause a denial-of-service attack on an Internet host from across the street or across the world.

Laws about computer evidence, computer crime, degree of legality of encryption, and so on, vary widely from country to country and change rapidly. Because of the transnational nature of the Internet and of computer crime involving the Internet, there is a strong push led by the United States to make uniform most countries' laws pertaining to computer crime. One may recall the spectacle of the individual who was arrested in the Philippines in mid-1999 for allegedly having been responsible for the infamous "I love you" virus, only to be released shortly thereafter because there was no law in the Philippines at the time against what he had been arrested for.

The Organization for Economic Cooperation and Development (OECD) and the Council of Europe, as well as numerous other organizations around the world, have created a plethora of "guidelines" intended to harmonize criminal laws on computer crime around the world. Typically, the United Nations also got involved, with the "Proposals for Concerted International Action Against Forms of Crime Identified in the Milar Plan of Action" (E/AC.57/1988/16), in which paragraphs 42–44 deal with computer crime.

Not surprisingly, the problems associated with constructing international guidelines have been formidable, since different societies have different laws and different perceptions of what "crime" is, let alone different procedures for such related issues as appeals. For example, some countries value privacy more than others and criminalize the compromises of privacy, whereas others don't. The ongoing dispute between the United States and Europe on this issue is a case in point (see Section 15.12). Then there is the jurisdiction issue, and each nation jealously guards its prerogatives.

Numerous excellent references on these issues, such as the "International Review of Criminal Policy: United Nations Manual in the Prevention and Control of Computer-Related Crime," are available on-line from http://www.ifs.univie.ac.at/.

15.6   Defining "Computer Crime"

Computer crime, like any crime, is time- and location-dependent. What is a crime in one location is not a crime in another; what is a crime in one location may not have been a crime in that same location in the past and may not be a crime in the future. Computer crime is basically any act that is illegal in some location and time, and that involves a computer in some manner.

The term "computer crime" can be subdivided into two broad categories:

1. Crime that involved a computer only in a tangential or peripheral manner, such as for composing a libelous message;

2. Crime the commission of which required the use of a computer. Examples of this class of crimes include but are not limited to:

a. Stock market manipulation by posting knowingly false messages on Usenet, with the intent of driving the price of a stock up or down for personal gain or revenge.

b. Wholesale theft of credit card numbers stored in the Web host of an on-line retailer, and fraudulent use of these stolen numbers for personal gain.

c. Attacks on a targeted computer through such means as remote "hacks" or "denial of service."

d. Identity theft made possible by the ease with which one can use the Internet to obtain vast amounts of ostensibly confidential information about anyone, especially in the United States.

e. Use of computers to negate means for protecting copyrighted work and distributing it on a large scale for personal profit or simply as a sociopolitical statement.

Contrary to popular belief, computer crime is not hard to prosecute, but only as long as law enforcement has the specialized training, the tools, the budget, and the equipment to pursue computer forensics. The ancillary societal problem associated with giving law enforcement carte blanche to monitor computers and networks is that it would give law enforcement unprecedented powers to access individual data that in most cases has nothing to do with any suspected crime; this is so because it is the nature of computers and networks to store and relay massive amounts of data, only an infinitesimally small percentage of which has any relevance to crime.

15.7   What a Business Can Do to Protect Itself

A good reference publication for providing guidance to businesses to minimize their legal exposure to liability is "E-Policy—How to Develop Computer, E-Mail, and Internet Guidance to Protect Your Company and Its Assets," by M. R. Overly, American Management Association, 1601 Broadway, New York, New York, 10019, also found at http://www.amanet.org.

If served with any variant of a legal demand that a company produce documents for the opposition's "discovery," a defense attorney may consider such options (if applicable) as:

- The qualifications and precise methods to be used by the plaintiff in handling the defendant's data;

- Identifying data residing in the hard disks sought by the plaintiff that are confidential, proprietary, or otherwise privileged or protected from the plaintiff's viewing;

- Obtaining comparable access for discovery of data in the plaintiff's possession.

15.8 Criminal Evidence Collection Issues

15.8.1 Collection

The investigator meeting a suspect for the first time should establish up front in a nonthreatening manner and before a suspect becomes defensive that the suspect is the sole user of the computer in question. This can eliminate any subsequent claim to the contrary as a defense. Even so, a savvy defense attorney can legitimately point out that it is eminently possible for files in one's computer to have been placed there without the defendant's knowledge:

- In the case of a computer connected to the Internet or any other network, by a remotely located hacker or hostile Web site. There is ample factual evidence of software and malicious mobile code (meaning, in this case, software sent by a remote Web site to a user's computer) doing exactly that.

- In the case of a computer that has never been connected to either the Internet or any other network (and this is becoming a smaller and smaller percentage of computers), software of suspicious origin (such as assorted shareware and freeware files), there is ample evidence of cases in which such software modified a computer without the computer owner's knowledge or permission.

Additionally, the collection of the computer evidence should be done in a manner that can be shown to have precluded the possibility that the collection process itself may have contaminated what was being collected. For example, there may be software that can do just about anything a user wants it to if the computer is turned on by an unauthorized user. Also, every time Windows is turned on, it actually writes new information on a disk and overwrites some older information.

About the only way to achieve this requirement of noncontamination is for the targeted magnetic media to be electrically disconnected from the computer they are using, and to be connected to another computer that will not boot that disk or run any software in it, but merely make a magnetic duplicate of the targeted disk.

That magnetic duplicate should then be retained as the new "uncontaminated master copy" and should not be "analyzed," as such analysis may contaminate it. Instead, additional copies must be made from that "uncontaminated master copy," and it is those additional copies that can be analyzed forensically.

15.8.2 Handling

The key issues associated with the handling of any forensic evidence, including computer forensics, are that the procedures used should be such that they can withstand any challenge by the defense as to their legitimacy and admissibility as evidence. This means that the handling of the evidence should be such that:

- There is a clear and fully documented chain of custody of the evidence with no gaps whatever;
- Each custodian of the evidence is in a position to have precluded any possibility that the evidence could have been modified in any way, either intentionally or unintentionally;
- What is presented in court can only have been what was collected.

15.9   U.S. Federal Guidelines for Searching and Seizing Computers

What is "computer crime"? As any new technology becomes popular enough to be adopted by a significant percentage of the population, it is inevitable that it will also be used in ways that violate existing laws.

- Automobiles, normally intended to transport persons to work or other locations, can also be used for illegal purposes (to escape from the scene of a crime, in the furtherance of a kidnapping, to store contraband, or to run over someone), and have been.
- Kitchen knives, normally intended to carve turkey and peel oranges, can also be used to maim and to kill, and have been.

- Electricity, normally intended to convey energy, can also be used to kill, or to torture, and has been.

- Potassium tablets, normally intended to sustain life by replacing potassium lost as a result of severe dehydration, can also be lethal to the heart if administered in high doses, and have been.

- Telephones, normally intended to exchange social and personal pleasantries and to conduct legitimate business, can also be used for every conceivable nefarious purpose, and have been.

- Computers, normally intended to increase the efficiency of a variety of human tasks, can also be used to store evidence of a crime or as instruments of a crime (e.g., to steal others' credit card numbers or identities), and have been.

All rational societies in the world have decided that, on balance, the beneficial uses of practically all technological and other advances of mankind outweigh the disadvantages of their occasional abuse. As a result, automobiles are legal everywhere, and so are kitchen knives, electricity, medicines, and telephones.

Computers, however, seem to rub governments the wrong way, by virtue of the fact that, in conjunction with the Internet and encryption, they allow individuals to create, store, and communicate ideas that individual governments find threatening. This is hardly surprising from a historical perspective. The totalitarian regimes of yesteryear required the individual licensing of typewriters and photocopying machines. In some regimes (e.g., the Communist regime in Cambodia under Pol Pot) even doors were banned; houses were not allowed to have any, so that the regime could look into each house at any time it pleased. Today, even in the country most protective of individual rights, the United States, applicable laws allow federal agents to break the door down in a house—even when a judge has refused to give a warrant for a "no-knock entry"—and enter the residence; all they need to have is an opinion that breaking the door down was essential to prevent the destruction of evidence.[7]

As with any technology, computers can be used to store "evidence" of what a regime may consider against existing laws—or preferences—or as an "instrumentality" of a violation of such laws—or preferences. Given that

7. See "Computer Crime and Intellectual Property Section (CCIPS): Searching and Seizing Computers and Obtaining Electronic Evidence in Criminal Investigations" at http://www.cybercrime.gov/searchmanual.htm#Ic.

computers, small and big, are now used by nearly every organization and individual, it is hardly surprising that the absolute amount of ways in which they have been used for something a regime does not like is correspondingly higher than when there were fewer computers around.

A list of ways that a computer (or an automobile or a kitchen knife) can be used in ways that either violate existing laws or simply are contrary to parochial preferences[8] of groups with financial and political clout, is limited only by one's imagination. It would be pointless to list such obvious analogs to conventional crime as keeping double books (for tax evasion), creating and sending ransom notes, writing and/or sending prose or imagery that is libelous or politically or otherwise offensive to some subculture(s) or to the regime itself, and so on.

Then there is the related capability of most modern computers to allow communications between individuals and groups to which many governments take justifiable offense, such as communications between terrorists,[9] drug dealers, and spies.[10] Amusingly, the very same Internet and the use of computers that law enforcers vilify are in fact a gift from the gods to law enforcers anywhere in the world; computers and the Internet are the most effective media for wholesale surveillance ever popularized. Whereas in the past, security services had to think creatively, to use physical surveillance, and to engage in many of the tricks we have all enjoyed in movies of that genre, today all they have to do—and they do—is to monitor as much of the worldwide Internet traffic as possible and to do computer forensics on all computers suspected of involvement in what a state may not like. Given that most

---

8. Is the thorough assessment of a purchased piece of security-related software for the purpose of identifying its security weaknesses so that the buyer will know whether to depend on it or not "illegal"? Amazingly, in the United States it is illegal if it includes the—essential—step of defeating means inserted by that software maker to prevent such assessment, according to the U.S. Digital Millennium Protection Act, which was recently railroaded through Congress into law.

9. This can be a big intellectual discussion in itself. Certainly the maiming or killing of innocent civilians is a reprehensible and cowardly act that nobody should condone. But the term "terrorism" is also used by repressive totalitarian regimes to apply to what most of us would consider the activities of "freedom fighters."

10. Spying, the world's second oldest profession, has existed since the dawn of recorded history. Spies were able to communicate long before computers or electricity were even discovered. The often-heard assertion by national law enforcement groups worldwide that the control or elimination of the Internet will prevent spies' communications is laughable and is intended for consumption by the gullible in order to apply pressure to legislative bodies to inch (or gallop) closer to Orwellian societies.

terrorists, spies, drug dealers, and others are not technologically savvy and will eventually and inevitably "slip," law enforcers should actually be the most vocal supporters of widespread use of computers and the Internet.

Just as there are countless colorful stories of how a particular suspect was apprehended and convicted in the precomputer days—Arthur Conan Doyle's Sherlock Holmes and Agatha Christie's Hercule Poirot detail some particularly challenging fictitious ones—there is a plethora of ones involving computer-related crime. For what it is worth, here is a sampling of some, taken from authoritative sources; the reader has to filter out the understandably self-congratulatory air that permeates them.

According to the *Computer Crime and Intellectual Property Section* document published by the U.S. Department of Justice, made publicly available by that government organization at http://www.cybercrime.gov/search-manual.htm#lc, there was an incident

> In *United States v. Roberts,* 86 F. Supp.2d 678 (S.D. Tex. 2000), [when] United States Customs Agents learned that William Roberts, a suspect believed to be carrying computerized images of child pornography, was scheduled to fly from Houston, Texas to Paris, France on a particular day. On the day of the flight, the agents set up an inspection area in the jetway at the Houston airport with the sole purpose of searching Roberts. Roberts arrived at the inspection area and was told by the agents that they were searching for "currency" and "high technology or other data" that could not be exported legally. After the agents searched Roberts' property and found a laptop computer and six Zip diskettes, Roberts agreed to sign a consent form permitting the agents to search his property. A subsequent search revealed several thousand images of child pornography. When charges were brought, Roberts moved for suppression of the computer files, but the district court ruled that the search had not violated the [U.S.] Fourth Amendment. According to the court, the search of Roberts' luggage had been a "routine search" for which no suspicion was required, even though the justification for the search offered by the agents merely had been a pretext. *See Whren v. United States,* 517 U.S. 806 (1996). The court also concluded that Roberts' consent justified the search of the laptop and diskettes, and indicated that even if Roberts had not consented to the search, [the] search of the defendant's computer and diskettes would have been a routine export search, valid under the Fourth Amendment.

According to this same official document, despite the U.S. Constitution's Fourth Amendment protection against unreasonable search, *agents may search a place or object without a warrant or even probable cause* in a number of cases:

- "If a person with authority has voluntarily consented to the search."
- "It is common for several people to use or own the same computer equipment. If any one of those people gives permission to search for data, agents may generally rely on that consent, so long as the person has authority over the computer. In such cases, all users have assumed the risk that a co-user might discover everything in the computer, and might also permit law enforcement to search this 'common area' as well." As such, "Most spousal consent searches are valid."
- "Parents can consent to searches of their children's rooms when the children are under 18 years old. If the children are 18 or older, the parents may or may not be able to consent, depending on the facts."
- "*Implied Consent...* For example, in *United States v. Ellis,* 547 F.2d 863 (5th Cir. 1977), a civilian visiting a naval air station agreed to post a visitor's pass on the windshield of his car as a condition of bringing the car on the base. The pass stated that '[a]cceptance of this pass gives your consent to search this vehicle while entering, aboard, or leaving this station.'... During the visitor's stay on the base, a station investigator who suspected that the visitor had stored marijuana in the car approached the visitor and asked him if he had read the pass. After the visitor admitted that he had, the investigator searched the car and found 20 plastic bags containing marijuana. The Fifth Circuit ruled that the warrantless search of the car was permissible, because the visitor had impliedly consented to the search when he knowingly and voluntarily entered the base with full knowledge of the terms of the visitor's pass."
- "*Plain View.* Evidence of a crime may be seized without a warrant under the plain view exception to the warrant requirement."
- "*Search Incident to a Lawful Arrest.* Pursuant to a lawful arrest, agents may conduct a 'full search' of the arrested person, and a more limited search of his surrounding area, without a warrant. *See United States v. Robinson,* 414 U.S. 218, 235 (1973); *Chimel v. California,* 395 U.S. 752, 762-63 (1969). For example, in *Robinson,* a police officer conducting a patdown search incident to an arrest for a traffic offense discovered a crumpled cigarette package in the suspect's left

breast pocket. Not knowing what the package contained, the officer opened the package and discovered fourteen capsules of heroin. The Supreme Court held that the search of the package was permissible, even though the officer had no articulable reason to open the package. *See id.* at 234–35. In light of the general need to preserve evidence and prevent harm to the arresting officer, the Court reasoned, it was *per se* reasonable for an officer to conduct a 'full search of the person pursuant to a lawful arrest.'... If agents can examine the contents of wallets, address books, and briefcases without a warrant, it could be argued that they should be able to search their electronic counterparts (such as electronic organizers, floppy disks, and Palm Pilots) as well. *Cf. United v. Tank,* 200 F.3d 627, 632 (9th Cir. 2000) (holding that agents searching a car incident to a valid arrest properly seized a Zip disk found in the car, but failing to discuss whether the agents obtained a warrant before searching the disk for images of child pornography)."

- Breaking down the door (no-knock warrants). "As a general matter, agents must announce their presence and authority prior to executing a search warrant. See *Wilson v. Arkansas,* 514 U.S. 927, 934 (1995); 18 U.S.C. § 3109. This so-called 'knock and announce' rule reduces the risk of violence and destruction of property when agents execute a search. The rule is not absolute, however. In *Richards v. Wisconsin,* 520 U.S. 385 (1997), the Supreme Court held that agents can dispense with the knock-and-announce requirement if they have a reasonable suspicion that knocking and announcing their presence, under the particular circumstances, would be dangerous or futile, or that it would inhibit the effective investigation of the crime by, for example, allowing the destruction of evidence. When agents have reason to believe that knocking and announcing their presence would allow the destruction of evidence, would be dangerous, or would be futile, agents should request that the magistrate judge issue a no-knock warrant. The failure to obtain judicial authorization to dispense with the knock-and-announce rule does not preclude the agents from conducting a no-knock search, however.... In some cases, agents may neglect to request a no-knock warrant, or may not have reasonable suspicion that evidence will be destroyed until they execute the search. In *Richards,* the Supreme Court made clear that 'the reasonableness of the officers' decision [to dispense with the knock-and-announce rule] ... must be evaluated as of the time they entered' the area to be searched. *Richards*, 510 U.S. at 395. Accordingly, agents may 'exercise independent judgment' and decide to conduct a no-knock search when they execute the search, even if they did not request such authority or the magistrate judge specifically refused to authorize a no-knock search. The question in all such cases is whether the agents had 'a reasonable suspicion that knocking and announcing their presence, under the particular circumstances, would be dangerous or futile, or that it would inhibit the effective investigation of the crime by, for example, allowing the destruction of evidence.'"

Things must be appreciated in context. The point of the foregoing is that, even in a country known for its respect for individual rights and with a Constitution that protects those individual rights, courts and law enforcement have carved elaborate paths whereby they can essentially get around what average citizens may consider to be their constitutional rights protecting them from governmental intrusion. In countries where there are no written constitutions and/or where the legal protection for individual rights is minimal or nonexistent, the individual can only depend on his or her own resources for protection from unwelcome intrusion by an oppressive regime.

15.10   The Law Surrounding Decryption Keys

Whether one can be forced to reveal a decryption key depends on the country and on the circumstances. The Regulation of Investigatory Powers (RIP) law was enacted in October 2000 in the United Kingdom; it empowers some within the British law enforcement community to demand that an individual either decrypt an encrypted file or provide law enforcement with the key for decrypting it; refusal to do so is reportedly punished by a two-year jail sentence; astonishingly, disclosure to most any third party that this demand has been made by law enforcement upon one carries a five-year jail sentence.

An interesting situation comes about if the encryption used involves the increasingly popular public-key encryption crypto-system, such as is used in the popular PGP software (see Section 14.3), which is freely available worldwide. If properly configured, the sender who encrypts a message for an intended recipient is physically unable to decrypt that same message; only the intended recipient can do so.

It follows that one can only provide authorities with the decryption key for incoming encrypted messages and not for outgoing encrypted messages; it is hard to see how an individual can be held liable for the content of messages that others have sent him or her, unless they are particularly explicit in regard to that recipient's involvement or culpability.

In the United States it is believed that the Fifth Amendment to the U.S. Constitution, which empowers one to be able to legally refuse to incriminate oneself, allows one to refuse to provide the decryption key upon demand by any authority *if* that decryption key resides (or can be credibly claimed to reside) solely within that person's mind [3]. If, however, the decryption key is recorded in some media such as paper or magnetic storage media, then such media have to be surrendered upon demand under possible penalty of "contempt of court" or "obstruction of justice."

An interesting situation exists in the case of public-key encryption (see Section 13.2.3), in which keys are notoriously long, are usually created by a machine, and are very random and nearly impossible to remember. In public-key encryption, however, implementations are such that the mere possession (or confiscation) of a decryption key (known as one's "private key," versus the public key that is used to encrypt) is not enough to decrypt a document; one needs to "activate" the private key with a pass phrase that is supposed to reside solely in one's mind. It appears, therefore, that one would have to surrender the private key even in the United States, but should be able to invoke one's Fifth Amendment rights and refuse to provide the pass phrase needed to activate that key.

In other countries, laws vary widely. In the worst case, authorities have been known to resort to "rubber hose cryptanalysis" (beating individuals with a rubber hose until they reveal the decryption key). A detailed country-by-country list of the local laws with respect to encryption can be found in:

- http://www.2.epic.org/reports/crypto2000/;
- http://cwis.kub.nl/~frw/people/koops/lawsurvy.htm;
- http://strategis.ic.gc.ca/SSG/mi06318e.html.

Information can also be obtained by searching for the keywords "crypto law survey." See also Chapters 12 and 13 on encryption.

Basically, an individual or organization must adopt defensive strategies before becoming embroiled in any investigation of litigation. The reader is referred to Part II of this book for recommended defensive strategies.

15.11 Destruction of Electronic Evidence

Clearly, if a defendant can be shown to have destroyed data after being sub-poenaed to produce the data or even after having been informed not to destroy any data in anticipation of a forthcoming subpoena, then such a defendant is likely to face additional penalties for having destroyed potential evidence. Even if a defendant who has destroyed data can be shown to have known or reasonably expected that this data would be sought by a litigant or a prosecutor in connection with an ongoing civil or criminal case, it is possi-ble that this defendant will face additional penalties.[11]

15.12 United States–Europe Data Privacy Disputes

European privacy regulations (the European Union's Omnibus Data Protec-tion Directive, which has been in effect since October 1998) are far more strin-gent than U.S. ones (see Sections 8.2 and 13.3.1 on privacy). This has become a major point of contention in connection with commercial efforts on both sides of the Atlantic to access one another's databases through the Internet.

As of July 6, 2000, the European Parliament, representing the Euro-pean Union's 15 member nations, had rejected a data-privacy "deal" made between the European Commission and the United States that would shield U.S. companies from the European regulations on privacy. In particular, the European Parliament wanted new provisions that would allow Europeans to appeal any perceived violations of their privacy to some independent body, and also the right to sue U.S. companies for damages for privacy violations.

Even so, it appears that this rejection by the European Parliament will have no impact, because the Parliament's role was only to determine if the European Commission had acted within the scope of its authority in coming up with the above agreement with the United States, and the Parliament did not state that this authority had been exceeded; the Parliament has no statu-tory authority to veto this deal.

15.13 New International Computer Crime Treaty

In its zeal to attack computer crime that is transnational in nature, a new international computer crime treaty, known as the Draft Convention on

---

11. *Carlucci v. Piper Aircraft Corp.* 102 F.R.D. 472 (S.D. Florida, 1984). Also: *ABC Home Health Services Inc. v. IBM Corp.,* 185 F.R.D. 180 (S.D. Georgia, 1994).

Cybercrime, goes beyond attacking computer crime and gives law enforcement unprecedented powers to attack privacy and possibly violate the Fifth Amendment to the U.S. Constitution. It is a treaty involving the 41-nation Council of Europe and the United States. It went through 19 drafts before its existence was revealed in public.

This treaty is viewed by some (e.g., U.S. Libertarian Party presidential candidate Harry Brown in the November 2000 elections) as an "end run" attempt by U.S. law enforcement to pressure the U.S. Senate into approving measures that it is unlikely to have otherwise approved by asserting that the United States would need to conform to "international standards" (on cybersnooping). Typically:

- The treaty would enable U.S. law enforcement to order U.S. persons to reveal passwords and decryption keys, something that appears to be in violation of the U.S. Constitution's Fifth Amendment against self-incrimination.
- The treaty would do away with anonymous remailers (something already treated as illegal in some countries, such as France), and would require ISPs to surveil customers' Internet usage and store at least 40 days' worth of customer data.

The treaty would make illegal some common and legitimate software, such as software used by practically every large commercial organization to test their own respective systems for security; the rationale given is that such software, which it calls "hacker tools," can also be used by criminals. As a result, corporate and commercial cybersecurity will suffer a serious and lasting blow (see the November 1, 2000, editorial by Weld Pond at http://www.zdnet.com/zdnn/stories/news/0,4586,2647940,00.html).

15.14 Legal Limitations

The laws are not clear in most countries as to whether or not "passive interception" requires a warrant by law enforcement, or if this practice is lawful even with respect to average citizens. A U.S. Supreme Court decision at the turn of the twentieth century stated that wiretapping is legal without a warrant because it did not involve a physical trespassing into anyone's property; this was subsequently reversed. Until very recently, however, the former perception persisted; it had been ruled that interception of the radio signals of cordless phones did not require a warrant in the United States.

The laws become very nebulous at this stage everywhere in the world as to just exactly which forms of surveillance require a warrant and which do not.

- Can law enforcement (without a warrant) or even a regular citizen set up shop across the street and use a voyeur's telescope (also known as a "star-gazer's telescope") to watch a targeted room that happens not to have curtains? How about commercially available light-amplification night-imaging devices? Can these images be video-taped? Can they be used as legally obtained evidence in a court of law?

- Can law enforcement (without a warrant) or even a regular citizen go through someone else's trash placed by the curbside for collection by the trash collector? U.S. laws seem to make the subtle distinction that this is OK if the trash is at the curbside but not if the trash is right next to one's house (on one's property).

- Can law enforcement (without a warrant) or even a regular citizen monitor someone else's electricity or water meter and make inferences about the usage patterns of the targeted premises?

- Can law enforcement (without a warrant) or even a regular citizen use commercially available thermal-imaging devices to make educated inferences about the activities going on inside a targeted house? Recently law enforcement in the United States did exactly that and detected an unusually high amount of heat inside the house; a subsequent raid showed that the owners were cultivating plants for illegal drugs inside. As of June 2001, the U.S. Supreme Court ruled that police need a warrant in some cases to use high-tech means to collect information inside a private residence.

- Can law enforcement (without a warrant) or even a regular citizen use commercially available laboratory equipment (e.g., gas chromatography) to make chemical analyses of what comes out of a neighbor's chimney or vents to detect, for example, chemicals used in the production of illegal materials?

The laws are constantly evolving as lawmakers try to keep pace with the rapidly evolving commercialized technology. Some have argued that the founding fathers of the United States never dreamed that one's house could be monitored without a physical trespass, or they would have prohibited all such nonphysical trespasses in the U.S. Constitution. We will never know.

References

[1] *Reichmann v. Toronto Life Publications Co.*, 66 O.R. 2d 65, 1988 O.J. No. 1727, 30 C.P.C. ed 280.

[2] Gillespie, D., "E-Mail—The Clayton Deletion," available on-line at http://www.lawnet .com.au/.

[3] *Doe v. United States*, 487 US 201 1998, footnote 9, p. 210, and the dissent on p. 219.

16

Security Aspects of Evolving Internet Technologies

16.1 Merging of Conventional and IP Telephony

Less than a decade ago, Internet enthusiasts realized that the Internet could be used to handle live conversations if one was willing to settle for some degradation in the quality of service (QoS) that we have come to expect of conventional telephony. And conversations could be free, too, even across the world. Software, such as Internet Phone,[1] appeared on the market—some of it free—which allowed any two Internet-connected individuals to converse at no cost, regardless of distance. This merging of voice and data traffic into a single system is depicted in Figure 16.1.

This merge was pure anathema to the established telephone companies, all of which initially ran to their respective governments asking to have this option made illegal.[2] In countries in which the telephone service was a government-provided monopoly, there was that much more of an incentive to put this genie of merging voice and data traffic back into the bottle.

The problem was that, even if Internet Protocol (IP) telephony, as it came to be known, was made illegal—and it was in some countries, initially—the law prohibiting it was unenforceable. IP telephony is also known

---

1. Other such software packages still available include products from VocalTec, Analogics, Lucent Technologies, and Netscape's CoolTalk. They do not require anything other than a functioning Internet connection.

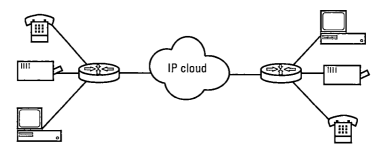

Figure 16.1 Merging voice and data traffic.

as "voice over IP" and, to a lesser extent, as VON (voice on the network). In a classic application of the adage "if you can't beat them, join them," many world-class telephone companies started offering to their customers Internet-based telephony at a reduced cost.

The reason for the reduced cost of IP telephony is not technology; a substantial portion of the cost of telephone service is due to assorted regulatory fees that, in most cases, do not apply to circuits that carry data. IP telephony also has the potential to increase employee productivity by integrating voice, e-mail, teleconferencing, and white boarding into a single infrastructure. Having a single infrastructure is less expensive for companies to maintain, since it requires a single support staff rather than two (one for conventional voice and another one for handling data).

This is all heresy to the old way of thinking. Conventional telephony is "circuit switched," meaning that a circuit is established for any phone call between the calling and the called party, and bandwidth (the width of the electronic road that connects the two parties) is reserved for that call, whether it is needed throughout the call or not. Each type of standardized cable can

---

2. In March 1996, ACTA, a group representing most telephone companies in the United States, filed a petition with the FCC to classify IP telephony software as "common carriage" so as to ban its sale. It also petitioned the FCC to define "permissible uses" of the Internet. Charles H. Helein, then general counsel for ACTA, stated that "[t]here is something fundamentally wrong, from our members' perspective, that somebody can talk over the Internet for free. They are giving away our product." Amusingly, the ACTA petition wanted to regulate IP telephony and not to deregulate conventional telephony. The comment on record by the CEO of VocalTec, Elon Ganor, was as follows: "In a sense, what these guys are asking is to declare the entire software industry as a telecommunications carrier. I think that's a little far-fetched." On May 7, 1997, the FCC's final decision was announced; it legitimized IP telephony.

carry a fixed number of simultaneous phone calls; for example, a T1 line can handle 24 calls; this is clearly inefficient.

Data networks work altogether differently. IP data generated by any user is not sent out like a long spaghetti string, but is broken into "packets," each of which has:

- A header that shows the intended destination address of the packet;

- A sequence number, so that the packets can be put together in order at the intended destination even if they arrive out of sequence (as often happens when different data packets reach the destination by different routes due to network-related reasons);

- The information content of each packet.

Individual packets travel from the source to the destination through whichever path happens to be most promising at any one instant in time; a very small percentage of data packets are lost, due to any one of many reasons. Even so, packet-switched networks are inherently far more efficient than circuit-switched networks in terms of the utilization of resources, since no idle bandwidth is allocated unless it is needed at that instant in time.

In fact, even the telephone companies of the world saw the light. When a conventional telephone call is made today, the signal is digitized the moment it arrives at the telephone subscriber's local switching office (at a very inefficient constant rate of about 56 Kbps, regardless of instantaneous need), and from there on it is handled as a data packet all the way to the called party's own local switching office, where it is converted back into a plain old "analog" signal that is sent to the called party's home or office. The path that even these "conventional" modern telephone calls take in delivering the digitized voice from one end to the other often does change during a telephone call as more effective paths become available due to reduced traffic at any moment in time.[3]

This technology (also referred to collectively as Signaling System 7) is what has made ISDN (Integrated Services Digital Network, or "I Still Don't

---

3. One feels sorry for the old-time interceptor that has set up shop somewhere in the middle between two communicating parties. At best, he will get fragments of the digitized conversation. Worse yet, since the call setup information (who is calling whom) is going through a totally different physical path anyway, he won't know what he is listening to. Of course, a local law enforcement organization can always "tap" a subscriber's phone line and intercept all calls to and from it.

Need It") possible. In ISDN, the digitized signal from the telephone company's local switching office is brought as a digitized signal to the end user, and
not as a conventional analog signal; this requires significantly more expensive
"telephone sets" at the end user's place. This technology, which has been
somewhat popular in Europe and Japan, never caught on in the United
States because the prices charged for it made no economic sense to end users;
besides, it was "too little, too late," since it has already been made obsolete by
xDSL (various flavors of Digital Subscriber Line) that can carry much higher
bandwidths.

From a business perspective, one wants to have three classes of QoS:

Routing telephone calls through the Internet is not without its problems. Whereas a delay of a few seconds—or even minutes—in e-mail messages is acceptable, that same delay in a live conversation is totally
unacceptable, hence the increased importance of the QoS. Happily, more
and more resources are being devoted to Internet infrastructures worldwide,
and the QoS is steadily improving to the point where one can have a credible
IP telephony service. In fact, some companies sell IP telephony to individuals
and companies at a substantially reduced cost compared with conventional
telephony.

From a business perspective, one wants to have three classes of QoS:

1. "Good" for Internet applications that can function with some delay
   (e.g., e-mail);

2. "Better" for corporate VPNs (discussed in Section 12.4);

3. "Absolute QoS" for voice/video.

Technologically, this requires that each data packet have a "precedence" identifier that tells the network with which of these three classes of
QoS any particular packet is associated. This is already done in internal networks ("intranets") using numerous commercial vendors' equipment, but is
not possible with the existing Internet, which developed at a time when IP
telephony was not in its designers' minds.

There is a further cost advantage to IP telephony and it is associated
with physical moves. Moving a conventional phone from one physical location to another requires a lot of manual work to make and break assorted
wired connections. Since Dynamic Host Configuration Protocol (DHCP),
which allows the dynamic—on the fly—assignment of Internet protocol
addresses on a network, was popularized, physical moves within a network
are quite painless.

Today there are numerous commercial hardware products that allow companies to install IP telephony on a broad scale. Vendors include industry giants Cisco (http://www.cisco.com/), Lucent (http://www.lucent.com/), and Nortel/Micom (http://www.itweb.co.za/office/Micom/wp0004.htm), and other companies, such as Frontier Communications (which joined forces with Lucent on July 20, 1999, http://www.lucent.com/press/0799/990720 .nsa.html) and Micom Communications (http://www.micom.com/press/ VIPintro.html).

16.1.1 Security and Privacy Issues

As with respect to any new technology, law enforcement was slow to catch on. Interception of IP telephony, although technologically straightforward, was initially not within the capabilities of most law enforcement organizations; such organizations could always, however, serve a warrant on an Internet service provider demanding a copy of all IP telephony conversations to or from a specified customer. Today's aggressive law enforcement in the United States and the United Kingdom, and to a far lesser extent elsewhere, has changed this, and interception of IP telephony is increasingly probable if there is a desire to do so.

A digitized voice signal is no harder to intercept than a conventional analog telephone signal; in many ways it is far easier, because every data packet is clearly identified with its source and destination, is date/time stamped, and is easily stored in magnetic media. The "fly in the ointment" is that today it is also easy—and totally free—for any user to deploy strong encryption on IP telephony, thereby negating all interception efforts. Freely available products such as Speak Freely (http://www.speakfreely.org/), which is available worldwide for Windows 95/98/Me/NT/2000 and for Unix, allow one to use strong encryption to ensure the privacy of voice communications.

Even the United Kingdom's much heralded RIP Act would be of questionable value to that government in dealing with encrypted IP telephony, because the encryption keys used in a conversation can be permanently deleted at the end of that conversation and could not be surrendered upon demand.[4]

---

4. Of course, if the room in which one is sitting and using encrypted IP telephony is "bugged" with conventional devices commercially sold, then all the encryption in the world is defeated.

Setting up Speak Freely is not quite intuitive but, once the program is operative, it provides one with high encryption and high voice quality communications over the Internet. A recommended setup procedure is to first get it to work in the "local loopback" mode, as explained in the directions; this involves adjusting the levels of the microphone and speaker (or earphone, for privacy). The next step in bringing the product on-line is to establish a connection with any one of a handful of servers used by Speak Freely for echo, such as echo.fourmilab.ch. Once connected, one simply talks into the microphone, and the sound will echo back about 10 seconds later. This is shown in Figures 16.2 and 16.3.

To communicate effectively with another person, both individuals must have compatible settings with respect to the technical parameters; the default settings are recommended for most situations. For an interesting technical tutorial on the various advantages and disadvantages of different settings (such as GSM encoding), the interested reader will find a lot of information in the "help" option. Once communication has been established, the two communicating parties can initiate encryption in both directions; obviously, the same encryption must be used (i.e., both the same type[s] and the same key[s]). These are set up under Options, as shown in Figure 16.4.

For security purposes, it is obviously inadvisable to agree on the encryption and the keys while talking with no encryption; this must be prearranged before the connection, using PGP encrypted messages, for example. As a last resort, if the two communicating parties know each other very well, they can agree on encryption keys over an unencrypted line by referring to items they both know that others would not (e.g., "the last name of the girl with the red dress at your birthday party last year").

One can use all three encryption options shown in Figure 16.5 simultaneously. If this is done, and if the encryption keys have not been agreed beforehand, only the first encryption key should be agreed upon in the manner suggested in the previous paragraph; once an encrypted connection is established with this key, the second and third encryption keys should then be agreed upon.

Establishing the initial connection is similar to placing a conventional phone call; instead of the phone number, one "dials" the other person's IP address. This can be provided directly by the other party in an e-mail just prior to the voice call; alternately, it can be found by the calling party if the party to be called has first "registered" with a Speak Freely server, such as lwl.fourmilab.ch, as shown in Figure 16.6. The information need not be true; it can be anything at all as long as it involves a unique e-mail address

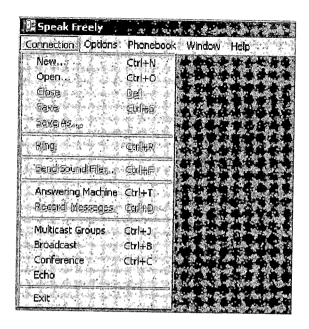

Figure 16.2 To initiate any new connection with Speak Freely, click on "new."

(which can be fictitious); hiding the e-mail address from the Speak Freely server is pointless, in this case, because the server will know the IP address—which is the whole point of going through this "registration" in the first place.

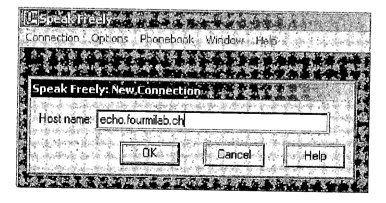

Figure 16.3 To test it, specify the echo server (among others).

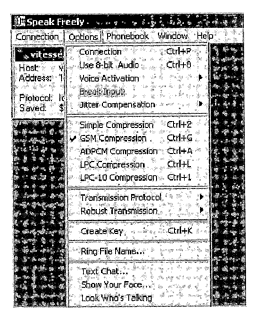

Figure 16.4 Ensure that the correct settings are used.

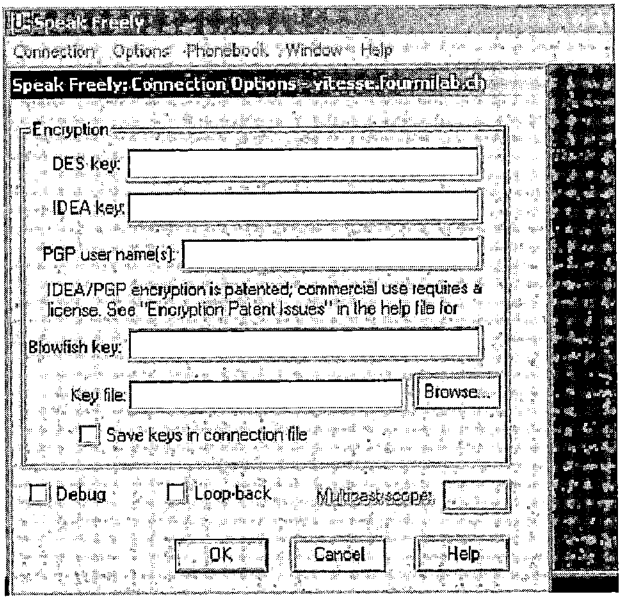

Figure 16.5 Setting up encryption for Speak Freely.

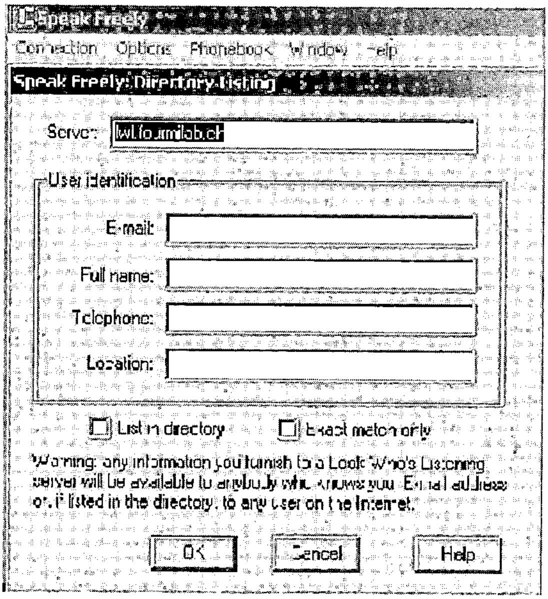

Figure 16.6 Registering with a Speak Freely server (optional) so that others can obtain the IP address.

In this case, the calling party (who is presumed to inquire *after* the party to be called has registered with such a server) will inquire from the server as shown in Figure 16.7. The calling party will contact the server and enter the preagreed-upon e-mail address that the party to be called has registered as. The server will then provide the calling party with the IP address of the party to be called, and the connection will be subsequently established.

16.2   Wireless Internet Access

The trend in most telecommunications, whether data or voice (and the two are merging as per Section 16.1), is away from wires and toward wireless, and it is motivated by convenience and decreased cost. Even within an office, the one-time expense of wireless local area network hardware is often less than the recurring expense of rewiring employees' network connectivity every time there is a reorganization or a shuffle of who sits where. For those whose work or lifestyle involves a lot of traveling, wireless connectivity is an obvious convenience, as the explosive growth of cellular telephony throughout the world has proved.

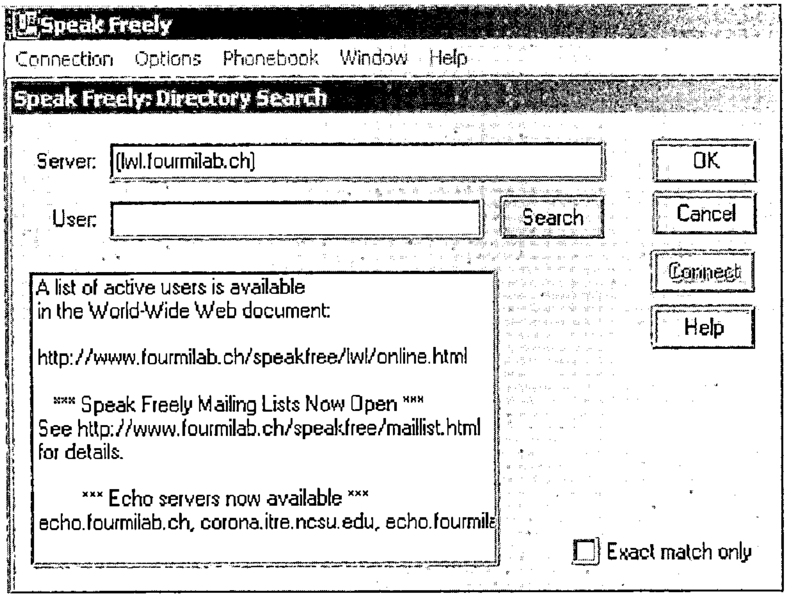

Figure 16.7 Determining the IP address of the party to be called if that party has registered with a preagreed Speak Freely server.

There is an additional advantage to wireless connectivity to the Internet, however: Unlike conventional wired connections in which the exact physical location of one's computer can be readily pinpointed, wireless connectivity allows a privacy-minded user a little more elbow room, in that his or her exact location can only be estimated to varying degrees of accuracy depending on the technology used and the resources of those who want to geolocate that person.

In general, having a wireless link in place of a wired link makes interception easier, simply because a wireless signal can always be intercepted from some distance away, whereas the wired signal requires the interceptor to physically access the wire that carries the information sought.

16.2.1   Distance Range of Wireless Interception

The propagation loss L of radio waves is proportional to the inverse square of the range R between the transmitter and the receiver under line-of-sight conditions; that is,

$$L \sim [\lambda / R]^2$$

This follows from simple geometrical arguments, because the surface area of a sphere is proportional to the square of its radius. The precise functional dependence is:

$$L = [\lambda / (4\pi R)]^2$$

where λ is the wavelength (in the same units as R; e.g., meters).

When there are intervening obstacles, however, such as walls, buildings, and trees, the attenuation can be vastly larger (often exceeding inverse range to the fifth power), and the corresponding range is much smaller. In practical terms this means that the intended receiver may be unable to receive the desired signal a mere 100 feet away, yet an interceptor located at a high-elevation vantage point may be able to receive that same signal from many miles away.

As an example, assume a wavelength of 1m (300 MHz). Urban attenuation loss even in the absence of intervening walls over a 1-km path could be as high as

$$L = [1 / (4\pi 1,000)]^5 = 3.2 \times 10^{-21}$$

or –204 dB, for those readers with an engineering background.

To get the same attenuation loss over a totally unobstructed line-of-sight path, one could be as far away as 1.5 million km! This shows quite clearly the advantage enjoyed by interception sites located in high-elevation-vantage locations. It also shows why walkie-talkies seldom get a mile of range in an urban environment, yet about the same transmitter power can reach a Globalstar or Iridium satellite just fine.

Because of this, the question "How far can I communicate?" or "How far away can I be intercepted?" can only be answered correctly by saying, "It depends"; any other answer is simply incorrect.

16.2.2 Connection Options

The basic options available to one who wants to connect to the Internet are outlined in the following sections; note that not all of them are available everywhere.

16.2.2.1 International Systems

1. *Cellular telephony.* Cellular service providers have been spending vast fortunes in "spectrum auctions"[5] (initially pioneered in the United States and now used in many nations as a way for governments to raise cash). As a result, cellular service providers have gone to extremes to market cellular services and to "cram" as many users as possible into the spectrum they bought. Adaptors exist for many cellular telephones and cellular systems.[6] A user is cautioned, however, that only a minimal amount of location privacy can be expected from the use of cell phones. In the United States, for example, the federal law CALEA (Communications Assistance to Law Enforcement) has mandated that cellular service providers be able to pinpoint the location of any one user within about 100 feet, ostensibly for emergency situations, for example, when one is having a heart attack in a car (which does not explain the law enforcement sponsorship of this law). Because of propagation anomalies, maintaining communications while in motion results in incessant interruptions of the connection.

   A myth has developed concerning the GSM system as somehow immune to interception. This is factually false for the following reasons:

   - There are three "flavors" of GSM encryption: none, A5/1, and A5/2. In their document "Real Time Cryptanalysis of A5/1 on a PC," Birukov, Shamir, and Wagner (http://216.167.120.50/a51-bsw.htm) show that A5/1 encryption is eminently cryptanalyzable; A5/2 is an even weaker encryption.

---

5. "Spectrum" here refers to a range of radio frequencies that are allocated to any one telecommunications service, such as TV, cellular, satellite communications, local emergency vehicle communications, and so on. As more and more services compete for the same commodity (interference-free radio frequencies), the price of that commodity (the spectrum) goes up.

6. With the exception of the United States, where Global System Mobile (GSM) market penetration is minimal, most of the world uses the GSM system. Adaptors for connecting numerous GSM handset models to computers range in price from around $100 to well over $500. In the United States, there are numerous competing systems; one of the most popular, a code division multiple access (CDMA) system used by Sprint PCS, allows users to buy such adaptors for around $100; other competing systems offer their own adaptors.

- In an October 21, 1999, e-mail to ukcrypto@maillist.ox.ac.uk, Mark Briceno, who reverse engineered the GSM algorithms, stated, "GSM security, to sum it up, is a joke. I know, because I am the person that reverse engineered the GSM algorithms. This includes COMP128, the authentication algorithm used by the overwhelming majority of GSM providers (not Vodafone, btw, though that fact should not be taken as an indication that the authentication Vodafone is using, but refuses to disclose, is any more secure than COMP128). GSM phones are subject to cloning. This includes cloning over the air."

- What is true is that, if one's GSM cell phone is registered in country X, country Y will not know the identity of the user who operates that phone in country Y; this is so because GSM is designed so that the only information that country Y's GSM service provider will get is that this particular phone is registered in country X (with which country Y has a reciprocal service arrangement), that country X's GSM service provider vouches that the bill for that call will be paid, and that the user can be identified by a temporary user ID which does not reveal his or her true identity.

- For out-of-country GSM users, one can rent a GSM phone from a small number of vendors; these phones are often "registered" in Switzerland or Singapore. Even for in-country GSM users, anonymity and privacy are easily achievable with the popular trend whereby anyone can purchase prepaid usage cards with no identification. One simply purchases, say, 1,000 minutes of airtime in a subscriber identification module (SIM) smart card, and nobody knows who that person is.

- In the case of non-GSM countries, for example, in the United States, anonymity is harder to come by, but still possible; many convenience stores sell a cell phone with a prepaid amount of airtime. Again, the privacy-minded person will still have to protect:

  - The fact that the ISP that he or she dials will likely know who that authorized subscriber is, unless one is using a new marketing concept, whereby a handful of companies are selling a fixed prepaid number of on-line minutes to their servers without requiring any identification from the purchaser;

- The fact that one's identity can be revealed indirectly through other telephone numbers (such as one's home or office telephone number) that one dials with that same telephone. This is so because today a record is kept of all telephone calls made by any telephone.

2. *Inmarsat Mini-M terminals.* These terminals look like briefcases, and are the descendants of much larger units used in years past; when an Inmarsat Mini-M unit's cover is opened, it serves as an antenna that must be pointed to the appropriate Inmarsat satellite. The units cost approximately $5,000 each, and each minute costs about $2 to $8. They can be used in most areas on Earth.

   Data rates are typically quite low (only 2,400 bps). As with cell phones, each Inmarsat unit must be licensed with some authorized service provider. As with any radio signal, it can be intercepted, but the content of the communication can be encrypted as is the case with any Internet data stream. Because of the pointing require-ments, these units can only be used on stable platforms; this excludes cars and small boats in motion.

   As with "satellite cellular" phones, discussed later, unless one has a justifiable business reason for using satellite telephony, it would be difficult to explain to a local security service why one is not using a much less expensive conventional phone line to connect to the Internet.

3. *Wireless local area network devices.* These are intended only for short ranges (within a few hundred feet from a transmitter; however, because of the uncertainties of radio wave propagation, the signal can often be received at considerably longer ranges). By and large, however, they offer no substantive location-privacy when com-pared with direct wireline connections.

   Caution: "802.11b" is the current standard for wireless home net-works; wireless networks are also catching on in the workplace; tens of millions of units are planned to be in use by mid-2002. The security implementation can be easily defeated as per some Febru-ary 2001 disclosures [1]. The 802.11b standard basically describes the communication that occurs in wireless local area networks (LANs). The Wired Equivalent Privacy (WEP) algorithm is used to protect wireless communication from eavesdropping. A secondary function of WEP is to prevent unauthorized access to a wireless network; this function is not an explicit goal in the 802.11b standard, but it is frequently considered to be a feature of WEP.

4. *Satellite cellular.* Systems such as the now-defunct Iridium, and Globalstar, which allow a subscriber to place and receive telephone calls practically anywhere on earth, can also accommodate data traffic at low data rates and with the proper adaptors.

   The privacy advantage is that, if data encryption is used, the host country will usually not be able to access either the data stream or any information about who is using such a phone. Although geolocation of such phones is technically straightforward, it is also unlikely in most countries. The disadvantage from a user's perspective is cost. Also, one may be hard pressed to explain why one is not using a much less expensive conventional phone (at home, or in a hotel if one is a visitor). Coverage for Globalstar is limited mostly by licensing issues (some countries do not like to forgo the revenue from international calls handled by government-owned Post, Telephone, and Telegraph, commonly known as PTTs).

5. *Airline telephones.* Most airlines today peddle the use of in-flight telephones with standard "RJ-11" receptacles for passengers' laptop computers; some cynics suggest that this is the main reason airlines ban the use of conventional cellular phones on board. Unless one is prepared for a very frustrating and expensive experience of drop-offs and disconnects and data errors, the use of such telephones for accessing the Internet is not recommended. Additionally, they offer neither privacy nor anonymity; the screen of one's laptop can readily be seen by all around; the telephone call itself must be charged to one's credit card; and one must have an account with whichever ISP to which one connects (or attempts to connect).

6. *Orbcomm radios.* Orbcomm is a U.S. firm based in Dulles, Virginia, that operates a number of low-orbiting small satellites used in numerous diverse applications, such as telemedicine and Internet access. A unit made by Magellan Company, model GSC100, looks like a walkie-talkie and costs around $1,000. It operates in the 150-MHz band—which means that it uses a half-meter-long telescopic conventional antenna that is not directional. The user enters a message on the unit and waits for the satellite to come overhead, at which time messages are sent to and from the satellite, to and from any Internet e-mail account. The system requires an unobstructed view of the sky.

7. *Teledesic* (http://www.teledesic.com/). This is a well-financed joint effort by McCaw Communications and Microsoft. Teledesic is building a global broadband Internet system using direct two-way satellite communications. It is still a few years from completion.

8. *Datafast.* An Australian two-way satellite-based system by Datafast Company (http://www.datafest.net.au/) is functionally similar to the popular U.S. system known as DirecPC.

16.2.2.2   United States–Only Systems

1. *Ricochet Network* (http://www.ricochet.net/). User equipment amount to a PCMCIA card with a small antenna, such as the one available from GoAmerica for wireless Internet access.

   Data rates are up to 128 Kbps. Service is available in select U.S. cities only, as well as in a handful of U.S. airports and hotels. In view of the limited power output of each unit, its geographical position can certainly be determined to within approximately half a mile. Individual "RF modems" must have corresponding accounts individually set up.

2. *DirecPC.* Until recently, Hughes Network Systems' DirecPC was a one-way satellite system; the user communicated his or her command to the Internet via a phone line, and received the Internet data from the satellite. The system requires a small elliptical inch dish on a roof, and the disk must be pointed at the satellite. A soon-to-be-released augmentation of the system allows full two-way satellite communications. Although wireless, this connectivity is not portable, as it requires a precisely pointed satellite dish. One could theoretically move the dish from its original location to another one, but the account holder would be known. A competing system is offered by Starband (http://www.starbanddepot.com/).

3. *Other systems.* A small assortment of competing wireless systems in the United States caters to the Internet user. These include the Palm network (which serves the Palm VII and Palm VIIx handheld devices that have a built-in radio and antenna). One needs to establish an account first, which requires the use of a credit card number.

16.2.2.3   Security Issues

Wireless connectivity to the Internet does not generally provide any more privacy or anonymity than a wired connection; if anything, it makes it less risky for an interceptor to "tap" the connection without the "smoking gun" trail of a physical connection to a conductor. If one wants to derive anonymity and privacy from the use of wireless connectivity to the Internet, one must also:

- Use a GSM cell phone that is registered in a third country, a prepaid airtime-usage SIM card for a GSM phone, or a prepaid non-GSM cell phone purchased with cash in a country that sells such phones. Alternately, use either a satellite cellular phone such as offered by Globalstar or an Inmarsat Mini-M terminal and have a good and believable explanation for such usage.

- Use an ISP that does not know the identity of the account holder, such as a handful of new ones in the United States that sell a prepaid amount of "connect time" without requiring any information from the purchaser.

Reference

[1] See, for example, http://biz.yahoo.com/rf/010205/n0599070_2.html and (for a technical discussion) see also http://www.issac.cs.Berkeley.edy/issac/wep-faq.html.

Selected Bibliography

For an extensive list of references on IP telephony, see:

Herlein, G., "The OpenPhone Project: Internet Telephony for Everyone!" *Linux Journal,* Vol. 69, December 1999, http://www.linuxjournal.com/lj-issues/issue69/3512.html.

Herlein, G. (gherlein@quicknet.net), and E. Okerson (eokerson@quicknet.net), IXJ-DRIVER-HOWTO, v.0.3.16, January 2000, ftp://ftp.quicknet.net/Developer/Linux/Drivers/Latest/IXJ-DRIVER-HOWTO.

Hersent, O., D. Gurle, and J. -P. Petit, *IP Telephony: Packet-Based Multimedia Communications Systems,* Harlow, England: Addison-Wesley, 2000.

http://techlibrary.wallstreetandtech.com/data/rlist?t=SYS_40_12_14_2 and http://www.cis.ohio-state.edu/~jain/refs/ref_voip.htm. This is an excellent list in that it identifies the numerous groups that deal with the subject (technical, regulatory, and advisory) in addition to providing a good taxonomy of technical references.

Afterword

Privacy of Computer-Related Activities: The Future

The future of privacy with respect to computer-related activities is bleak, for the following factual reasons:

1. Whistler, the new post-Windows-2000 operating system by Microsoft is—not surprisingly—dependent on the user's having an Internet connection. This means that data will be moving in and out of one's computer on a steady basis and, therefore, that there will be plenty of opportunities for sensitive data to leave one's computer. Additionally, the ISP will have increasing knowledge of each computer user's on-line and off-line activities.

2. Internet connections are steadily and rapidly shifting away from dial-up connections to high-speed ones, such as xDSL and cable modems. This means that a lot more data will be going in and out of users' computers; realistically, nobody has the time, equipment, or inclination to monitor all this data to ensure that it does not contain "snooped" information.

3. Most of us have tired of having to pay regular fees to software vendors to get each next upgrade of software, especially since such upgrades are often "bug fixes" that we should be getting for free. Once high-bandwidth (xDSL and cable) Internet access becomes the norm, the tendency will be to move away from having one's

own software; instead, many will be using a service provider's latest version of software for some minimal fee (say, 1 cent per hour to use the latest version of Microsoft Word or Adobe Photoshop). This will further increase the amount of data going into and out of our individual computers, making it that much harder to identify any remote snooping—not to mention the fact that a third party will know exactly what software we use, when, and how.

4. Many vendors, notably including Microsoft, have already shifted to a scheme whereby a buyer of their software has to "register" it on-line, or the software stops functioning after a set number of uses.

5. The use of adware (software that contacts sites through the Internet without the user's knowledge or approval) is likely to expand and become increasingly sophisticated. It is already next to impossible to detect such programs when they use legitimate ports to communicate while a user is on-line (e.g., using Web browsers' port 80).

6. As this book shows, computer forensics is really very simple to practice. Snooping on an on-line user who does not use anonymity and encryption (which are already banned in some countries) is even simpler, hence the deployment of such methods as the U.S. Carnivore, the technology behind the British RIP Act, and corresponding practices in other nations.

7. As this book also shows in great detail, the move from DOS to Windows created a vast increase in the vulnerabilities to computer forensics and remote interception. Moving from DOS to Windows 3.1x was bad enough, but one could still manage to control the system files (win.ini and system.ini) and the swap file. The move to Win95/98/NT/2000 has made security massively more complex because of the huge registry, which stores a lot of information and causes the computer to crash if one makes a misstep in editing it. The move to more complex operating systems—already in beta testing—will continue this trend.

8. As a larger percentage of citizens use computers and connect on-line, governments and profit-minded commercial entities will be increasingly motivated to monitor the citizenry; it is effective and cost-effective. If monitoring *can* be done (and it can be done easily nowadays), it will be done.

Additionally, existing laws (even in countries that respect the rule of law) offer no real protection to an individual from "snooping," because if security services and police want to snoop, they will often do it despite the law; they will only go through the legal process if they want to use the information they collect in court. This applies especially to countries where only lip service is paid to the rule of law.

Despite the foregoing, the informed user who uses the techniques detailed in this book will always be able to maintain the privacy of on-line and off-line data. Specifically:

1. Full-disk encryption (Section 14.2) will always protect against hostile computer forensics practiced by a repressive regime. At a minimum, encryption of individual files (Chapters 13 and 14) will always be an option, subject to the caveats identified herein.

2. The techniques described in Chapters 8 through 14 (secure installation, disk wiping, removal of files that record user activities, and so on) will always provide the protection inherent in their use. Again, the user is cautioned against sloppy use of such techniques, as they will result in a false sense of security.

3. End-to-end encryption while on-line (encryption between the user's computer and the eventual "host" on the Internet) will always remove the threat of interception by an ISP or a telephone tap.

4. For cases in which the use of encryption is in and of itself a crime (or at least a red flag), steganography (see Section 14.5), if (and only if) used properly, is always a viable option that defeats encryption-detection.

In summary, the odds are stacked in favor of only the rare computer user who is both well informed and security conscious. If a user is neither, then the odds will always be overwhelmingly in favor of the person or entity who wants to snoop into his or her computer-related activities. Remembering Cardinal Richelieu's admonition ("If you give me six lines written by the most honest man, I will find something in them to hang him"), and given how easy it is for an unethical competent prosecutor to present forensically obtained tidbits of computer data out of context to sway a technically challenged judge or jury, one would be well advised to use the information in this book to become both well informed and security conscious.

Appendix A
Providers of Computer Forensics and Training

A.1   Major Commercial Organizations in the United States

Here is a list of major commerical organizations in the United States.

- TASC Corporation, Herndon, Virginia. Now part of SAIC.
- New Technologies Inc. (NTI), http://www.forensics-intl.com/, Gresham, Oregon.
- Per-Se Technologies (a unit of the Atlanta-based Medaphis Corpo-ration). Many of Per-Se's analysts are former employees of the U.S. government.
- SAIC's Center for Information Security Technology. It makes Computer Misuse Detection System (CMDS), a computer foren-sics tool, and provides expertise in computer forensics to its U.S. government clients.
- Perot Systems Corporation, Atlanta, Georgia. In partnership with ISS (Internet Security Systems), PSC is implementing ISS's detec-tion software.
- Electronic Data Systems Corp. (EDS) has formed a joint venture with the National Technical Information Service agency to provide

public-key infrastructure, intrusion detection, and computer forensics services.

A.2   Smaller Commercial Organizations

The list below is only a partial list.

- Digital Detective Services, Falls Church, Virginia.
- META Security Group, Atlanta, Georgia. Offers post-attack-investigations computer forensics.
- Computer Forensics and Forensic Computing. Computer forensics expert: Judd Robbins, http://knock-knock.com/expert/forensic.htm.
- Computer Forensics Inc., http://www.forensics.com/.
- 21st Century Computer Forensics and Services, http://www.com-pukirk.com/.
- Computer Forensics Expert Witness Network, http://computer-forensics.net/.
- LJK Computing, Inc., Tampa, Florida.
- SDC & Associates Consultants, http://www.sdcassociates.com/litigation.htm.
- I-Net Inc., Bethesda, Maryland. Headed by a former head of the FBI's National Computer Crime Squad.
- Berryhill Computer Forensics, http://www.computerforensics.com/index/htm.
- Presentation Dynamics Inc., http://www.computrade.net/.
- Rehman Technology Services, Inc., http://www.fdle.org/computer.htm.
- STP Computer Forensics, http://home.earthlink.net/~telling/.
- Data Recovery Rehman Technology Services, Inc., http://www.datadiscovery.com/.
- Data Recovery Richmond, Chester, Virginia.
- M Corby and Associates Inc., http://www.mcorby.com/training.htm.
- Rios Computer Associates, http://www.rios.org/.
- ICSC Computer Forensics Company, http://www.netside.net/~lasuarez/serv01.htm.

- Price Waterhouse Coopers, New York, http://www.pricewater-housecoopers.com/.
- CompuForensics, http://www.compuforensics.com.
- Rehman Technology Services, Inc., http://www.surveil.com.
- Casey Key PI & Computer Forensics, Inc., Orlando, Florida, http://www.caseykey.com/CKlink.htm.
- Data Recovery Richmond, http://www.computer-evidence.com/servicelvl.htm.
- Forensics, http://www.bergen.org/AAST/ComputerAnimation/App _Forensics.html.
- J.B. Kraft, http://www.jbkraft.com/.
- Computer Forensics Inc., http://www.forensics.com/annce/events.htm.
- Ernst & Young LLP, http://www.ey.com/aabs/isaas/forensics.asp.
- Sheldon Soltis, sheldon@evidence.finder.com/.
- Dockery Associates, L.L.C., http://evidence.finder.com/sheldon.html.
- Data Recovery Labs, http://www.datarec.com/~nmajors/forensic services.html.
- Electronic Evidence Discovery, Inc., http://www.eedinc.com/company/.
- Sydex Company, http://www.sydex.com/sydex.html.

A.3 Official U.S. Entities Renowned for Computer Forensics

Here is a list of offical U.S. entities renowned for computer forensics.

- King County Sheriff's Office Fraud & Computer Forensics Unit, http://www.metrokc.gov/sheriff/fraud.htm. This is the largest unit of its kind.
- High Tech Crimes Unit, San Jose Police Department. Considered to have the best such capability of all police departments in the United States.[1]
- Florida Association of Computer Crime Investigators (FACCI).
- Rome Air Force Labs. Defensive Information Warfare Branch.
- High Technology Crime Investigation Association (HTCIA).

---

1. According to L. Curtis, Silicon Valley President of the International High Technology Crimes Investigation Association.

- Computer Incident Advisory Capability Board.
- International Association of Computer Investigations (IACIS), http://www.iacis.com/.
- National White Collar Crimes Center (NWCCC), http://www.iir.com/nwccc.htm.
- High Technology Crime Unit, Santa Clara, California, District Attorney's Office.
- U.S. Secret Service, Office of Investigation.
- FBI Computer Analysis and Response Team, at the National Infrastructure Protection Center (NIPC), Washington, D.C.
- FBI Computer Investigations and Operations Center (CIOS) under the NIPC. Coordinates intrusion.
- AF OSI, at Bolling AFB, Washington.
- Oregon State Police Computer Crime Unit. Considered one of the best in computer forensics.
- Computer Investigations and Technology Unit, New York Police Department.
- Office of Criminal Enforcement Forensics and Training, Environmental Protection Agency.

A.4   Foreign Entities in Computer Forensics

A.4.1   United Kingdom

- Computer Forensics Ltd., http://www.computer-forensics.com.
- S. B. Bates and Associates, http://www.rg-av.com/reviews.htm.
- Ernst & Young, London, England.
- U.K. Serious Fraud Office; IT Investigations.
- Computer Security Research Center, London School of Economics, http://csrc.lse.ac.uk/csrc/evidsem.htm.
- Lee & Allen, Forensic Accountancy, London.
- Computer Crime Unit, Scotland Yard.
- QCC Consulting, London, England.

A.4.2 Australia and New Zealand

- Serious Fraud Office, New Zealand Police Electronic Crime Unit.
- About Us Company, http://www.vividinsights.com.au/html/about _us.htm.
- Network Security Ltd., Computer Forensics Division.

A.5 Computer Forensics Training Organizations

- Computer Sciences Corp., Falls Church, Virginia.
- Legal Aspects of Computer Crime (LACC), http://www.finder.com/ biblio.html, and by subscription, http://www.finder.com/subscribe .html. This is a moderated listserver that monitors developments in computer crime.
- Perot Systems Corporation, Atlanta, Georgia, in partnership with ISS (Internet Security Systems), is implementing ISS's detection software.
- Information Technology Association of America (ITAA) has formed a "Cybercitizen Partnership" with the U.S. Department of Justice.
- Mailing List and Discussion Forum of Computer Forensic Techniques, http://www.infowar.com/.
- National White Collar Crime Center (NWCCC), Federal Law Enforcement Training Center (FLETC). FLETC has been offering computer forensics courses since 1989.
- Forensic Association of Computing Technologists (FACT).
- International Association of Computer Investigative Specialists (IACIS), http://www.cops.org/.
- Financial Fraud Institute, Federal Law Enforcement Training Center, Glynco, Georgia.
- ESecurity Solutions, Ernst & Young Co.
- Forensic Technology Institute, University of New Haven, West Haven, Connecticut, has created a college-credit course and certification for computer forensics.
- Dockery Associates, LLC, http://evidence.finder.com/dockery/. Training in electronic media discovery. Publishes an "electronic evidence journal" available to subscribers.

- Office of Criminal Enforcement Forensics and Training, Environmental Protection Agency. At the National Enforcement Investigations Center (NEIC) in Denver, Colorado.
- Computer Forensics Online. An on-line Web magazine, popular with law enforcement. (Ref: http://www.shk-dlpc.com/cfo/editorial.htm.)
- New Technologies Inc. (NTI), http://www.secure-data.com/, Gresham, Oregon.

Appendix B
Ports Associated with Known Trojan Cyberthreats

B.1 Trojan Port Numbers

8	ICMP Ping Attack
9	UDP Chargen
19	UDP Chargen
21	TCP FTP service
23	TCP TELNET Service
25	TCP Several Trojans use this port
31	TCP (Agent 31, Hacker's Paradise)
41	TCP Deep Throat
53	TCP DNS service
58	TCP DM Setup
79	CP Firehotcker
80	TCP Executor
99	CP Hidden Port 2.0
110	TCP ProMail Trojan
113	TCP Kazimas

121	TCP Jammer Killah
129	TCP Password Generator Protocol
135	TCP UDP Netbios Remote procedure call
137	TCP UDP Netbios name (DoS attacks)
138	TCP UDP Netbios datagram
139	TCP UDP Netbios session (DoS attacks)
146	TCP Infector 1.3
421	TCP Tcp Wrappers
456	TCP Hacker's Paradise
531	TCP Rasmin
555	TCP Stealth Spy, Phaze
666	TCP Attack FTP
911	TCP Dark Shadow
999	TCP DeepThroat
9400	TCP In Command
9999	TCP The Prayer 1.0–2.0
1000	TCP Der Spaeher
1001	TCP (Silencer, WebEx)
1011	TCP Doly Trojan
1012	TCP Doly Trojan
1015	TCP Doly Trojan
1024	TCP NetSpy
1025	UDP Maverick's Matrix
1027	TCP ICQ
1029	TCP ICQ
1032	TCP ICQ
1033	TCP ICQ Trojan
1033	TCP Exploit Descent Manager Module
1042	TCP Rasmin
1045	TCP Rasmin
1080	TCP Socks/Wingate
1090	TCP Xtreme

1170	TCP Voice Streaming Audio
1207	TCP SoftWar
1234	TCP Ultors Trojan
1243	TCP (Sub Seven)
1245	TCP (VooDoo Doll)
1257	TCP (Sub Seven 2.1)
1269	TCP Maverick's Matrix
1492	TCP Ftp 99CMP Trojan
1349	UDP BackOrifice DLL Comm
1394	TCP Gofriller, BackDoor
1492	TCP FTP99CMP
1509	TCP Psyber Streaming Server
1600	TCP Shivka-Burka
1807	TCP SpySender
1981	TCP (Shockrave Trojan)
1999	TCP (BackDoor Trojan)
2000	TCP Remote Explorer
2000	UDP Remote Explorer/CallBook
2001	TCP Trojan Cow
2023	TCP (Unknown Trojan)
2086	TCP Netscape/Corba exploit
2023	TCP (Ripper)
2115	TCP Bugs
2140	TCP (Deep Throat)
2140	UDP (Deep Throat)
2283	TCP Unknown Trojan
2583	UDP Unknown Trojan
2565	TCP (Striker)
2583	TCP WinCrash
2716	TCP The Prayer 1.2–1.3
2721	TCP Phase Zero
2801	TCP Phineas Phucker

2989	UDP Rat
3024	TCP WinCrash
3129	TCP Master's Paradise
3150	TCP Deep Throat
3150	UDP Deep Throat
3587	UDP Sh*tHead trojan
3587	TCP Sh*tHead trojan
3700	TCP Portal of Doom
4092	TCP WinCrash
4321	TCP SchoolBus
4567	TCP File Nail
4590	TCP ICQ Trojan
4950	TCP Unknown trojan
5000	TCP (Sokets de Trois v1.)
5001	TCP Sokets de Trois v1.
5011	TCP OOTLT
5031	TCP Net Metropolitan
5032	TCP Net Metropolitan
5321	TCP Firehotcker
5400	TCP (Blade Runner)
5401	TCP Blade Runner
5402	TCP Blade Runner
5501	UDP
5521	TCP Illusion Mailer
5550	TCP (X-Tcp Trojan)
5555	TCP ServeMe
5556	TCP BO Facil
5557	TCP BO Facil
5569	TCP Robo-Hack
5666	TCP (PC Crasher)
5742	TCP (WinCrash)
6400	TCP (The Thing)

6670	TCP	(Deep Throat)
6711	TCP	Sub Seven
6712	TCP	Sub Seven
6713	TCP	Sub Seven
6723	TCP	MStream (Attacker to handler)
6771	TCP	Deep Throat
6776	TCP	Sub Seven
6838	UDP	MStream (Agent to handler)
6939	TCP	Indoctrination
6969	TCP	(Gate Crasher, Priority)
6970	TCP	Gate Crasher
7000	TCP	Remote Grab
7028	TCP	Unknown Trojan
7028	UDP	Unknown Trojan
7300	TCP	Net Monitor
7301	TCP	Net Monitor
7302	TCP	Net Monitor
7303	TCP	Net Monitor
7304	TCP	Net Monitor
7305	TCP	Net Monitor
7306	TCP	Net Monitor
7307	TCP	Net Monitor
7308	TCP	Net Monitor
7309	TCP	Net Monitor
7323	TCP	Sygate Backdoor
7323	UDP	Sygate Backdoor
7789	TCP	ICKiller
7983	UDP	MStream (handler to Agent)
8783	TCP	Trojan
9325	UDP	MStream (agent to handler)
9872	TCP	Portal of Doom
9873	TCP	Portal of Doom

9874	TCP	Portal of Doom
9875	TCP	Portal of Doom
9989	TCP	iNi-Killer
10067	TCP	Portal of Doom
10067	UDP	Portal of Doom
10167	TCP	Portal of Doom
10167	UDP	Portal of Doom
10498	UDP	(Handler to Agent)
10520	TCP	Acid Shivers
10607	TCP	Coma
10666	UDP	Ambush
11000	TCP	Senna Spy
11223	TCP	Progenic Trojan
12076	TCP	GJamer
12223	TCP	Hack'99, KeyLogger
12361	TCP	TCP Whack-a-mole
12362	TCP	TCP Whack-a-mole
12345	TCP	(Netbus, Ultor's Trojan)
12346	TCP	(Netbus)
12361	TCP	TCP Whack-a-mole
12362	TCP	TCP Whack-a-mole
12456	TCP	NetBus
12631	TCP	WhackJob
12701	TCP	Eclipse 2000
12754	TCP	MStream (Attacker to handler)
13000	TCP	Senna Spy
13700	TCP	Unknown Trojan
15104	TCP	MStream (Attacker to handler)
16660	TCP	Stacheldraht
16969	TCP	Priority
18753	TCP	Shaft Handler to agent(s)
20000	TCP	Millennium

20001	TCP	Millennium
20034	TCP	(NetBus 2 Pro)
20432	TCP	Shaft Client to handler(s)
20433	UDP	Shaft Agent to handler(s)
21544	TCP	Unknown Trojan
21554	TCP	GirlFriend
22222	TCP	Prosiak
20203	TCP	Logged!
20331	TCP	Unknown Trojan
23456	TCP	EvilFTP, UglyFTP
24680	TCP	Trojan
24680	UDP	Trojan
26274	TCP	Delta Source
26274	UDP	Delta Source
27665	TCP	Trin00/TFN2K
27374	UDP	(Sub-7 2.1)
27374	TCP	Sub-7 2.1
27444	UDP	Trin00/TFN2K
27573	UDP	Sub-7 2.1
27573	TCP	Sub-7 2.1
27665	TCP	Trin00 DoS Attack
29891	TCP	The Unexplained
30029	TCP	AOL Trojan
30999	TCP	Kuang2 Trojan
30100	TCP	(NetSphere)
30101	TCP	NetSphere
30102	TCP	NetSphere
30303	TCP	Sockets de Troie
31335	UDP	Trin00 DoS Attack
31337	UDP	(Backorifice/BO-2K)
31337	TCP	(Netpatch)
31338	TCP	NetSpy DK

31338	UDP	Deep BO
31339	TCP	NetSpy DK
31666	TCP	BOWhack
31785	TCP	(Hack'a'Tack)
31789	UDP	(Hack'a'Tack)
31790	UDP	(Hack'a'Tack)
31791	UDP	Hack'a'Tack
32418	TCP	Acid Battery
33333	TCP	Prosiak
33390	UDP	Unknown trojan
34324	TCP	(BigGluck, TN)
34555	UDP	Trin00 Ping/Pong Response
33911	UDP	Trojan Spirit 2001
40421	TCP	(Master's Paradise Trojan)
40412	TCP	(The Spy)
40422	TCP	Master's Paradise
40423	TCP	Master's Paradise
40425	TCP	Master's Paradise
40426	TCP	Master's Paradise
47252	TCP	Delta Source
47262	UDP	Delta Source
49301	UDP	Online KeyLogger
50505	TCP	Sokets de Trois v2.
50766	TCP	Fore 1.0 Trojan
50776	TCP	Fore
53001	TCP	(Remote Windows Shutdown)
54320	TCP	(Back Orifice 2000)
54320	UDP	Back Orifice
54321	TCP	School Bus, Back Orifice
54321	UDP	Back Orifice 2000
57341	UDP	Net Raider Trojan
57341	TCP	Net Raider Trojan

60000	TCP	Deep Throat
61603	TCP	Bunker-Hill Trojan
61348	TCP	Bunker-HillTrojan
61466	TCP	(Telecommando)
63485	TCP	Bunker-Hill Trojan
65000	TCP	(Devil)
65000	TCP	Stacheldraht

Perhaps a more useful list is the following one, from a "helpfile" from http://www.mcafee.com/myapps/firewall/ov_firewall.asp, which shows which ports are used by various known Trojans.

Trojan Name(s)	Port
Blade Runner, Doly Trojan, Fore, Invisible FTP, WebEx, WinCrash, FTP Trojan	21
Tiny Telnet Server	23
Antigen, Email Password Sender, Haebu Coceda, Shtrilitz Stealth, Terminator, WinPC, WinSpy, Kuang2, ProMail Trojan	25
Hackers Paradise, Agent	31
Masters Paradise	31
DeepThroat	41
DMSetup	58
Firehotcker	79
Executor	80
ProMail Trojan	110
JammerKillah	121
TCP Wrappers	421
Hackers Paradise	456
Rasmin	531

Ini-Killer, Phase Zero, Stealth Spy	555
Satanz Backdoor, Attack FTP	666
Dark Shadow	911
DeepThroat	999
Silencer, WebEx	1001
Doly Trojan	1011
Doly Trojan	1012
NetSpy	1024
Rasmin	1045
Xtreme	1090
Psyber Stream Server, Voice	1170
Ultors Trojan	1234
BackDoor-G, SubSeven	1243
VooDoo Doll	1245
BO DLL	1349
FTP99CMP	1492
Shivka-Burka	1600
SpySender	1807
Shockrave	1981
BackDoor	1999
Trojan Cow	2001
Ripper	2023
Bugs	2115
Deep Throat, The Invasor	2140
Striker	2565
WinCrash	2583
Phineas Phucker	2801
WinCrash	3024
Masters Paradise	3129
Deep Throat, The Invasor	3150
Portal of Doom	3700
WinCrash	4092

File Nai	4567
ICQ Trojan	4590
Sockets de Troie, Bubbel, Back Door Setup	5000
Sockets de Troie, Back Door Setup	5001
Firehotcker	5321
Blade Runner	5400
Blade Runner	5401
Blade Runner	5402
ServeMe	5555
BO Facil	5556
BO Facil	5557
Robo-Hack	5569
WinCrash	5742
The Thing	6400
DeepThroat	6670
DeepThroat	6771
BackDoor-G, SubSeven	6776
Indoctrination	6939
GateCrasher, Priority	6969
Remote Grab	7000
NetMonitor	7300
NetMonitor	7301
NetMonitor	7306
NetMonitor	7307
NetMonitor	7308
ICKiller, BackDoor Setup	7789
Portal of Doom	9872
Portal of Doom	9873
Portal of Doom	9874
Portal of Doom	9875
INi-Killer	9989

Portal of Doom	10067
Portal of Doom	10167
Acid Shivers	10520
Coma	10607
Senna Spy	11000
Progenic trojan	11223
Hack'99 KeyLogger	12223
GabanBus, NetBus, Pie Bill Gates, X-bill	12345
GabanBus, NetBus, X-bill	12346
Whack-a-mole	12361
Whack-a-mole	12362
WhackJob	12631
Senna Spy	13000
Priority	16969
Millennium	20001
NetBus 2 Pro	20034
GirlFriend	21544
Prosiak	22222
Evil FTP, Ugly FTP	23456
Delta	26274
SubSeven (new	27374
The Unexplained	29891
AOL Trojan	30029
NetSphere	30100
NetSphere	30101
NetSphere	30102
Sockets de Troie	30303
Back Orifice Client, Baron Night, B02, Bo Facil	31337
BackFire, Back Orifice, DeepBO	31337
NetSpy DK	31338

Back Orifice, DeepBO	31338
NetSpy DK	31339
BOWhack	31666
Prosiak	33333
BigGluck, TN	34324
The Spy	40412
Masters Paradise, Agent 40421	40421
Masters Paradise	40422
Masters Paradise	40423
Masters Paradise	40426
Delta	47262
Sockets de Troie	50505
Fore	50766
Remote Windows Shutdown	53001
School Bus	54321
DeepThroat	60000
Telecommando	61466
Devil	65000

Glossary

biometrics The collection of science-based techniques that abstract an individual's biological characteristics (such as fingerprint, retinal pattern, voiceprint, palm print) for the purpose of ensuring authentication.

BIOS Acronym for basic input output system. It is the set of instructions, stored in a computer chip (integrated circuit) that is used by the computer to interface the hardware with the operating system and facilitate the bootup (starting after power is applied) process.

booting up The sequence of steps involved in getting a computer to become functional after it is turned on. Some of these steps are automated (e.g., ones stored in CMOS, others on disk) and some are manual (e.g., entry of passwords).

caller ID A service offered by many telephone companies worldwide, made possible by the widespread use of a protocol called Signaling System 7, that sends the telephone number of the calling party to the called party. Most countries' telephone companies have this and use it for internal purposes, even though they may not offer it to their customers.

cluster A collection of a number of disk sectors that forms a disk's "allocation unit" for storing data; this is the smallest unit of storage that is handled by the particular operating system and disk being used.

CMOS memory   A small amount of battery-backed electronic memory in a computer circuit that stores a computer's configuration so that the computer can be started by merely pressing a switch.

cryptography   The process of converting a message into an equivalent version that is not understandable by unauthorized viewers (encryption), and the converse process of making it understandable (decryption).

e-mail   Abbreviation for "electronic mail"; the creation, transmission, reception, and viewing of messages using computers.

firewall   Generic name for any technique (software, hardware, or both) intended to reduce a network-connected user's vulnerability to security threats associated with being on that network (such as the Internet).

FTP   Acronym for File Transfer Protocol, the protocol for transferring files over the Internet or other network using TCP/IP.

hacker   Initially the term denoted a competent computer programmer. The term has degenerated to denote a person who performs a programming act that is illegal.

hashing   The software-based mathematical process of creating a short collection of digital symbols in connection with a digital file so that if that file were to be modified, a different set of digital symbols would result. Intended to ensure that digital files cannot be altered undetectably.

ICQ   Acronym for "I seek you." Israeli-developed software protocol (acquired by AOL) for teleconferencing over the Internet. Allows "chatting" (actually typing back and forth), e-mail, and even transfer of files. Its main claim to fame is that it alerts the user as to when anyone in his or her designated ("buddy") list is on-line.

Internet   A large network of smaller networks that was originally developed for the U.S. Advanced Research Projects Agency as a network intended to survive most any attack of any of its portions. Now the global network that links all countries for data communications.

IPX   Acronym for Internetwork Packet Exchange.

ISDN Acronym for Integrated Services Digital Network.

NetBIOS The standard networking protocol for DOS and Windows. It facilitates a programming interface for computer programs ("applications") for networking purposes over, for example, TCP/IP.

PBX Acronym for private branch exchange. A private telephone-switching system used in the conventional telephony world to connect numerous telephone instruments inside an office to a far smaller number of available telephone lines, on the premise that not all telephone instruments will be in use all the time.

PGP Acronym for Pretty Good Privacy. A hugely popular encryption software program using a combination of public and conventional key encryption, considered very secure if used properly. It was originally developed by Phil Zimmerman.

POTS Acronym for plain old telephone service.

POTS dial peer A software object that ties together a voice port and the telephone number of a device attached to the port (also called local dial peer).

PRI Acronym for Primary Rate Interface. Used in ISDN.

PSTN Acronym for public-switched telephone network.

public-key cryptography An encryption method using two keys (either one of which cannot be inferred from the other), whereby a file encrypted with one of these two keys can only be decrypted by the other. A user typically publicizes one key (labeled the "public key") so that anyone can encrypt files to that user, but only that user can decrypt the files, with the second key, labeled "secret."

QoS Acronym for quality of service. A measure of the level of performance needed for a particular application, such as a voice-over-IP connection.

registry A database file in a computer using Windows 95/98/NT/2000 that contains large amounts of information about a computer's entire configuration (including hardware and software).

remote dial peer   A software object that ties together an IP address and a telephone number at a remote site reached over the IP network (also called VoIP dial peer).

RSVP   Acronym for resource reservation protocol, a network protocol that enables routers to reserve the bandwidth necessary for reliable performance.

RTP   Acronym for real-time transport protocol, a network protocol used to carry packetized audio and video traffic over an IP network.

sector   A portion of a track.

session target   A remote IP or DNS address specified as one end of a voice connection.

slack   The colloquial commonly used term to denote the portion of a track of a disk that contains data after the "end of file" and before the "end of cluster."

SSL   Acronym for Secure Socket Layer. A protocol developed by Netscape that uses public-key encryption in conjunction with a browser that allows end-to-end encryption between an Internet user's browser and the Web site with which the user is communicating.

steganography   The process of hiding the existence of a sensitive file by using any one or more of a large collection of computer-related techniques. The modern-day equivalent of the microdot of World War II fame.

swap file   A file on a computer disk created by Windows and used as virtual (make-believe) memory; usually intended to allow a computer with limited conventional electronic volatile memory (RAM) to accommodate software that has higher RAM requirements.

TCP/IP   Acronym for Transmission Control Protocol/Internet Protocol. A protocol developed for the U.S. Department of Defense that has become the worldwide standard for data telecommunications; it includes functionality to ensure that the data arrives at its destination (verses UDP, which does not).

track   A concentric circle on a computer disk that is intended to store data. On magnetic tape, tracks are parallel to each other or, in some cases, such as with VCR tapes, helical.

VoIP Acronym for voice over IP, a feature that carries voice traffic, such as telephone calls and faxes, over an IP network, simultaneously with data traffic.

VoIP dial peer A software object that ties together an IP address and a telephone number at a remote site reached over the IP network (also called remote dial peer).

VPN Acronym for virtual private network. A way to enjoy private communications as if one had one's own private network, but by using a public network such as the Internet.

Web Abbreviation for World Wide Web (WWW). A user-friendly graphical way of connecting to other sites on the Internet for the purpose of receiving and sending information.

wiping Rendering data recorded on a disk unreadable by any known technical means intended to retrieve it.

About the Author

Michael A. Caloyannides earned his Ph.D. in electrical engineering, applied mathematics, and philosophy from the California Institute of Technology, in Pasadena, California, in 1972. He worked at the highest technical levels in the U.S. aerospace industry for 15 years, followed by another 14 years as senior scientist with the U.S. government, in which capacity he was awarded the Scientist of the Year award in 1987, along with numerous awards for exceptional accomplishment. In addition, he has taught classes in electrical engineering at California State University and at George Mason University, near Washington, D.C., and he has been a consultant to various corporations. He has also been an independent senior consultant to NASA, evaluating advanced technology proposals for work in deep-space exploration. He has published widely in professional journals and is a senior member of the IEEE.

Dr. Caloyannides' professional range of interests includes both of the two areas of explosive growth today: information technology and telecommunications. He is the appointed chairman of a federal advisory subcommittee working with the FCC on packet networks. He holds a U.S. patent on an adjustable digital filter for high-speed digital transmission. He is currently a Senior Fellow at Mitretek Systems, a Washington, D.C.- area think tank in information assurance, network security, computer forensics, and related aspects.

He can be contacted at micky@IEEE.org.

Index

2Mosaic_0.1, 52

Accessing e-mail, 165–66
Acquisition software, 66–73
   adware, 67–71
   "backdoor Santas," 71–73
   DIRT, 67
   Investigator, 67
   Mom, 67
   NoKnock E-Warrant, 67
   Silent Guard, 67
   SilentRunner, 67
   spyware, 67–71
   TSADBOT, 68–69
Additional decryption keys (ADKs),
      268–69
Adobe "Web Buy" feature, 125
Adware, 67–71
   legitimate ports and, 212
   protection against, 181–84
   use expansion, 348
   See also Spyware
AFS (Authentec Forensic Software), 22
Airline telephones, 343
Anadisk, 21
Analyzer.exe, 213

Anger.tar.gz, 213
Anonymicer, 188
Anonymity, 92–95
   flavors of, 93
   hostile computer forensics, 200–201
   in-country ISPs, 198–200
   Internet, 175
   as irritant, 93
   justification, 94
   practical, 95
   proxy servers for, 185–89
   Usenet, 198
Anonymizers, 159–61
   user interface, 159–60
   Web-based, 174
Anonymous remailers, 172–77
   concatenated, 173
   defined, 172
   See also Remailers
AOL Instant Messenger (AIM), 144–45,
      153, 195
Application proxy, 203
Application-software-created history files,
      36–37
Aps-0.14.tar.z, 213
Arms Export Control Act, 231

Related Artech House Titles

Advanced ANSI SQL Data Modeling and Structure Processing, Michael M. David

Advanced Database Technology and Design, Mario Piattini and Oscar Díaz, editors

Business Process Implementation for IT Professionals and Managers, Robert B. Walford

Configuration Management: The Missing Link in Web Engineering, Susan Dart

Demystifying the IPsec Puzzle, Sheila Frankel

E-Commerce Systems Architecture and Applications, Wasim Rajput

Electronic Payment Systems for E-Commerce, Second Edition, Donal O'Mahony, Michael Peirce, and Hitesh Tewari

Fundamentals of Network Security, John E. Canavan

Future Codes: Essays in Advanced Computer Technology and the Law, Curtis E. A. Karnow

Global Distributed Applications with Windows® DNA, Enrique Madrona

A Guide to Software Configuration Management, Alexis Leon

Guide to Standards and Specifications for Designing Web Software, Stan Magee and Leonard L. Tripp

Information Hiding Techniques for Steganography and Digital Watermarking, Stefan Katzenbeisser and Fabien A. P. Petitcolas, editors

Internet and Intranet Security, Rolf Oppliger

Internet Commerce Development, Craig Standing

Managing Computer Networks: A Case-Based Reasoning Approach, Lundy Lewis

Metadata Management for Information Control and Business Success, Guy Tozer

Multimedia Database Management Systems, Guojun Lu

Practical Guide for Implementing Secure Intranets and Extranets, Kaustubh M. Phaltankar

Practical Guide to Software Quality Management, John W. Horch

Practical Process Simulation Using Object-Oriented Techniques and C++, José Garrido

Secure Messaging with PGP and S/MIME, Rolf Oppliger

Security Fundamentals for E-Commerce, Vesna Hassler

Security Technologies for the World Wide Web, Rolf Oppliger

Software Verification and Validation for Practitioners and Managers, Second Edition, Steven R. Rakitin

Strategic Software Production with Domain-Oriented Reuse, Paolo Predonzani, Giancarlo Succi, and Tullio Vernazza

Systems Modeling for Business Process Improvement, David Bustard, Peter Kawalek, and Mark Norris, editors

Workflow Modeling: Tools for Process Improvement and Application Development, Alec Sharp and Patrick McDermott

For further information on these and other Artech House titles, including previously considered out-of-print books now available through our In-Print-Forever® (IPF®) program, contact:

Artech House	Artech House
685 Canton Street	46 Gillingham Street
Norwood, MA 02062	London SW1V 1AH UK
Phone: 781-769-9750	Phone: +44 (0)20 7596-8750
Fax: 781-769-6334	Fax: +44 (0)20 7630-0166
e-mail: artech@artechhouse.com	e-mail: artech-uk@artechhouse.com

Find us on the World Wide Web at:
www.artechhouse.com